THE SIXTH

MAD

SPY vs SPY

CASE BOOK

BY
ANTONIO
PROHIAS
EDITED
BY
ALBERT B.
FELDSTEIN

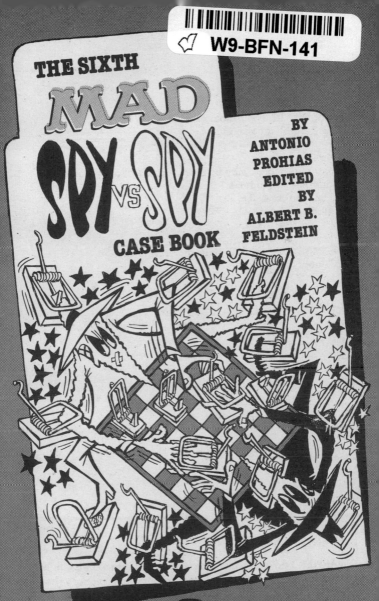

WARNER BOOKS
A Warner Communications Company

WARNER BOOKS EDITION

For information address:
E.C. Publications, Inc.
485 Madison Avenue
New York, N.Y. 10022

Title "MAD" used with permission of its owner,
E.C. Publications, Inc.

This Warner Books Edition is published by
arrangement with E.C. Publicatiions, Inc.

Warner Books, Inc.
666 Fifth Avenue
New York, N.Y. 10103

A Warner Communications Company

Printed in the United States of America

First Printing: August, 1982

Reissued: August, 1988

10 9 8 7 6 5 4 3

CONTENTS

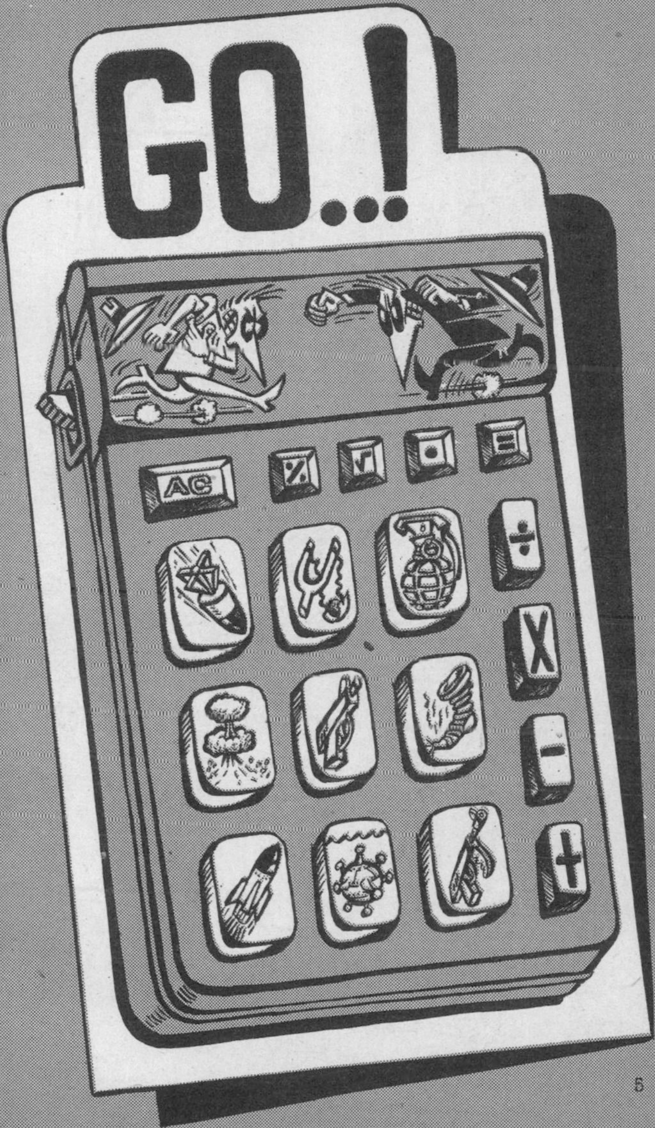
GO...!
AC

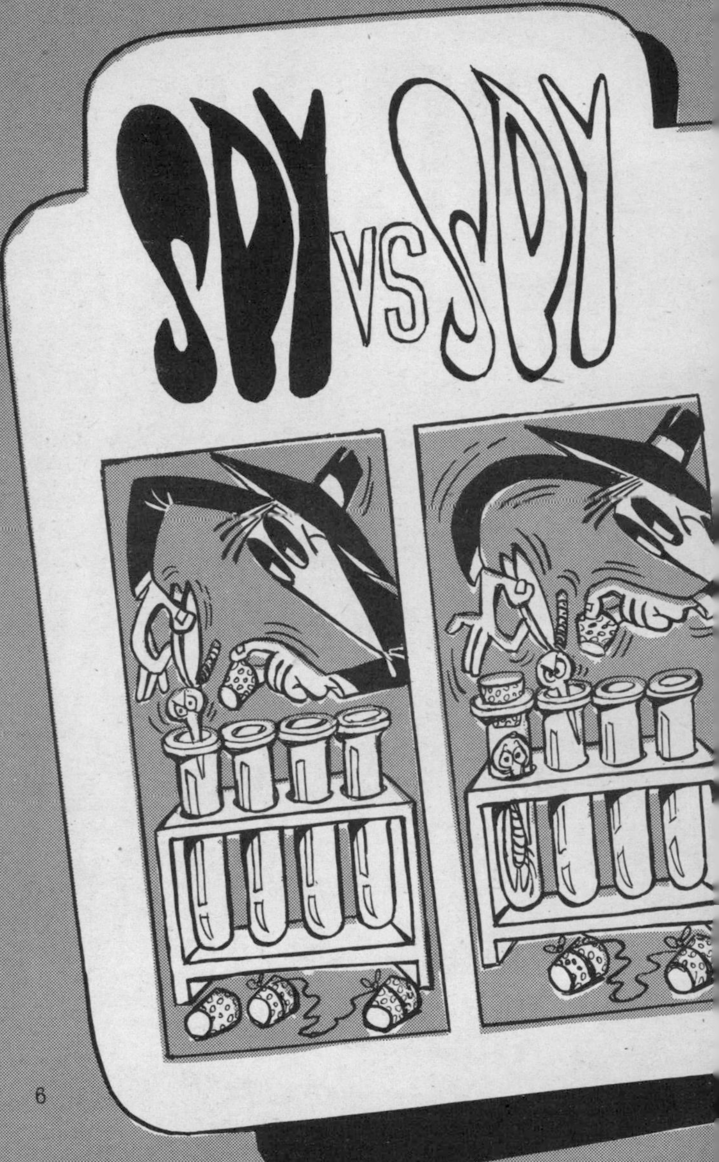
SPY VS SPY

the BUGGING INCIDENT

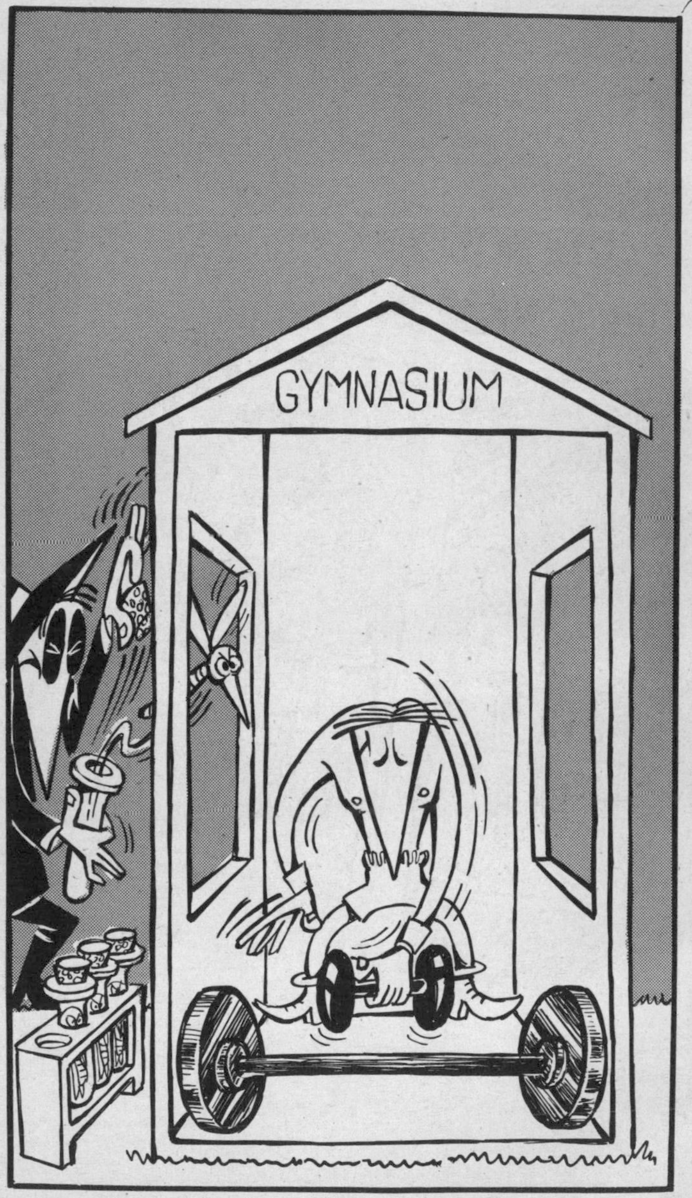
GYMNASIUM

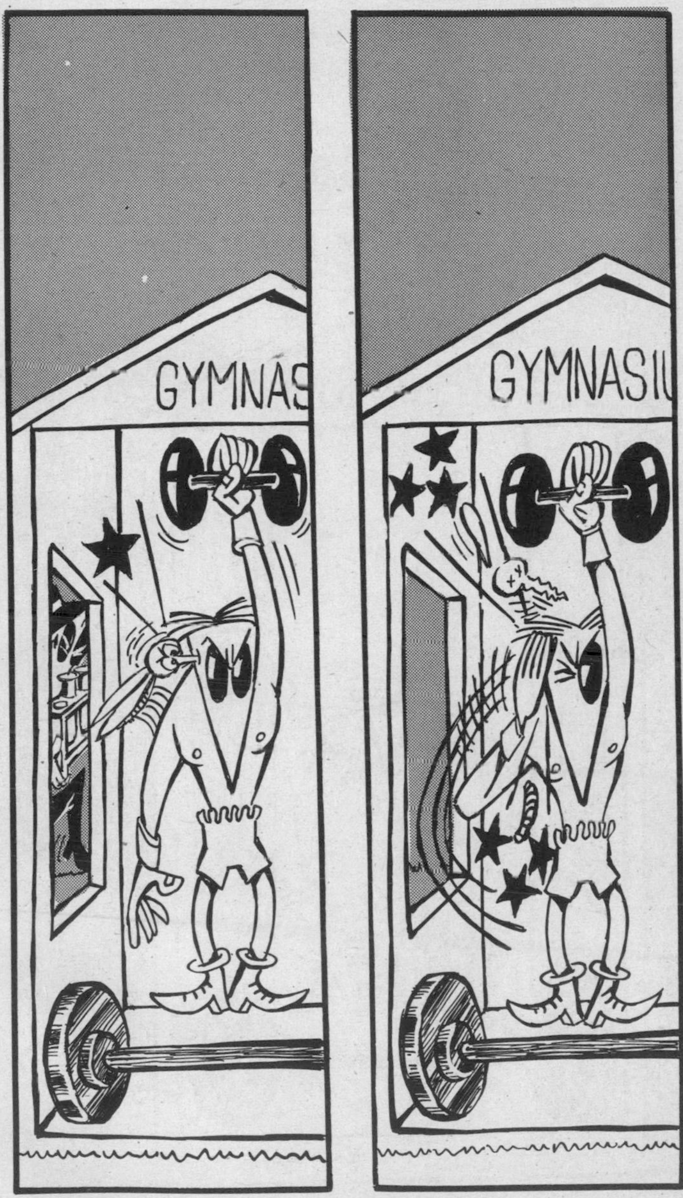
GYMNAS
GYMNASIU

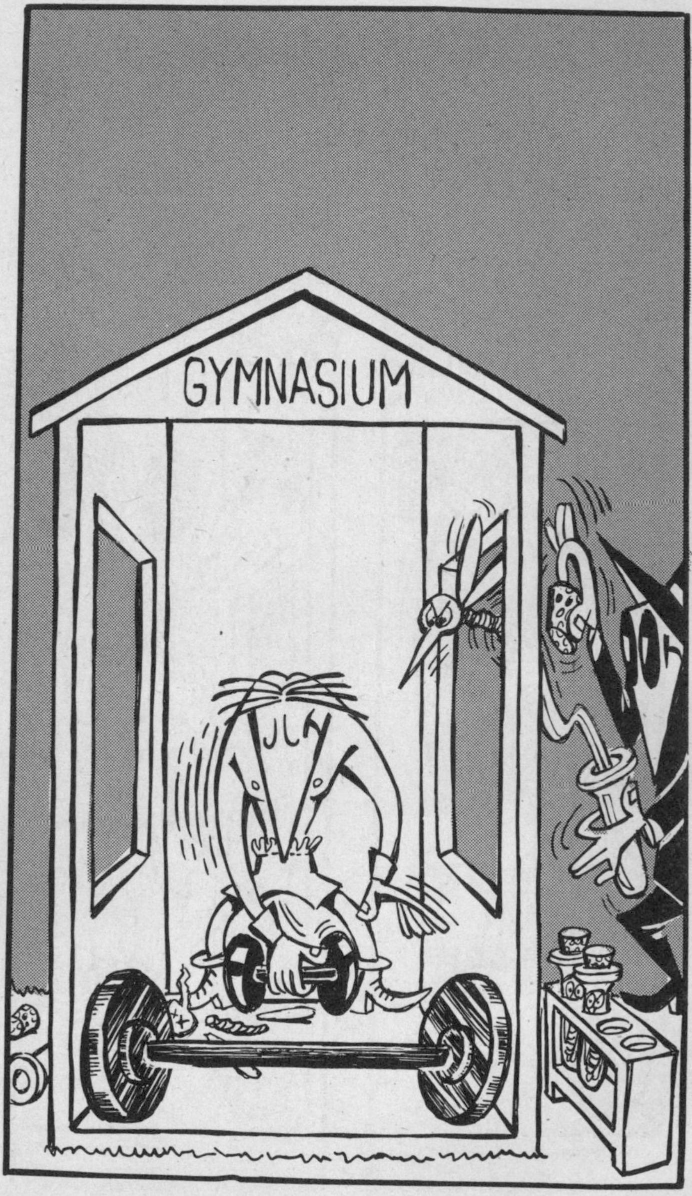
GYMNASIUM
JLH

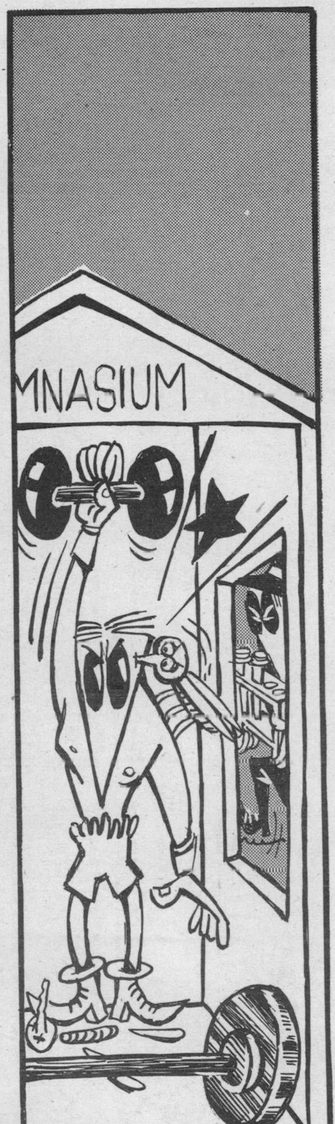
MNASIUM

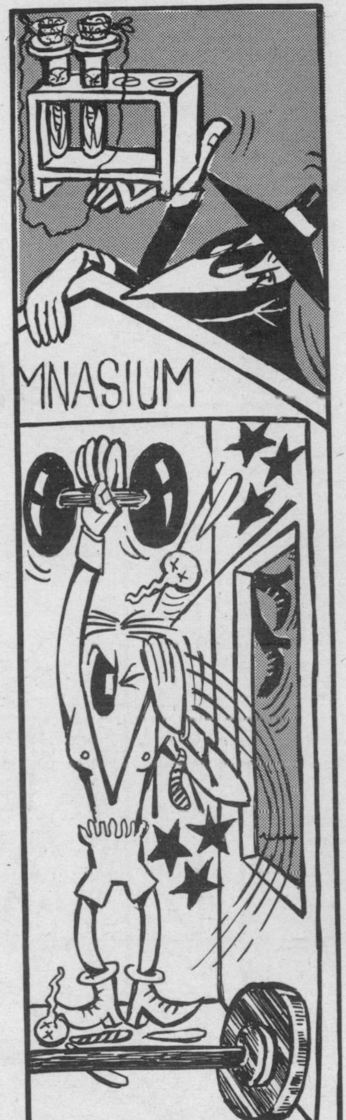
MNASIUM

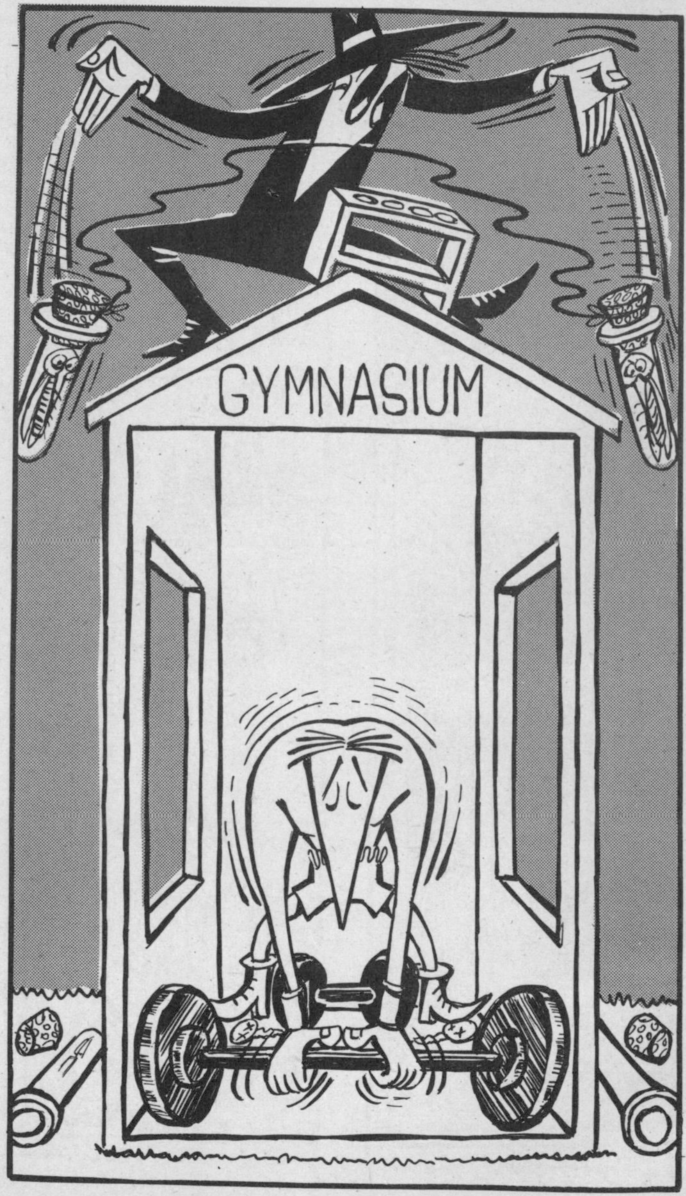
GYMNASIUM

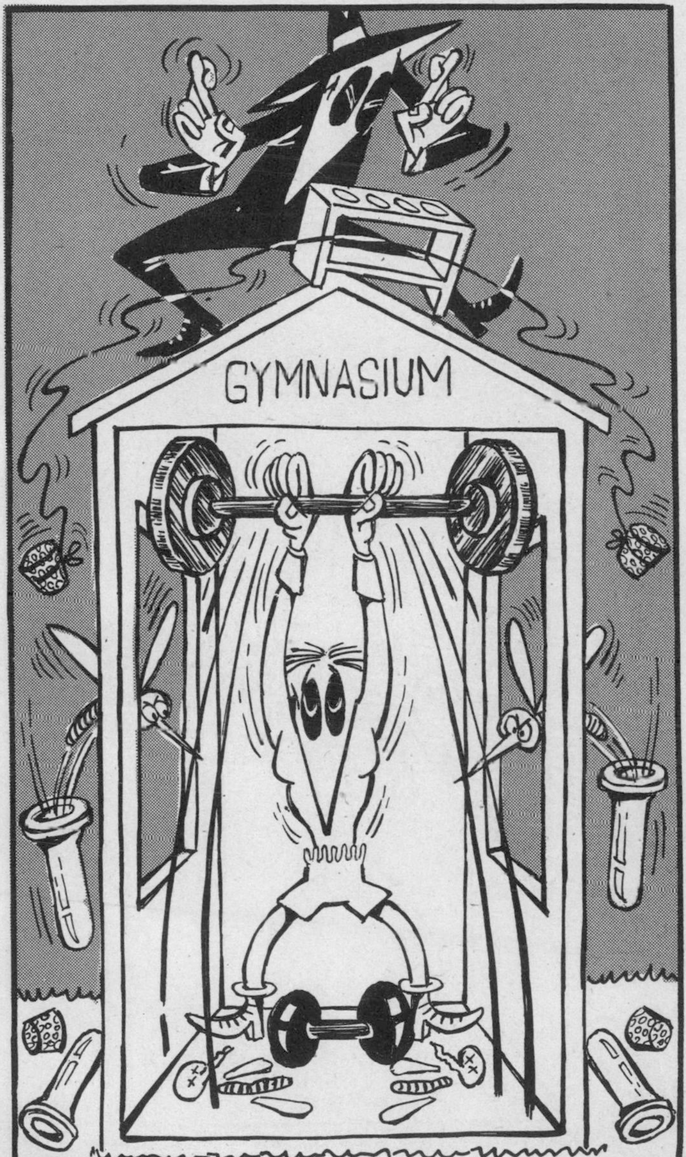
GYMNASIUM

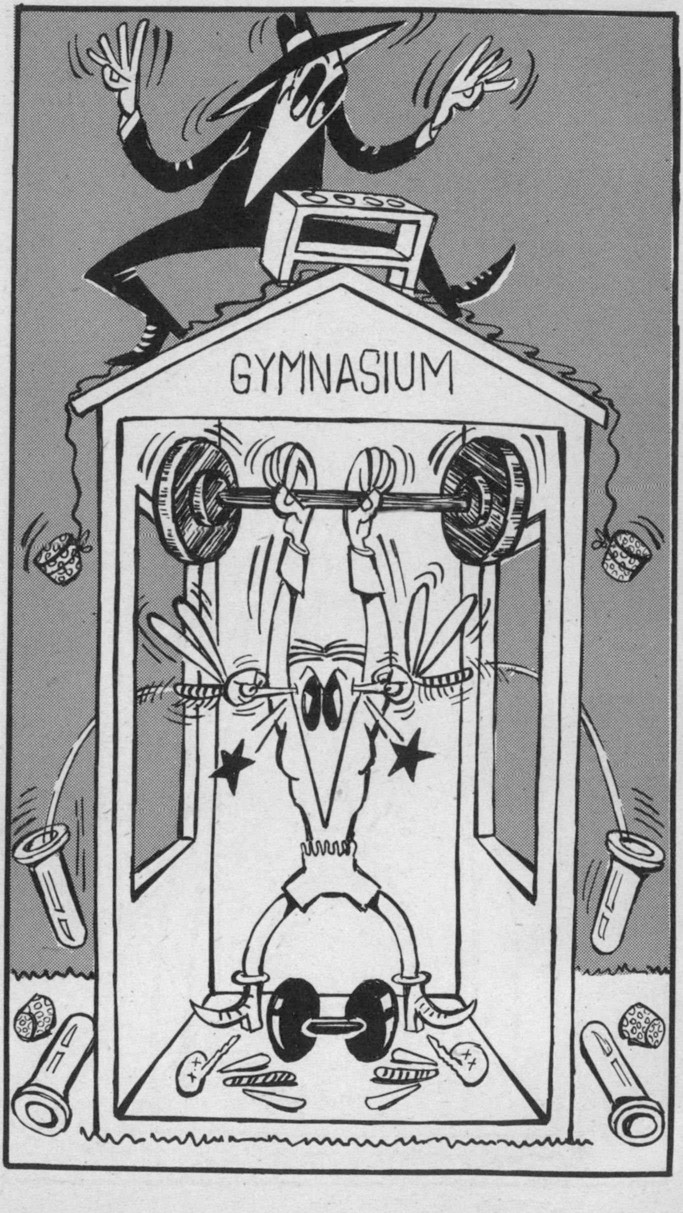
GYMNASIUM

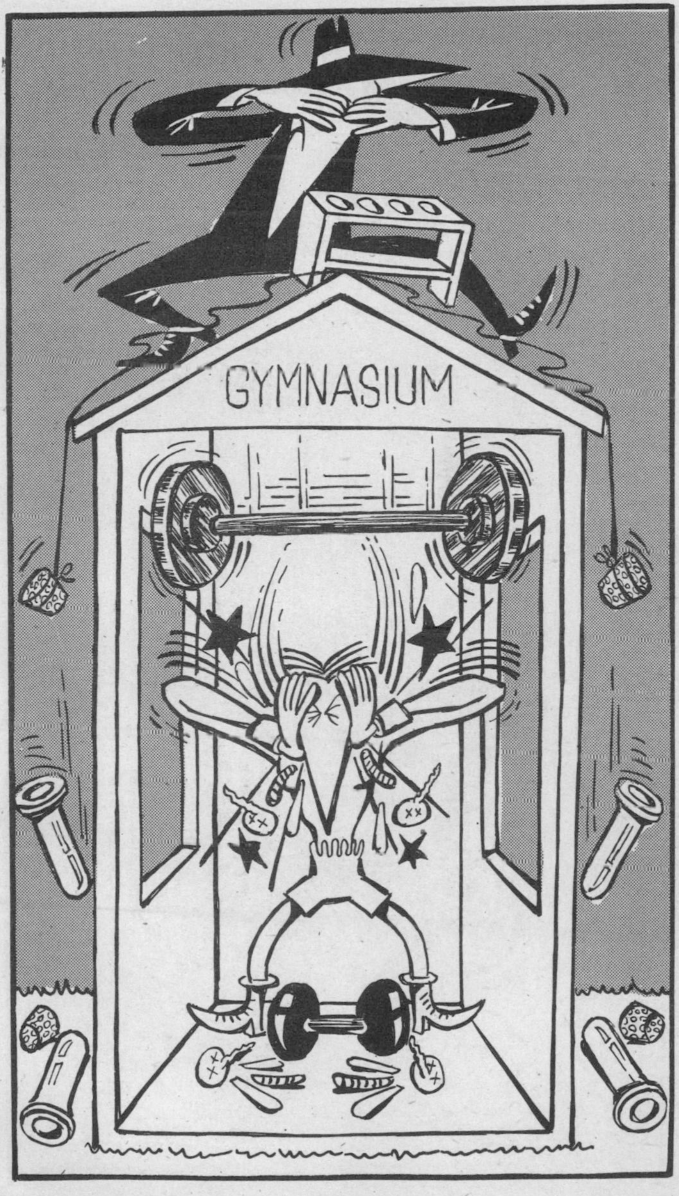
GYMNASIUM

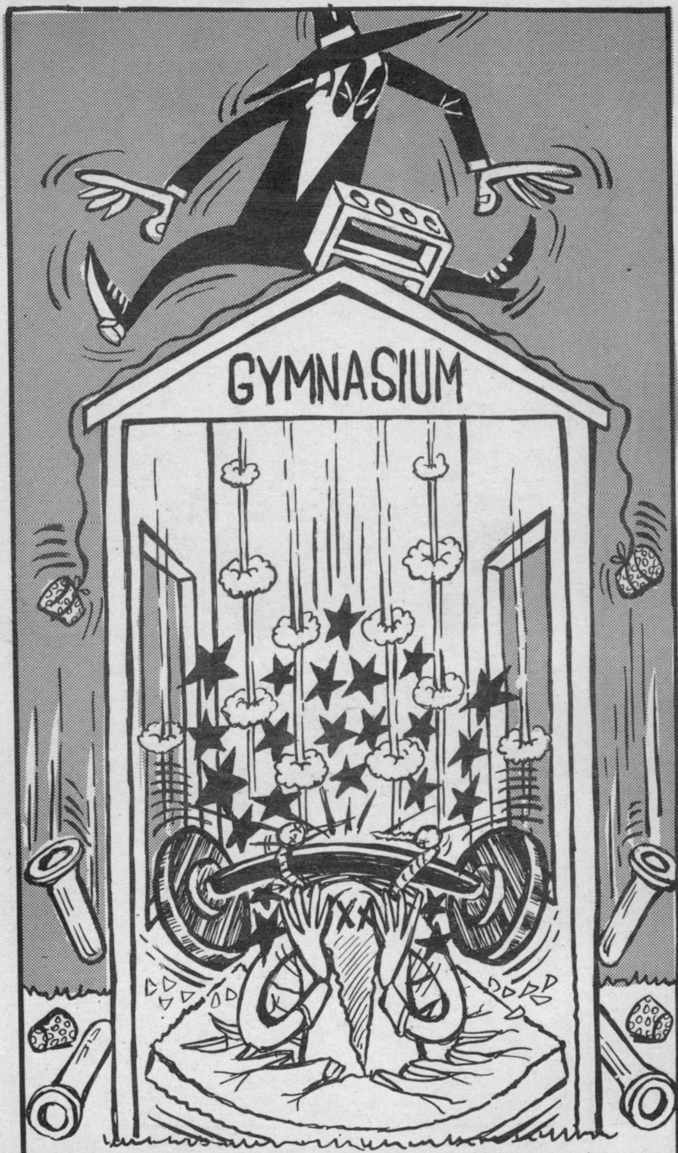
GYMNASIUM

SPY vs SPY

the CARRIER-PIGEON PLOY

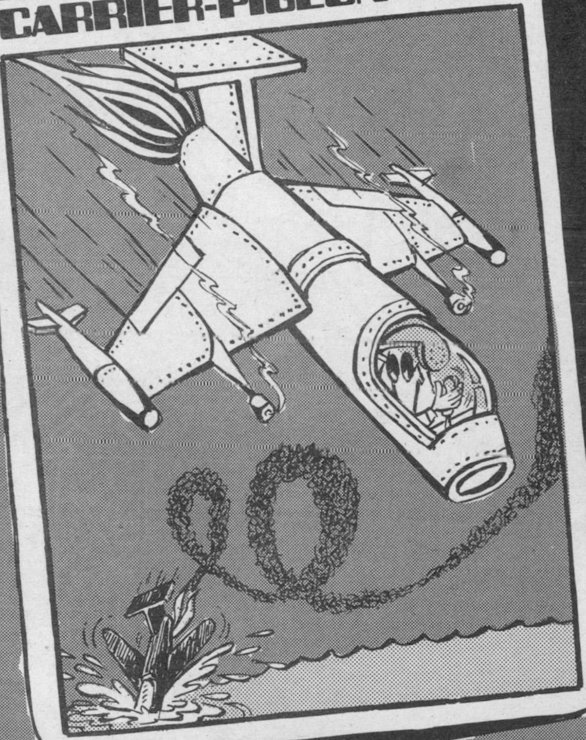

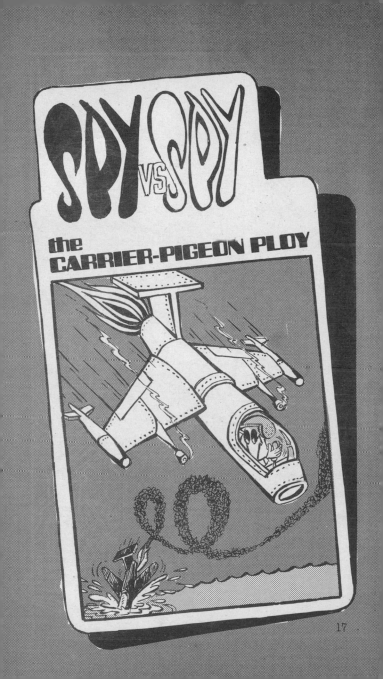

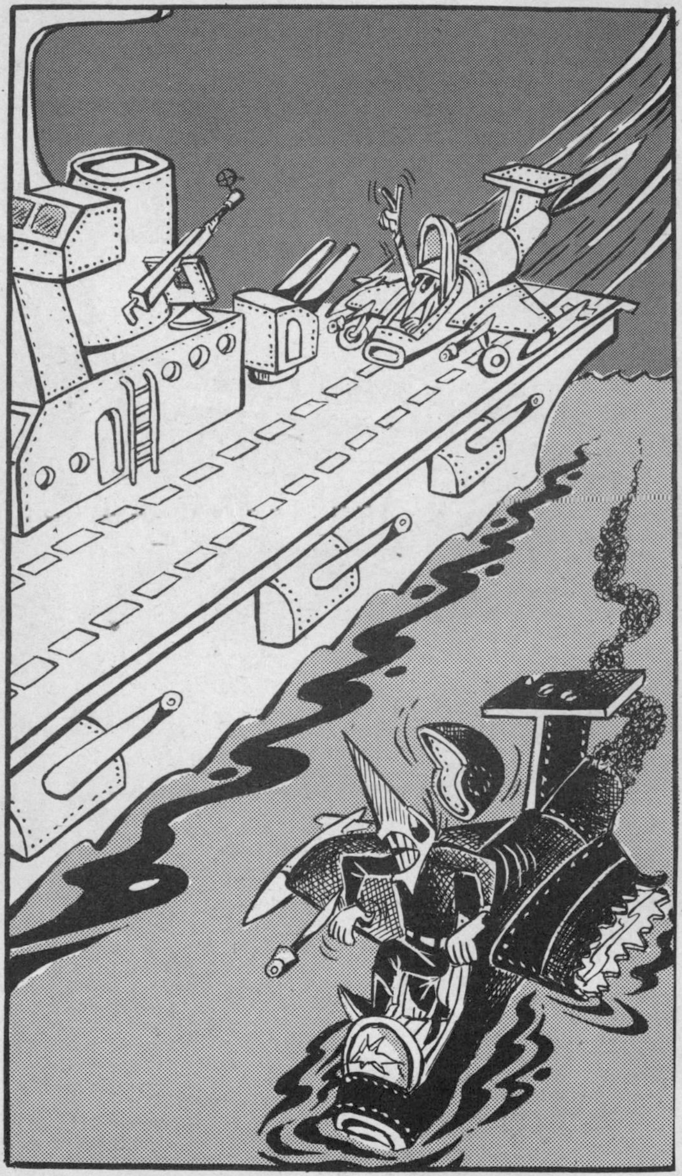

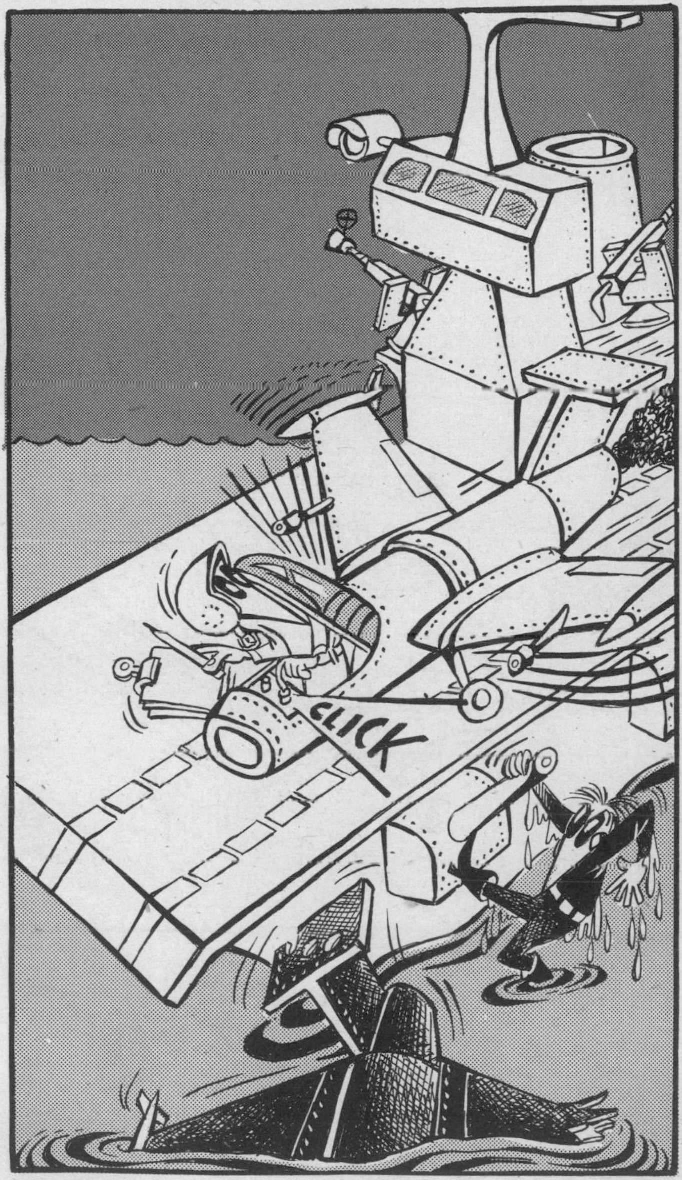
CLICK

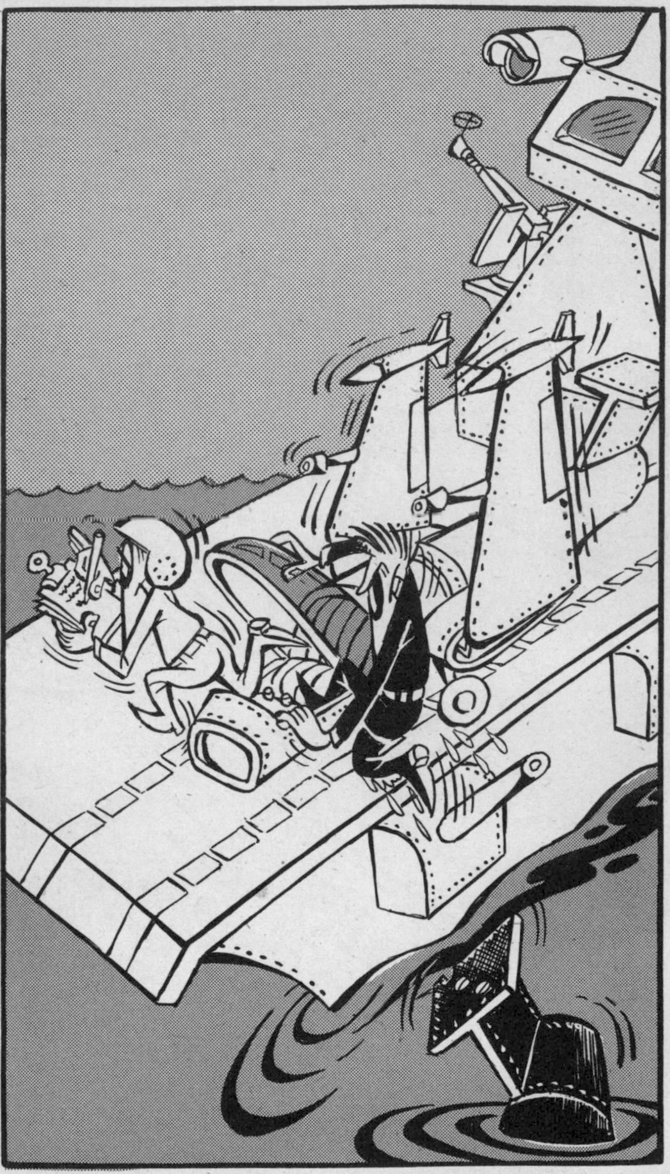

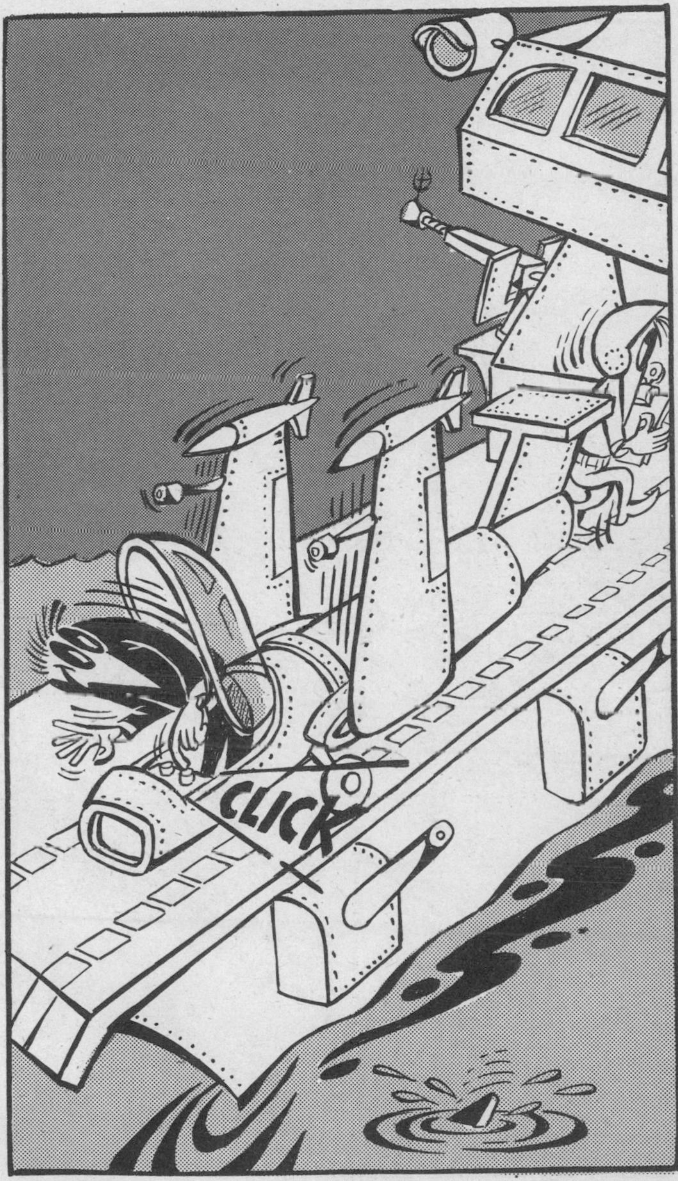
CLICK

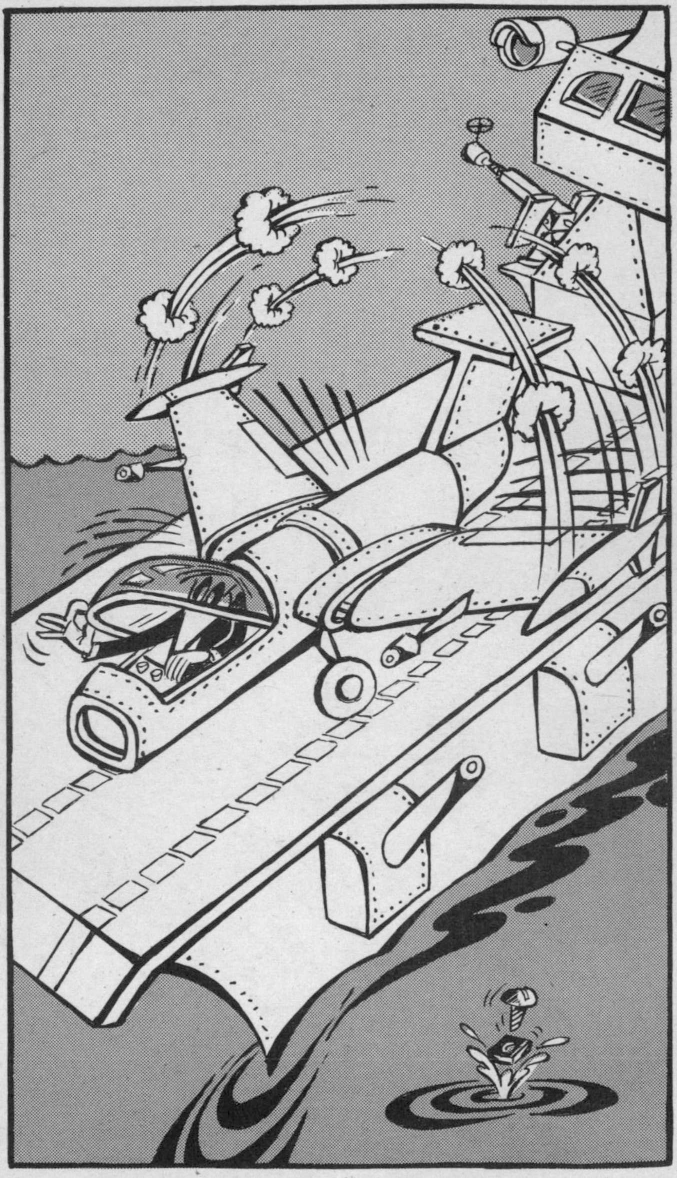

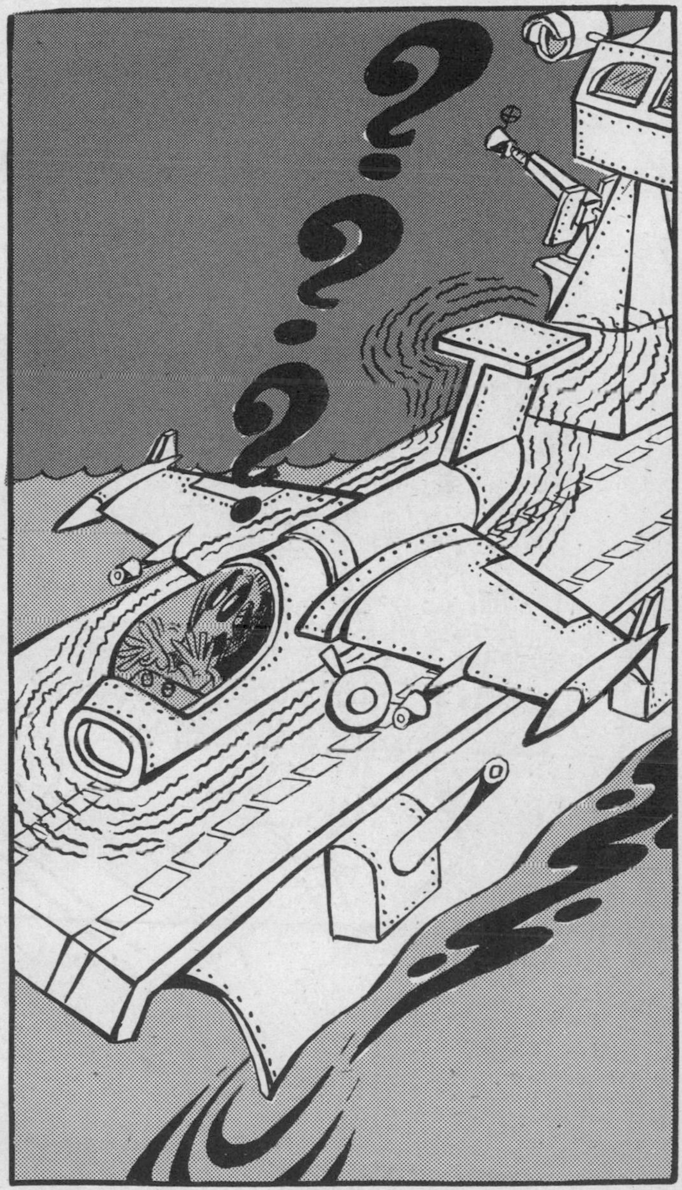

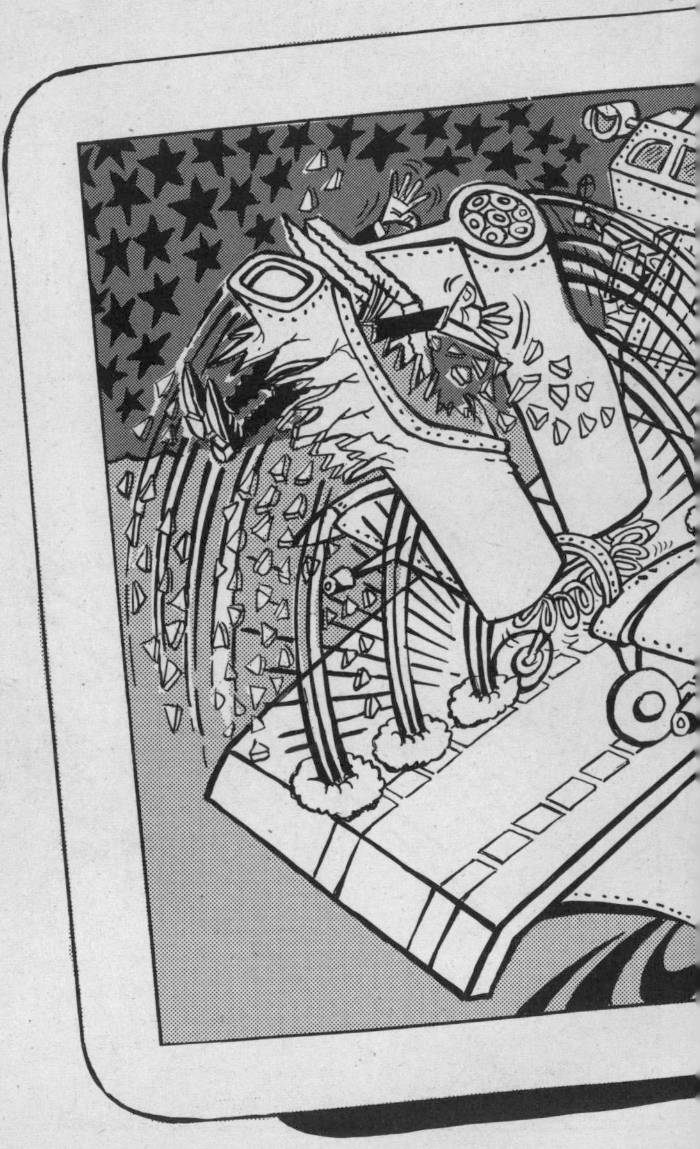

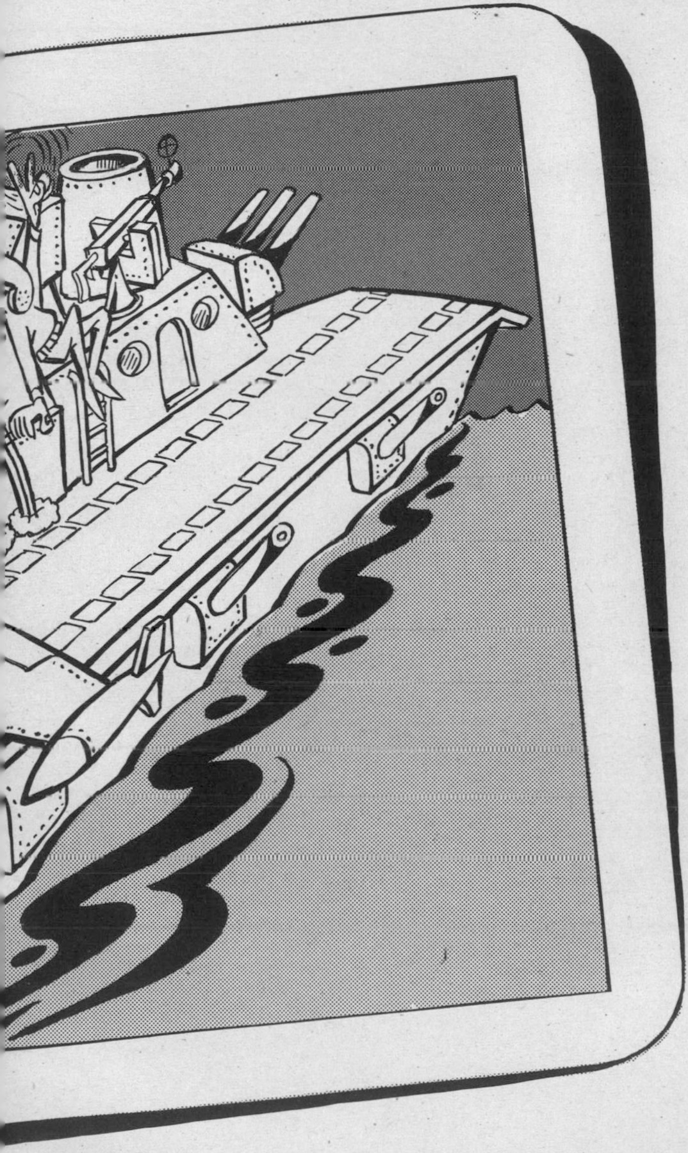

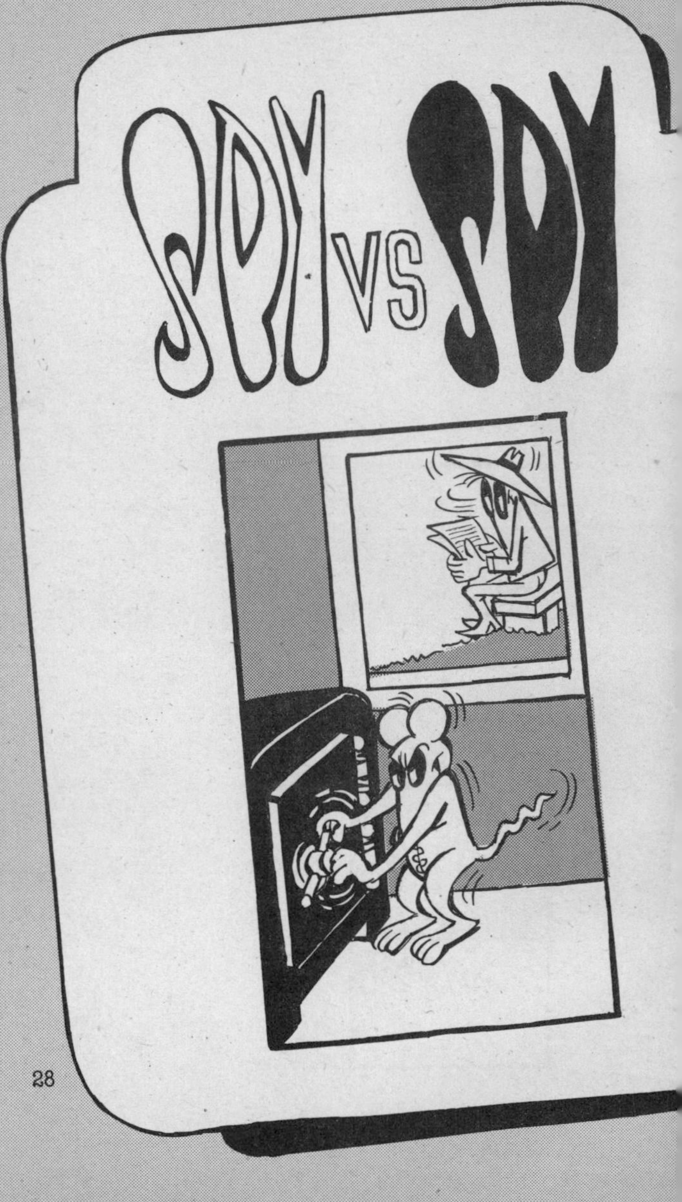
SPY VS SPY

THE RAT-FINK CASE

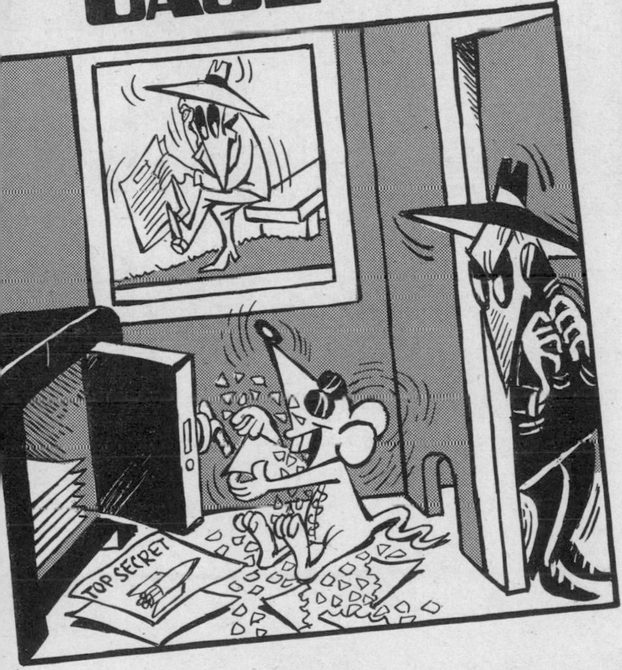
TOP SECRET

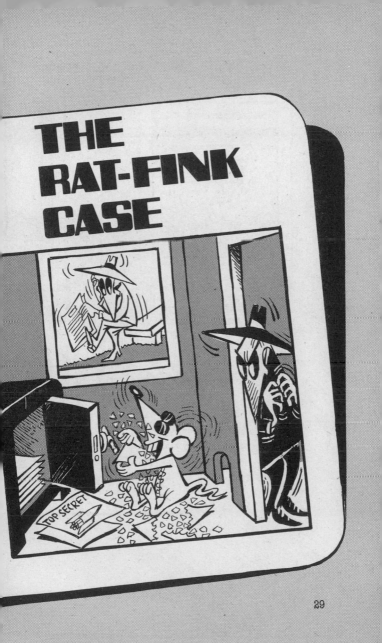

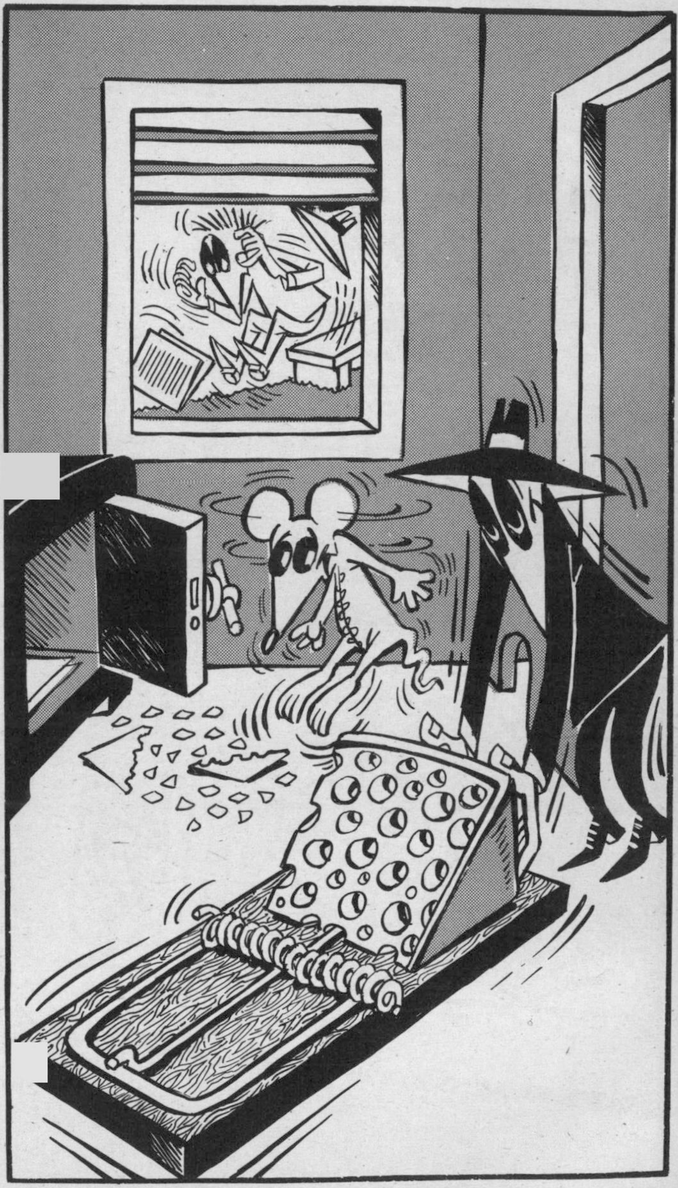

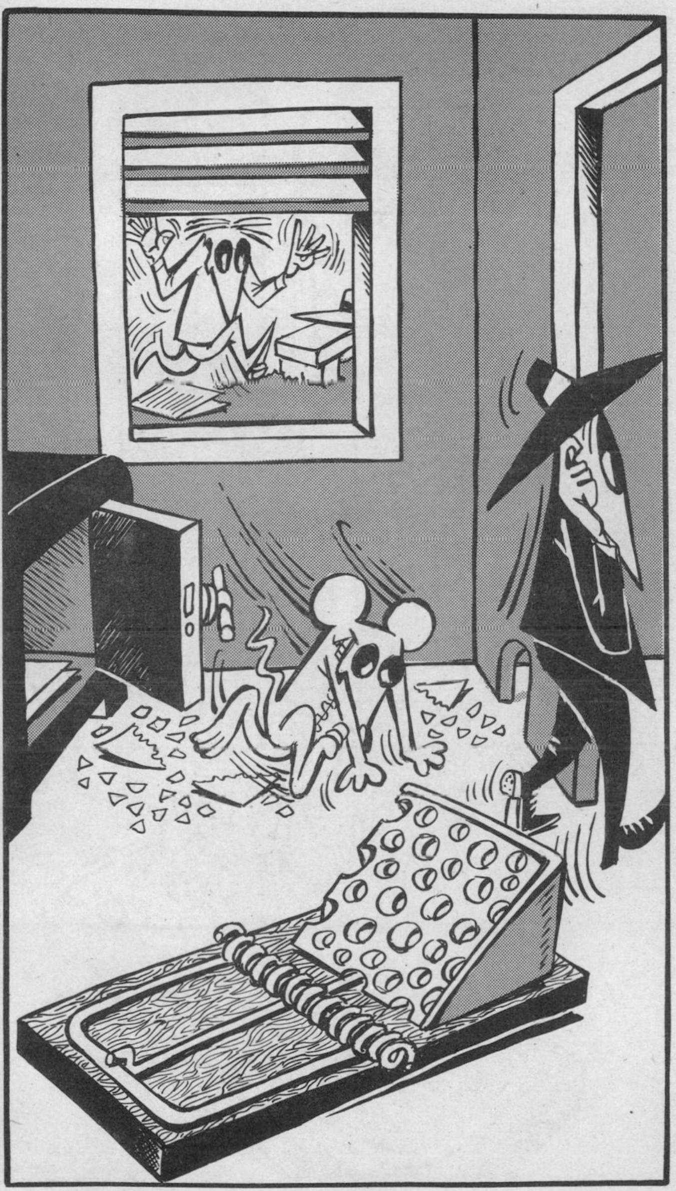

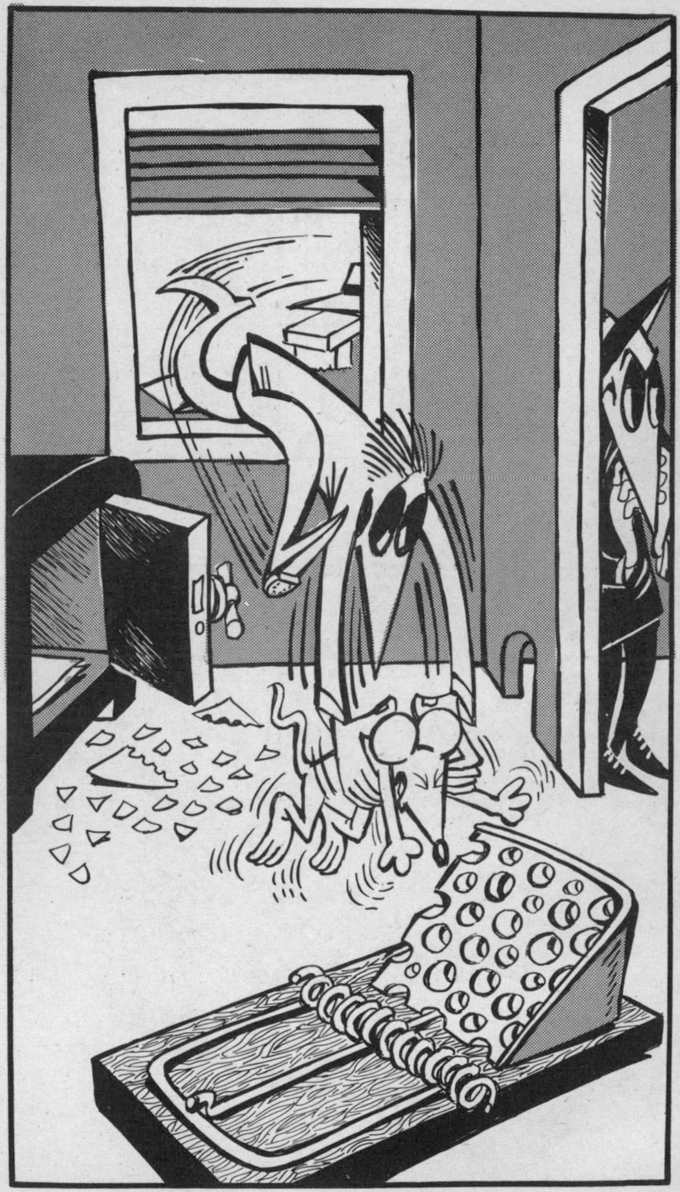

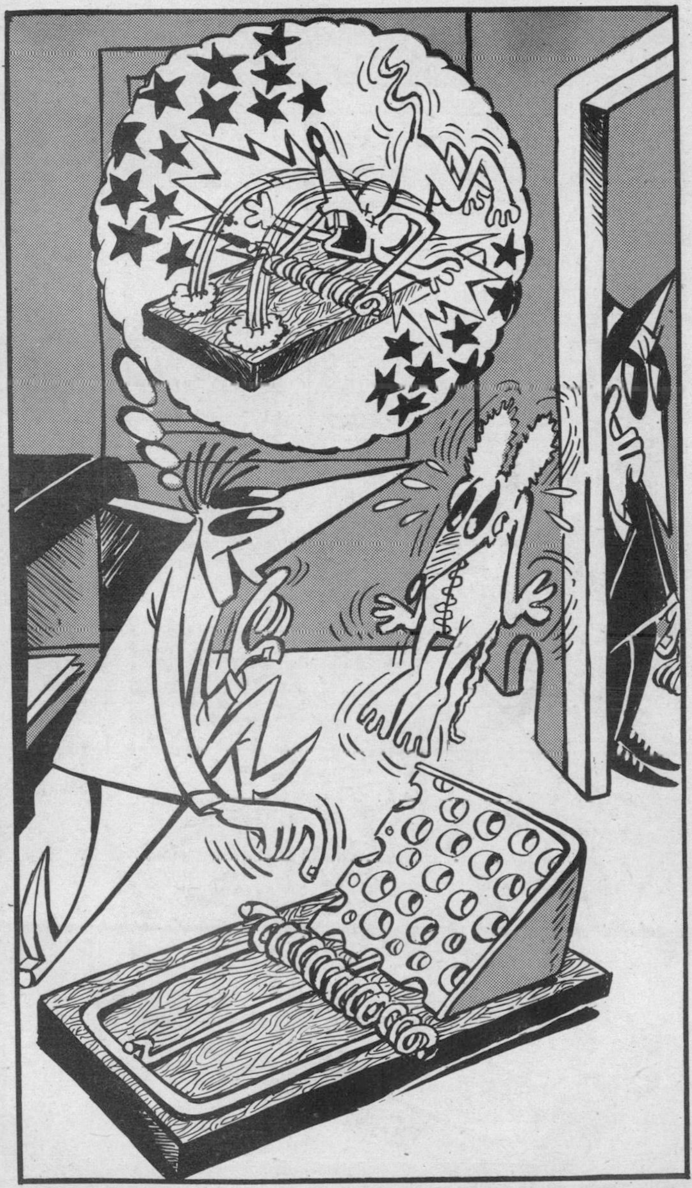

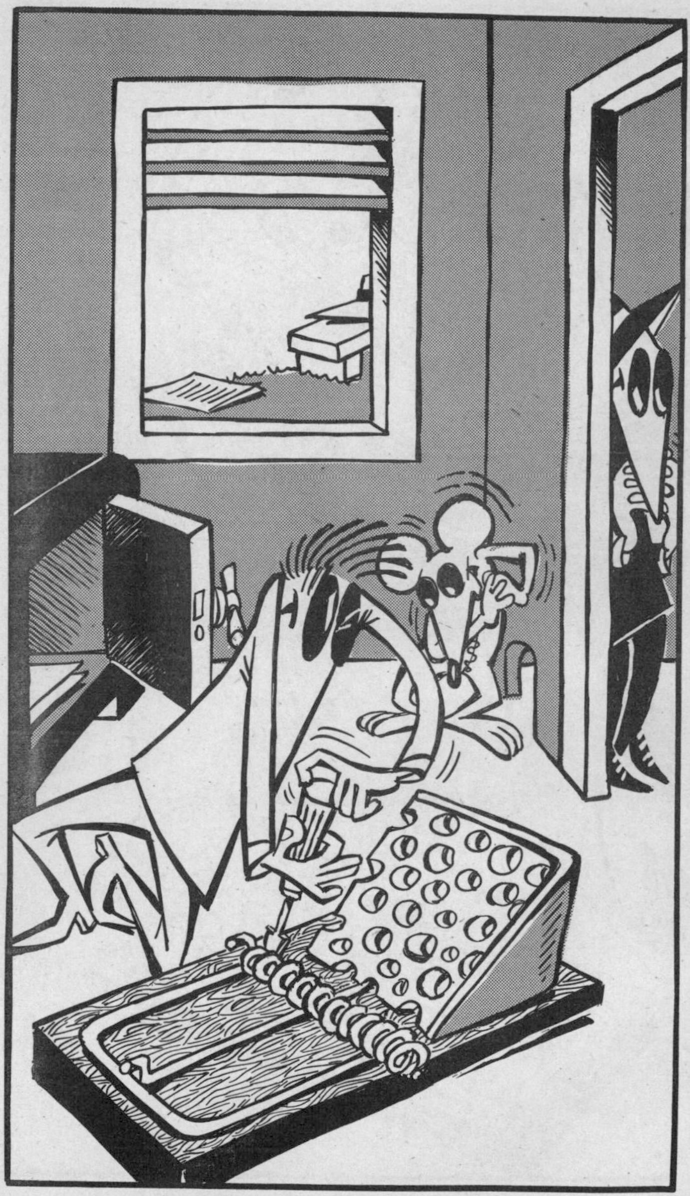

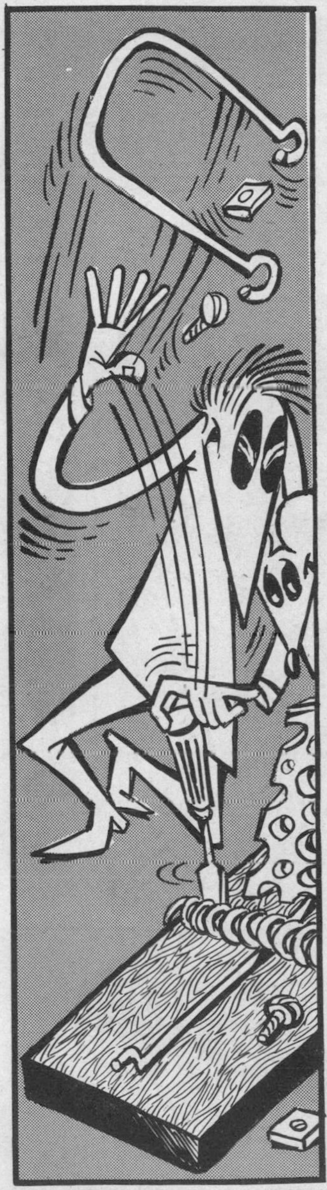

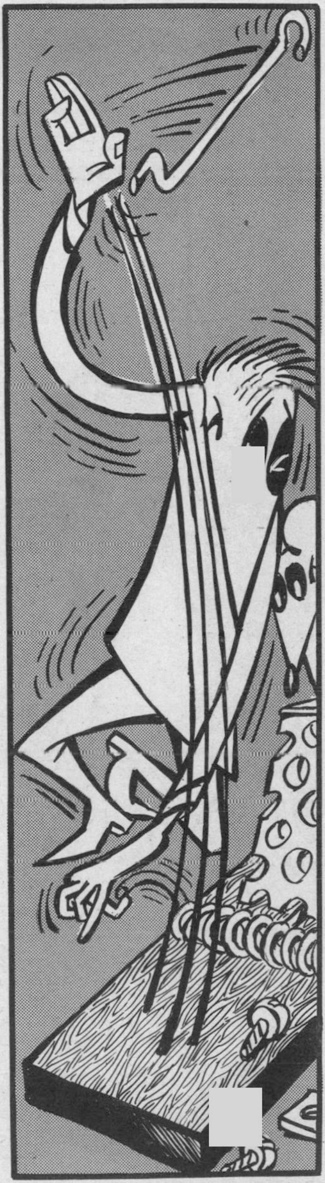

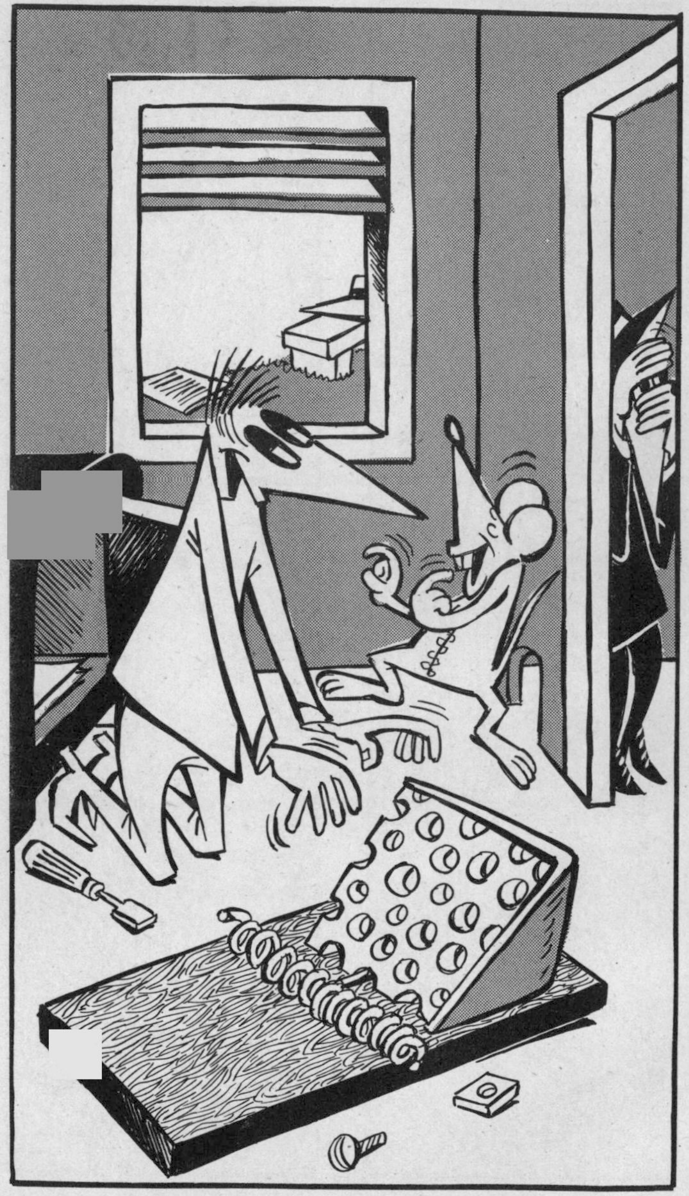

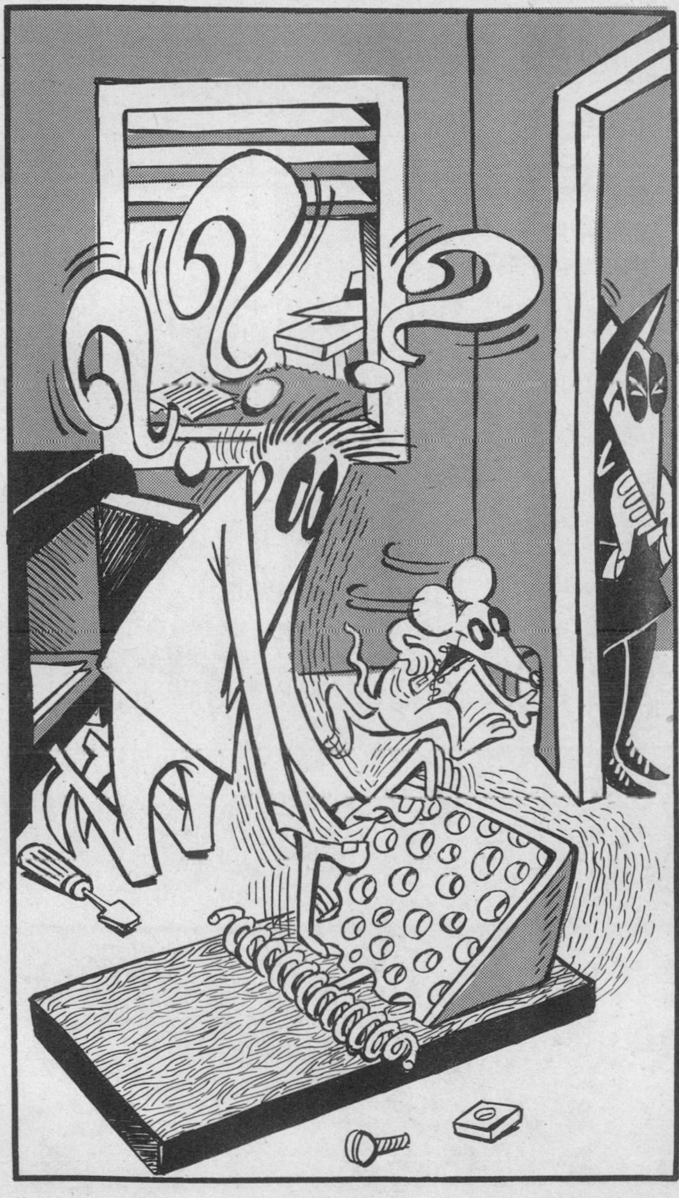

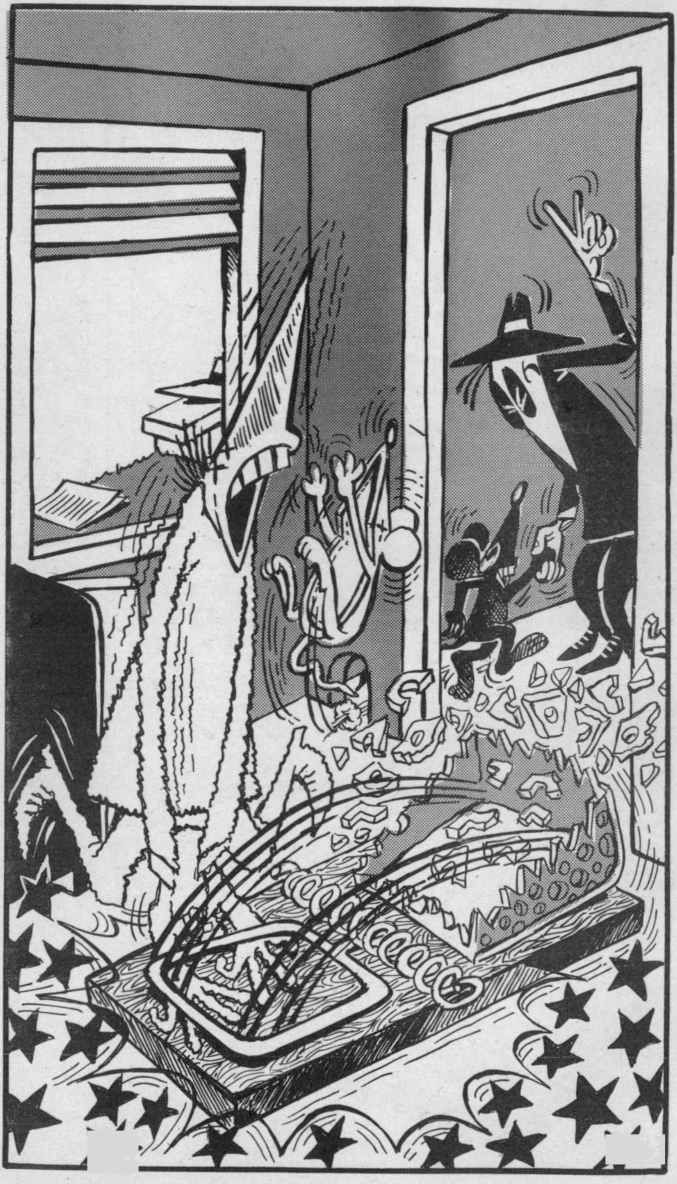

SPY vs SPY

the TWO ON THE ISLE FILE

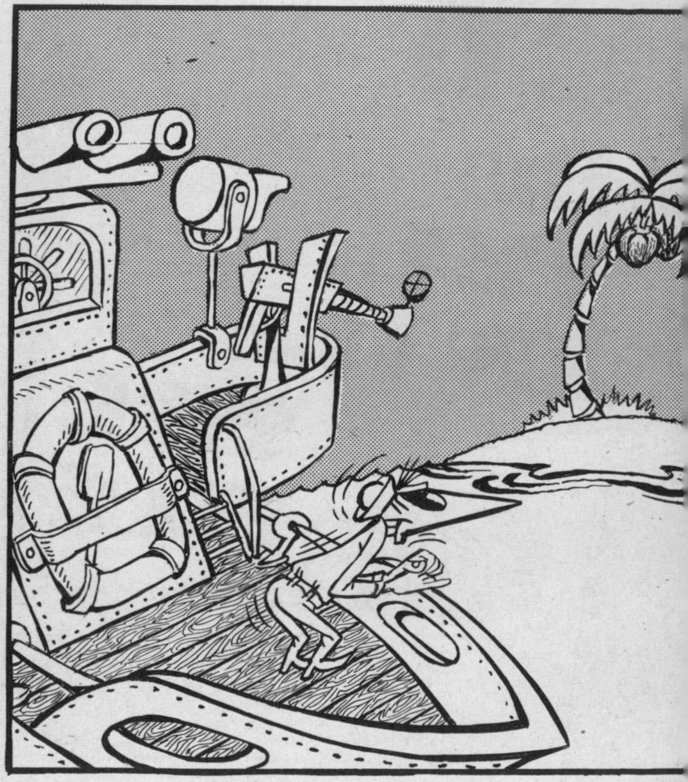

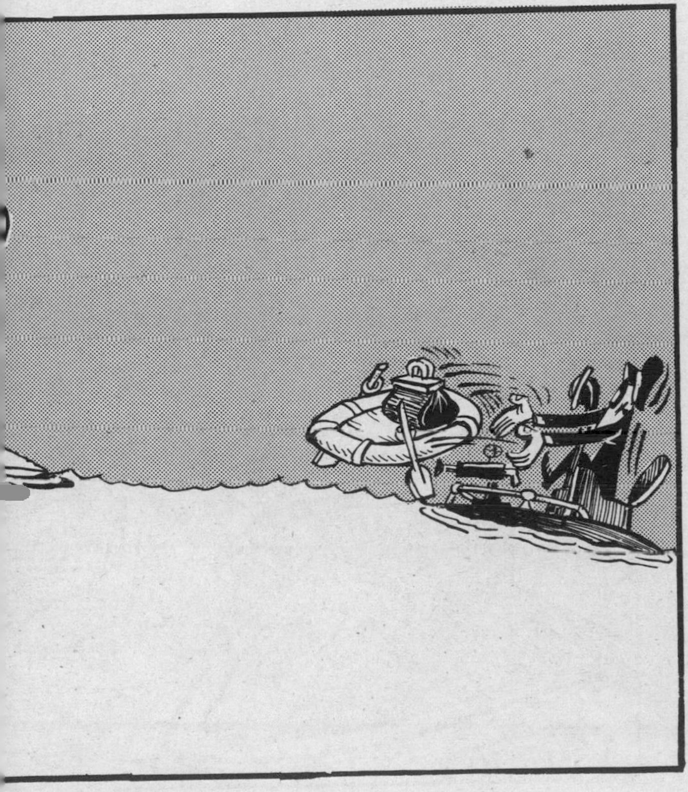

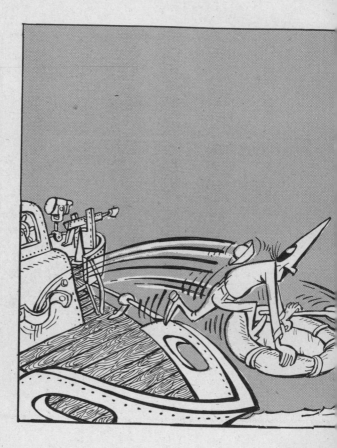

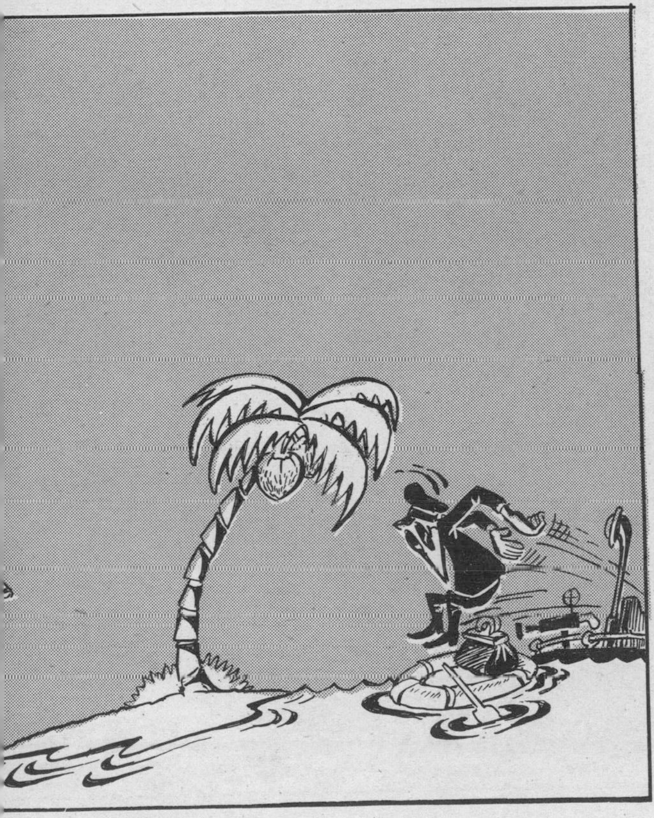

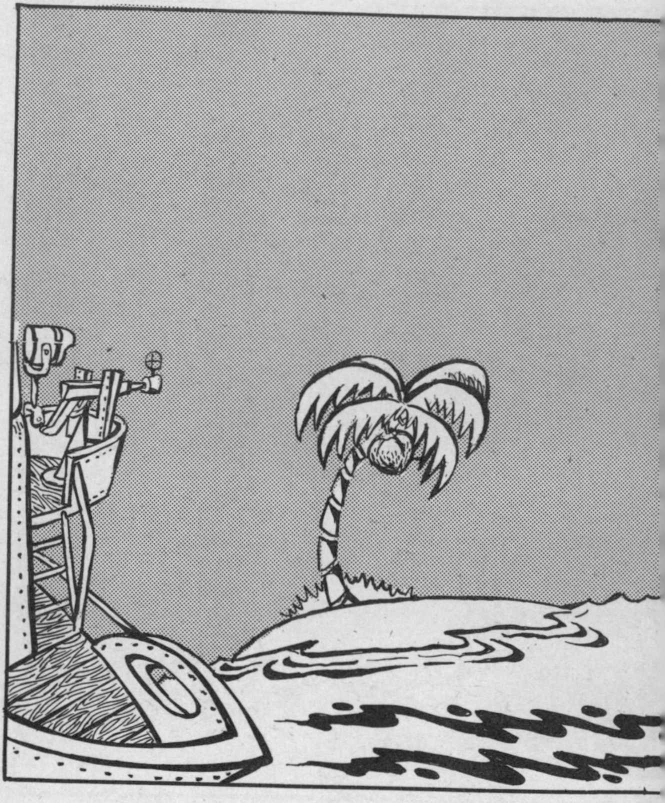

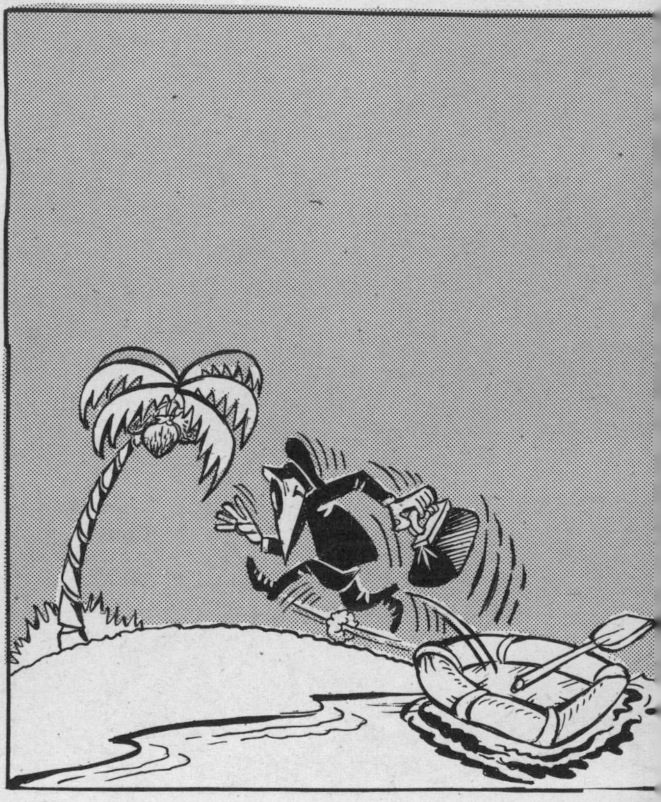

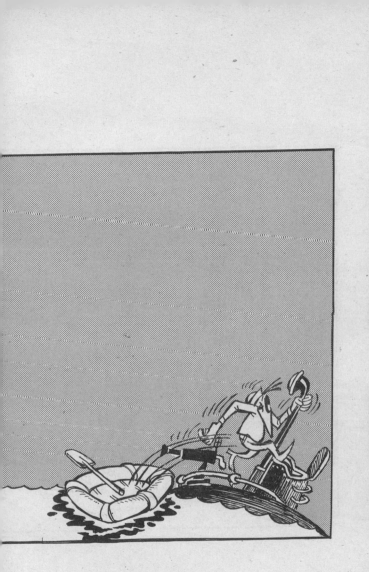

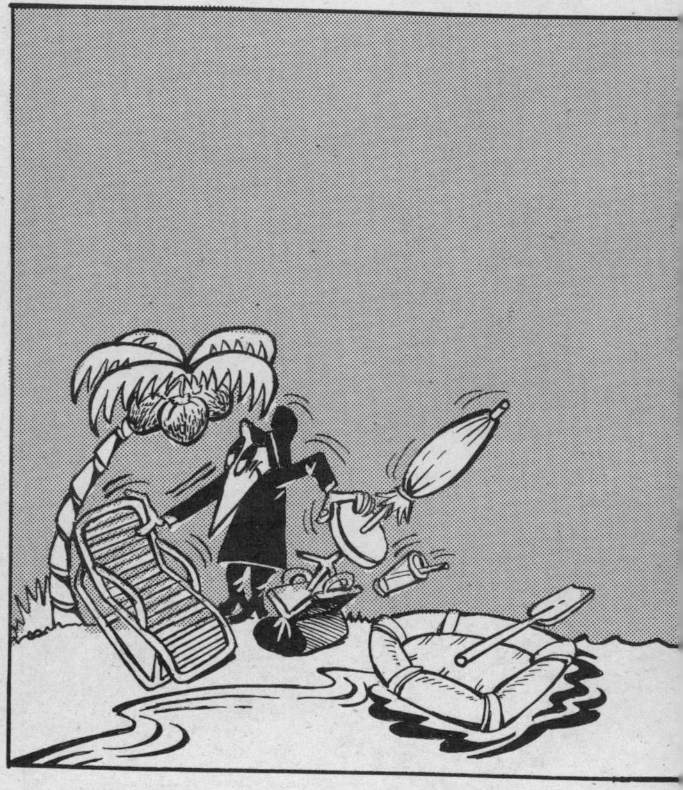

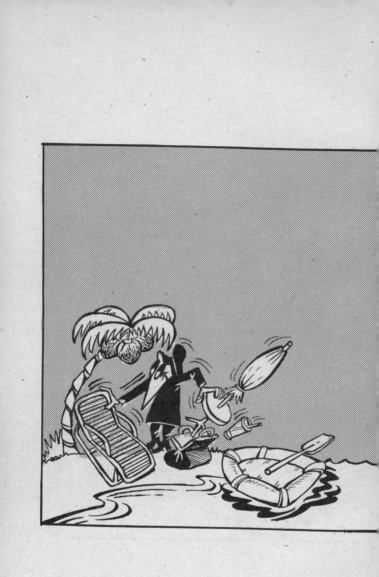

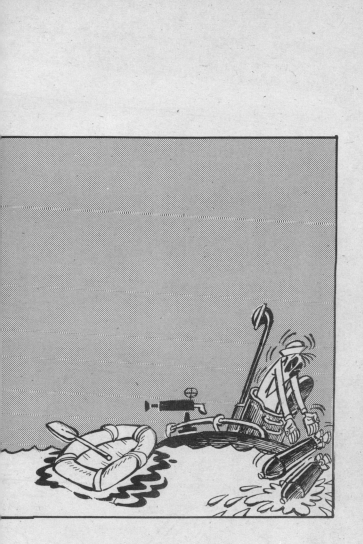

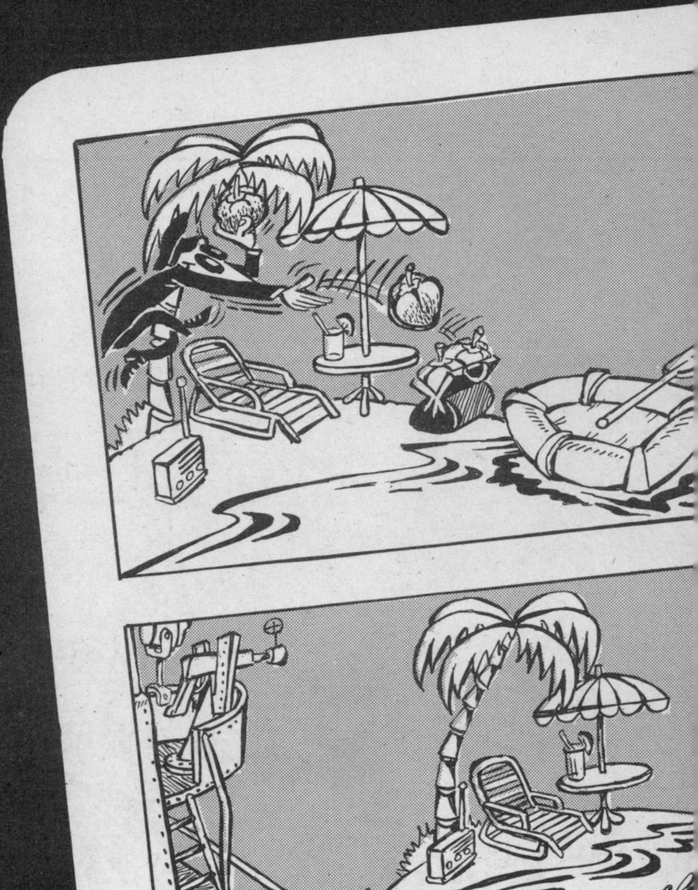

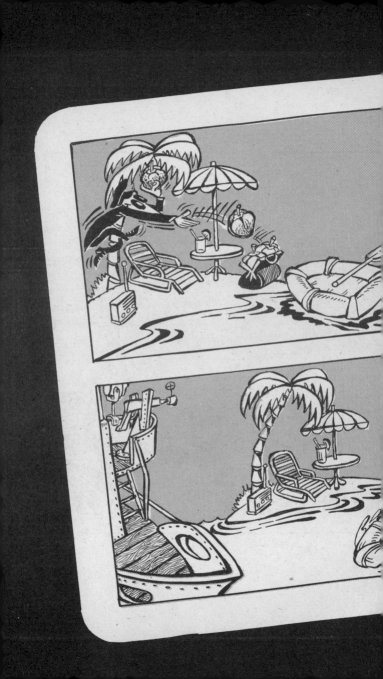

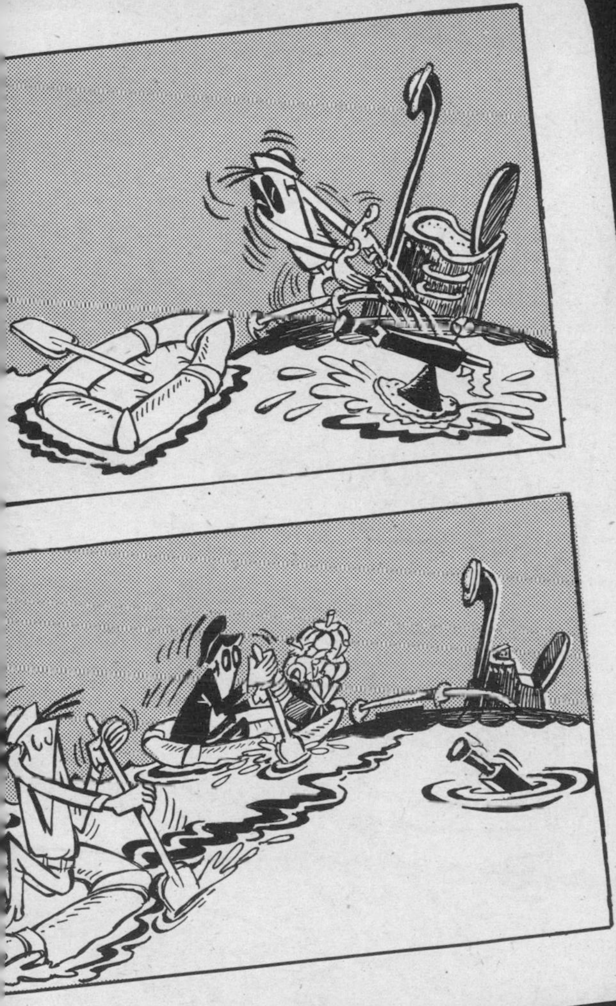

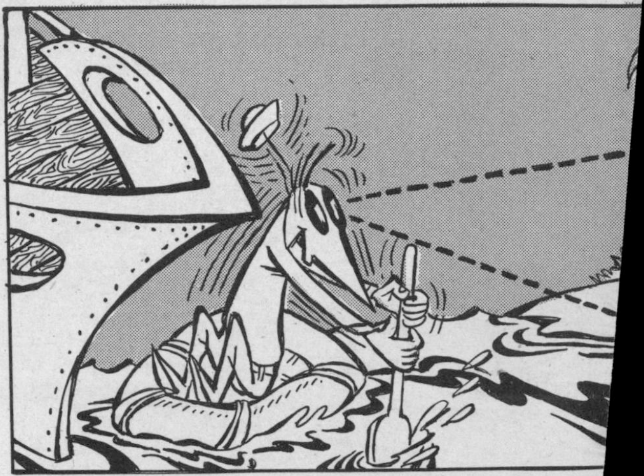

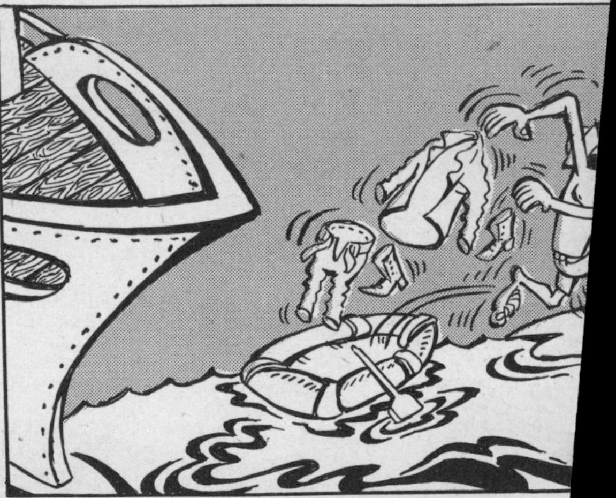

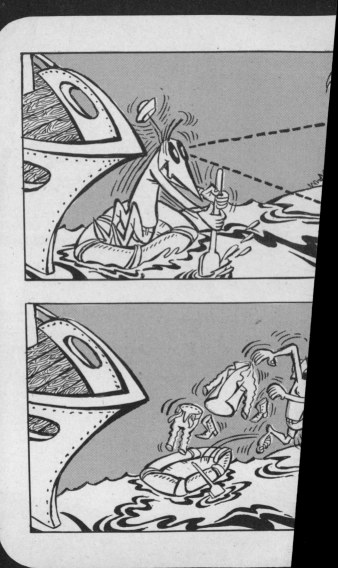

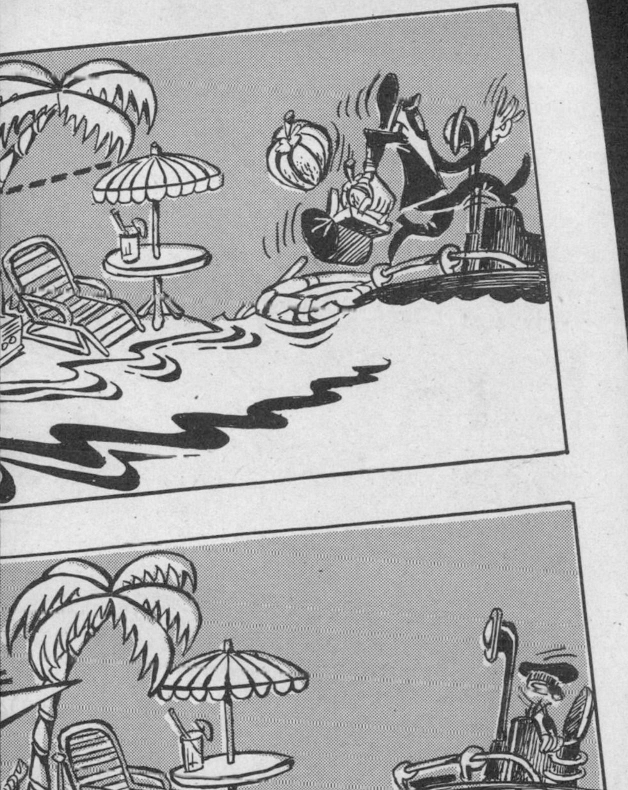

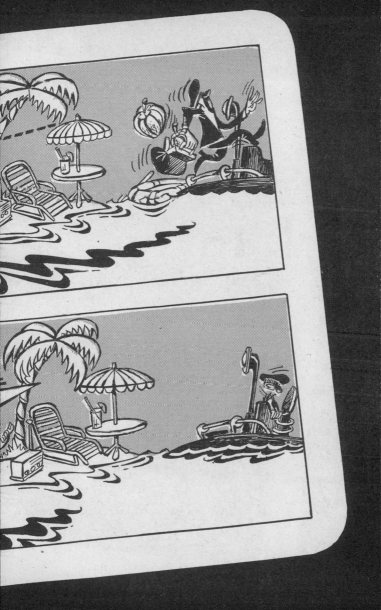

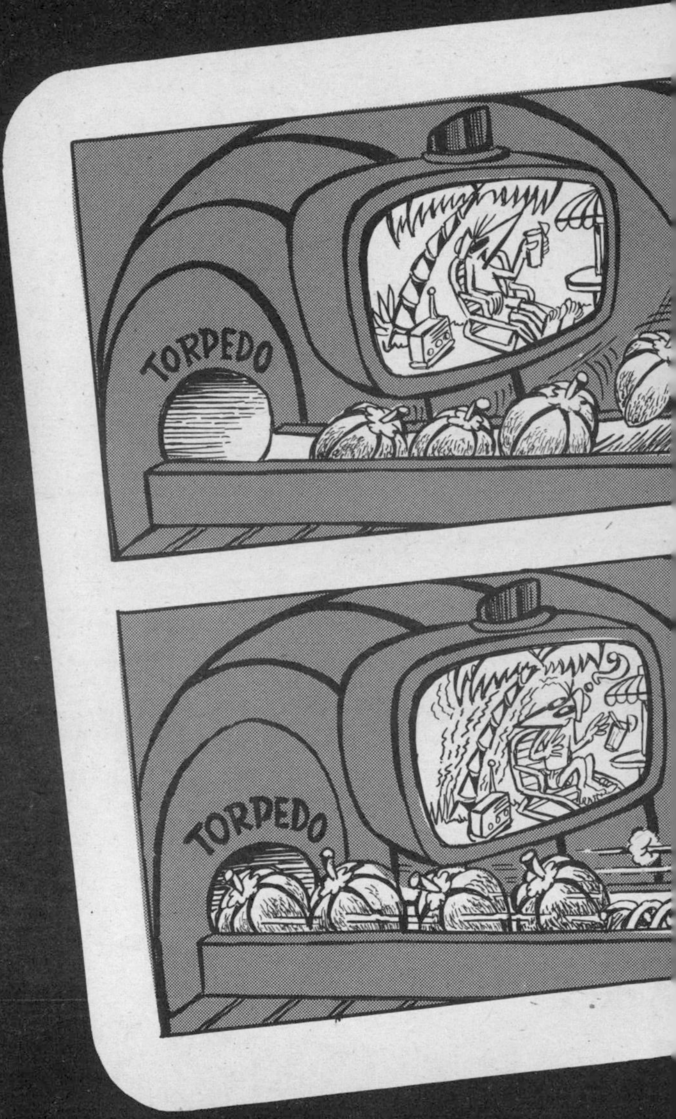
TORPEDO
TORPEDO

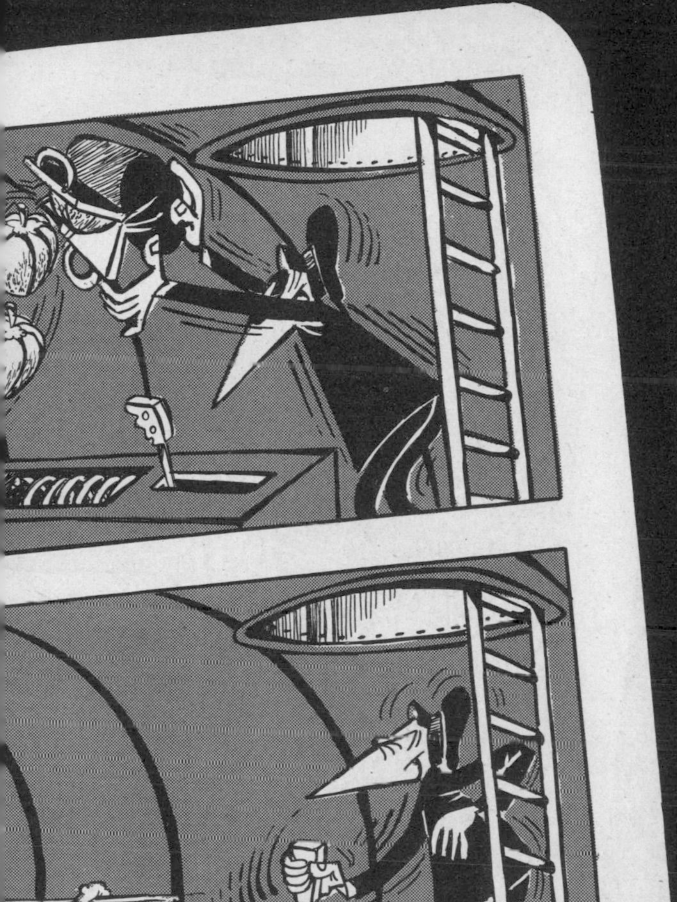

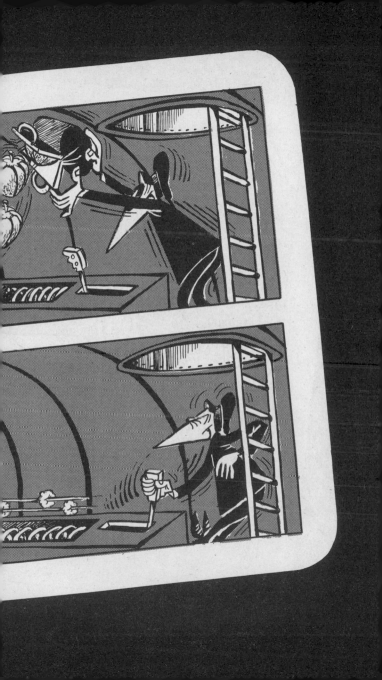

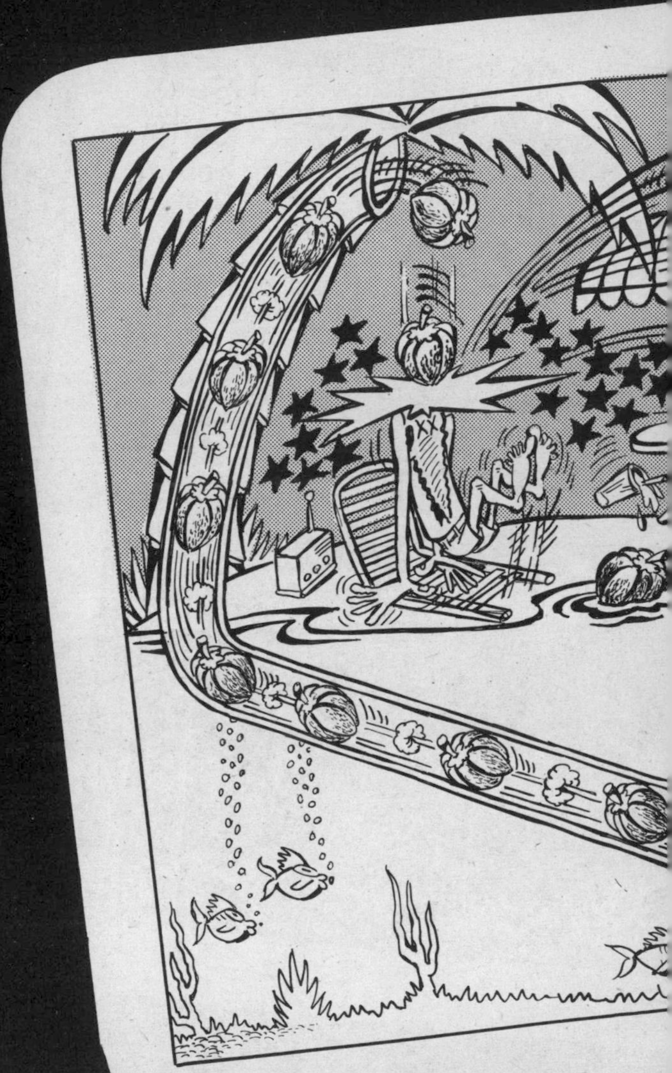

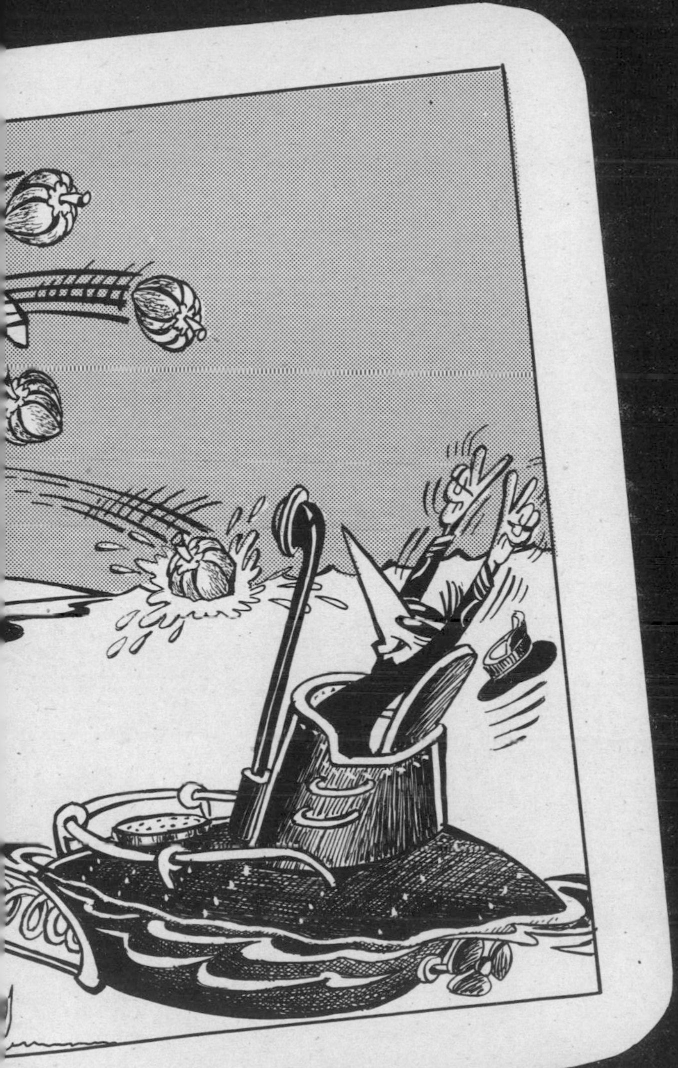

SPY vs SPY

THE SPLITSVILLE MEMORANDUM

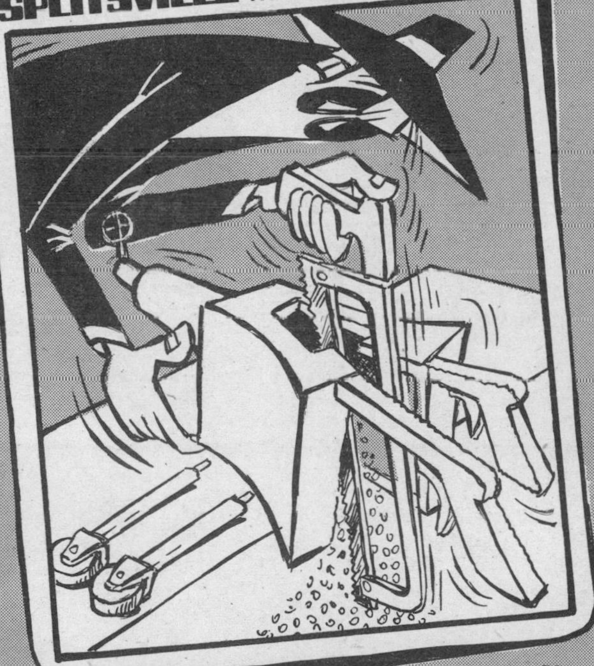

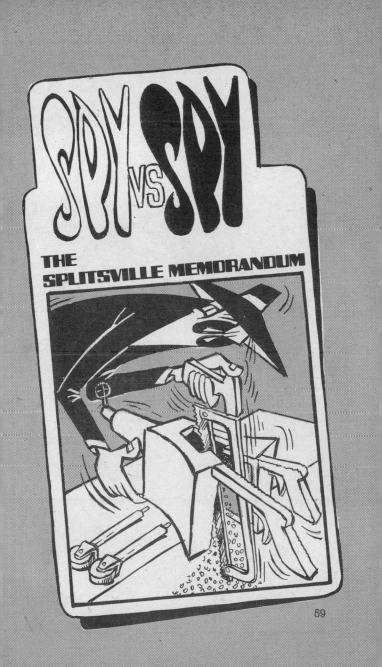

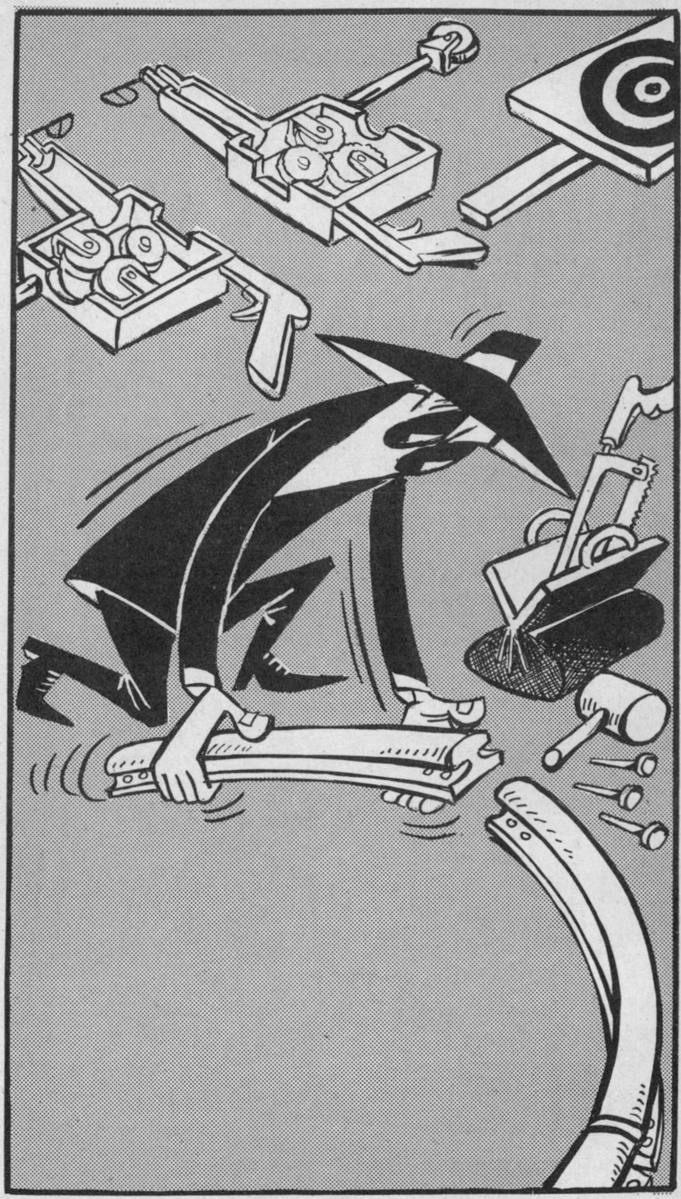

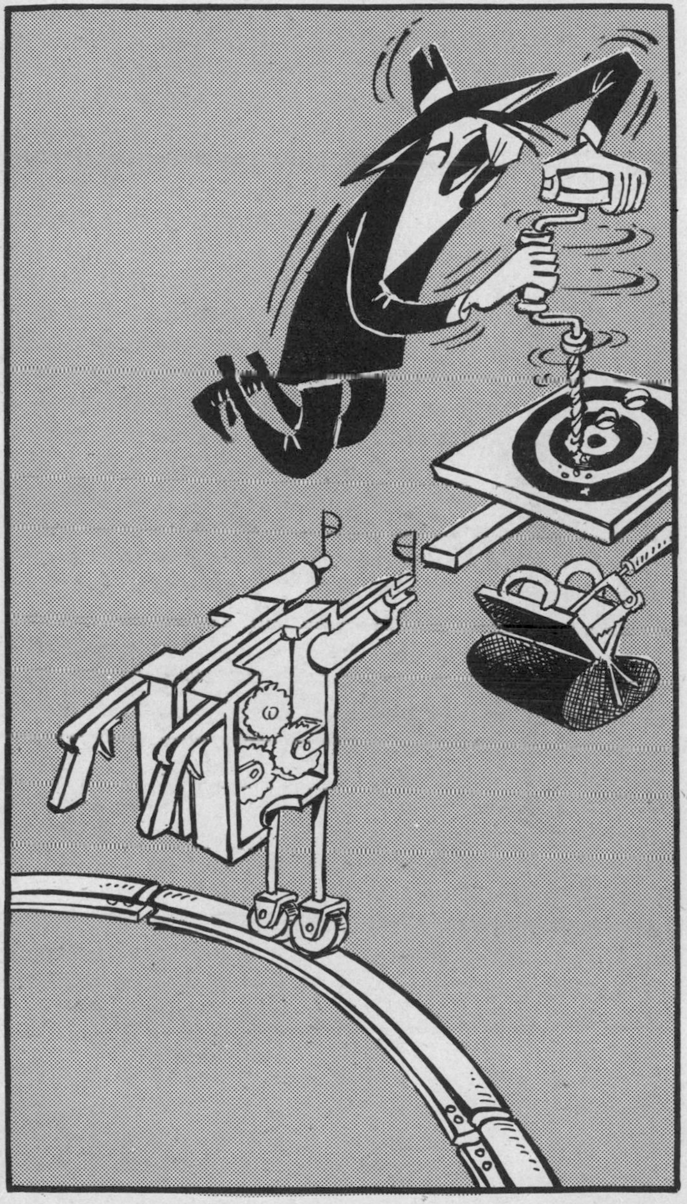

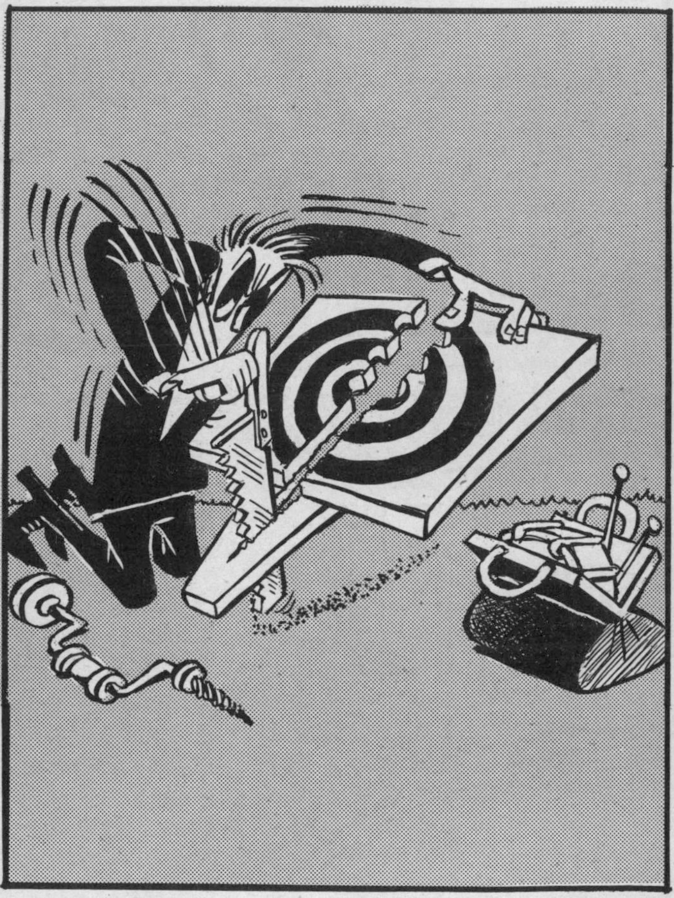

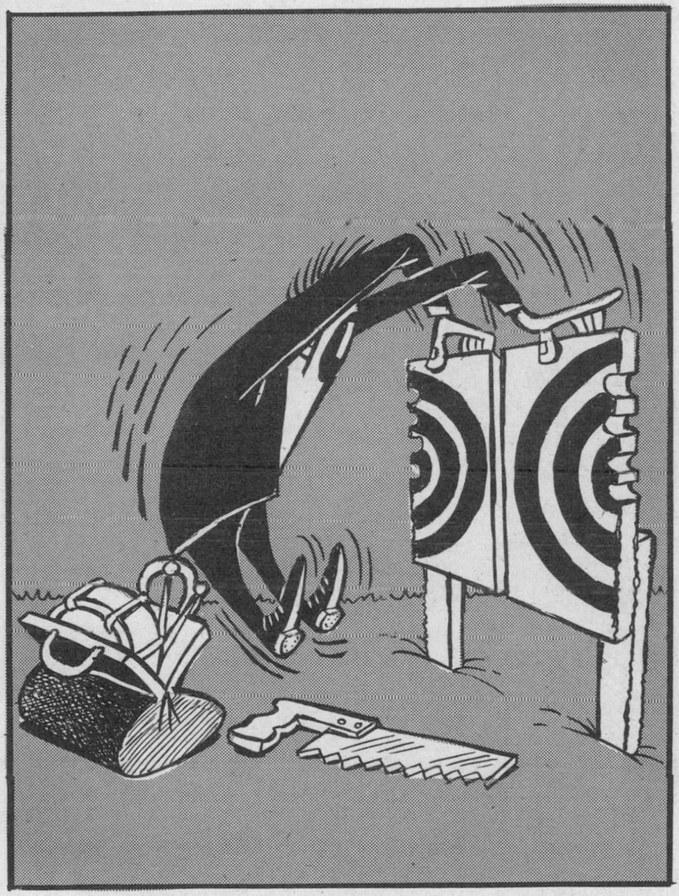

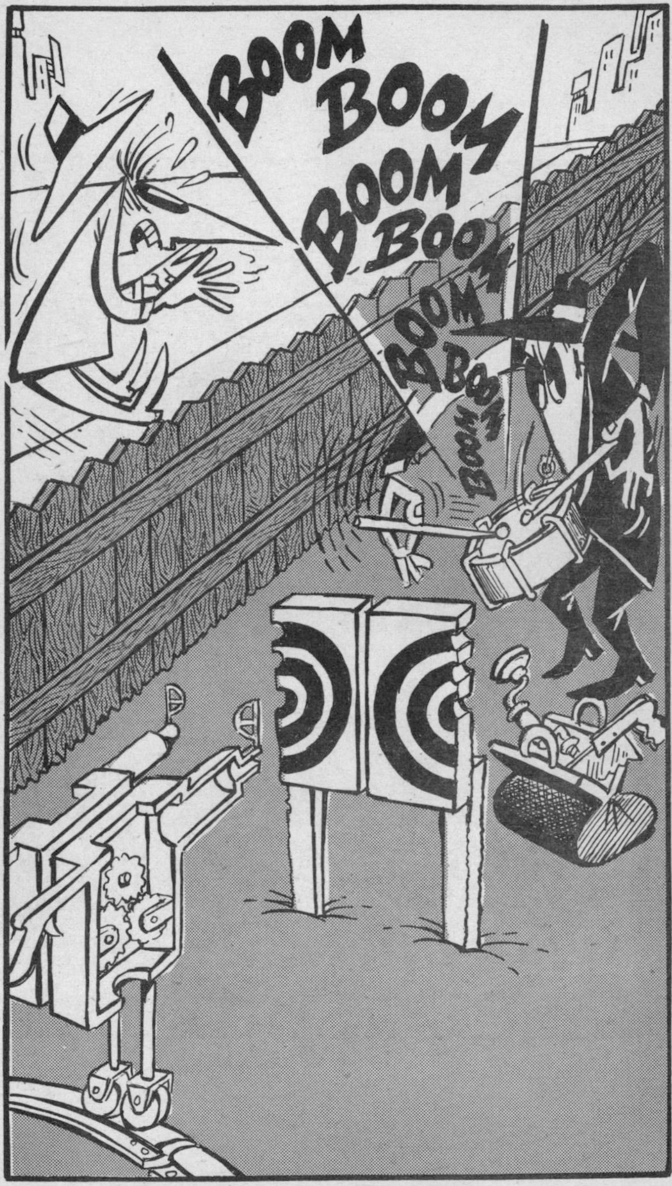

BOOM
BOOM
BOOM
BOOM
BOOM
BOOM
BOOM

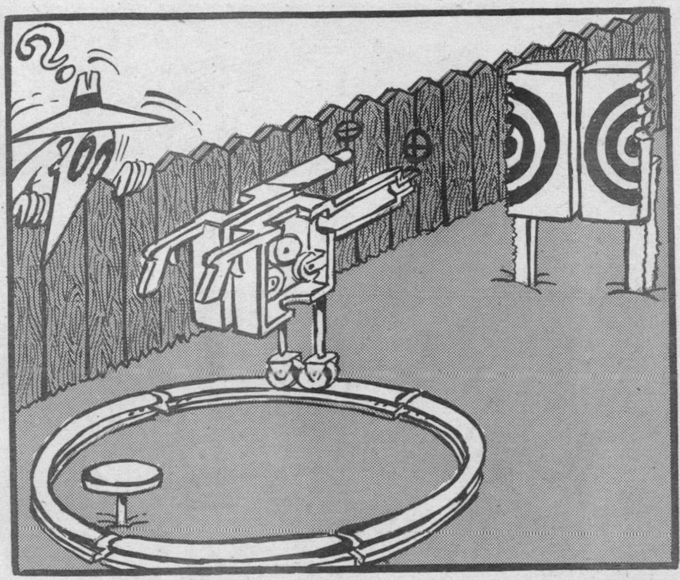

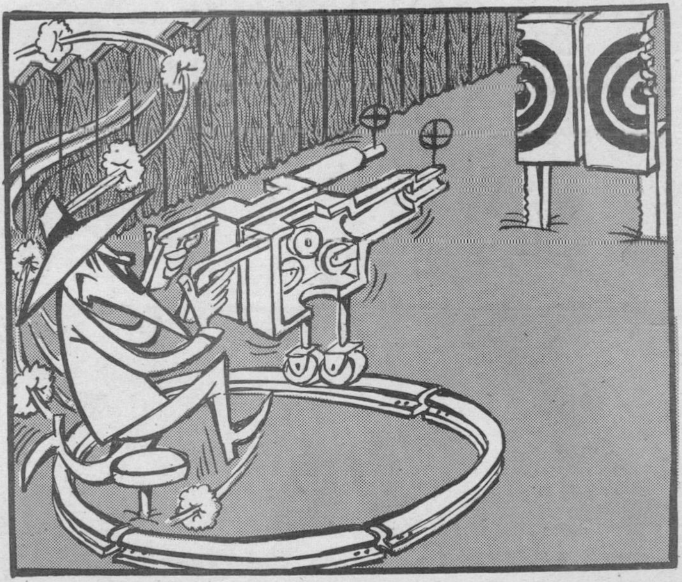

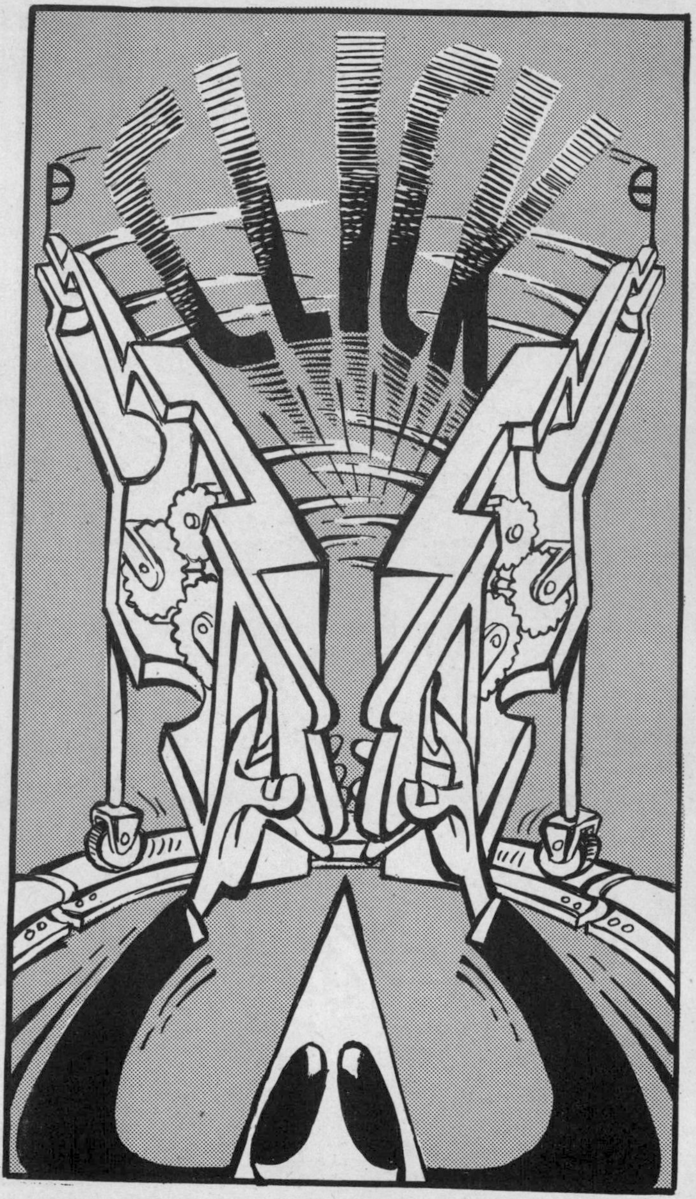
CLICK

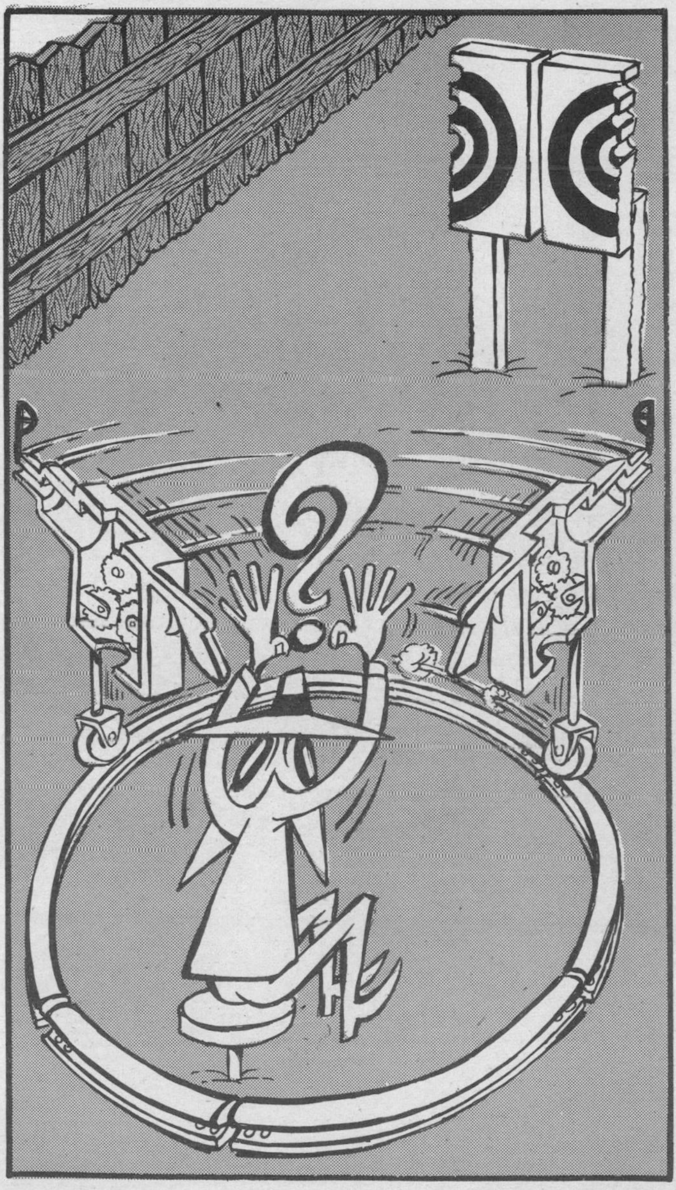

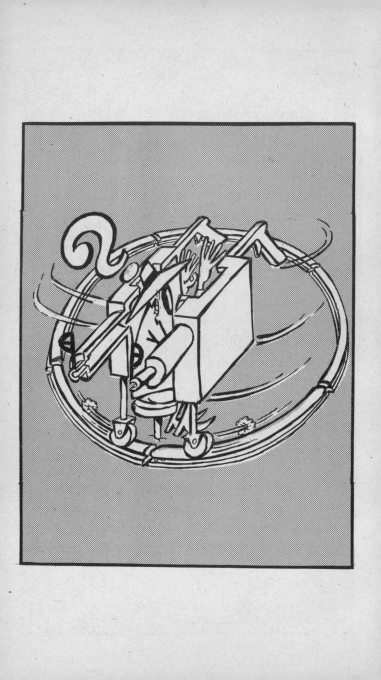

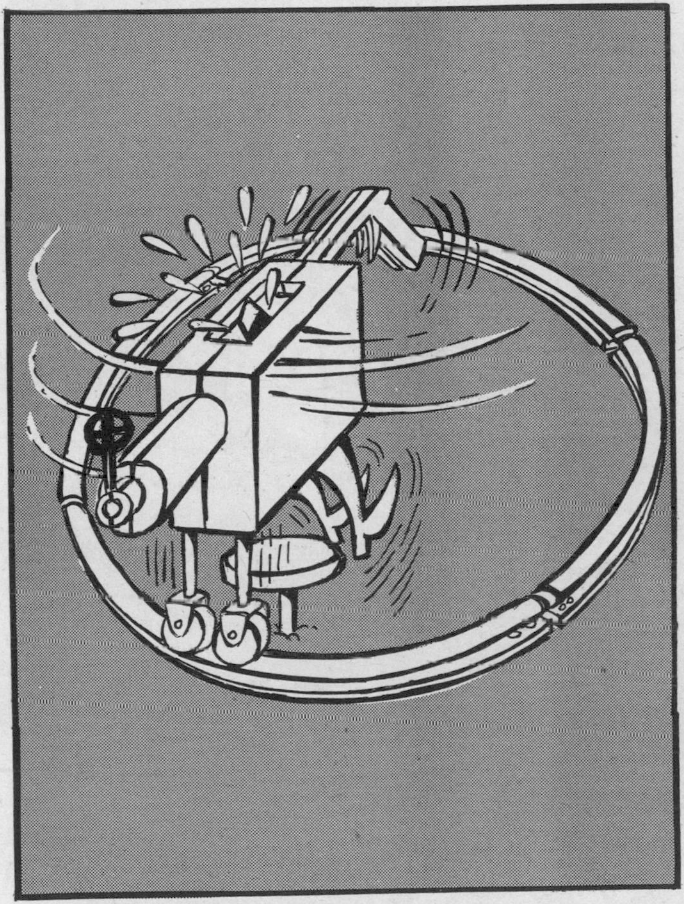

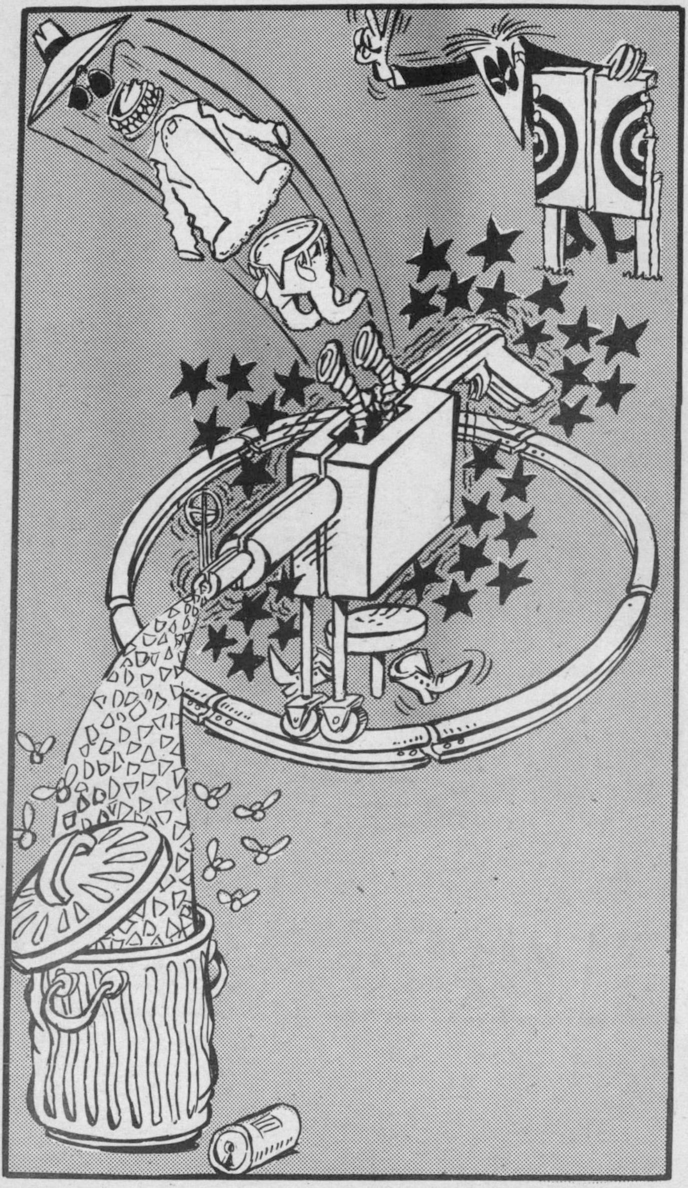

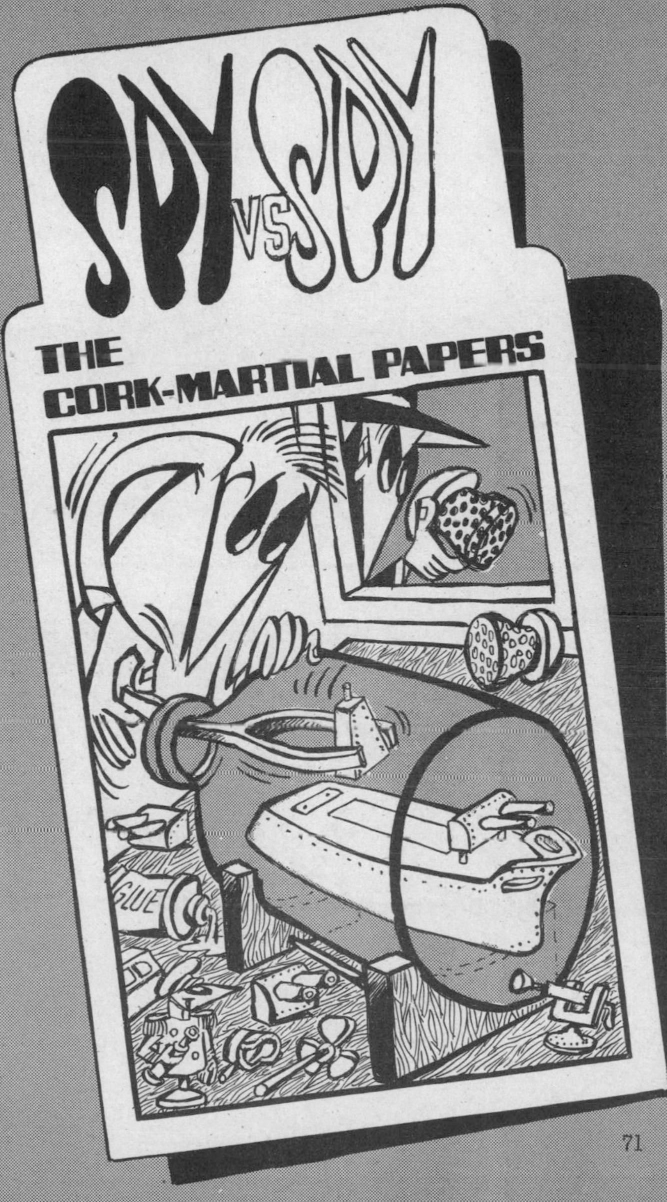
SPY vs SPY
THE CORK-MARTIAL PAPERS
GLUE

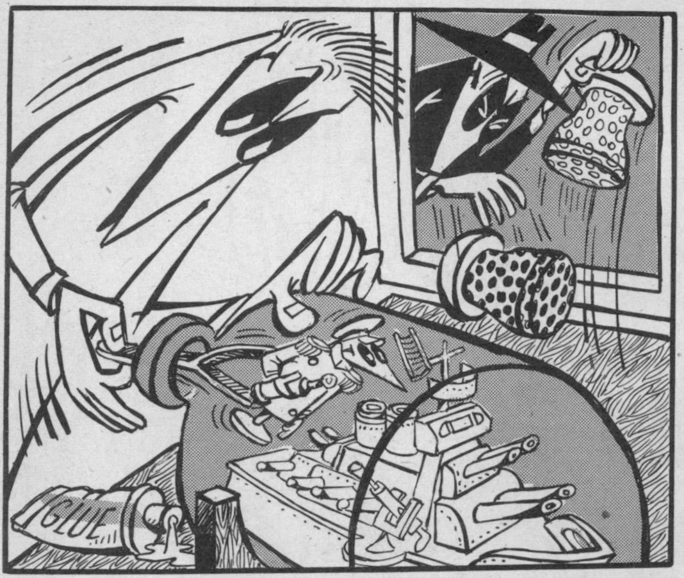
GLUE

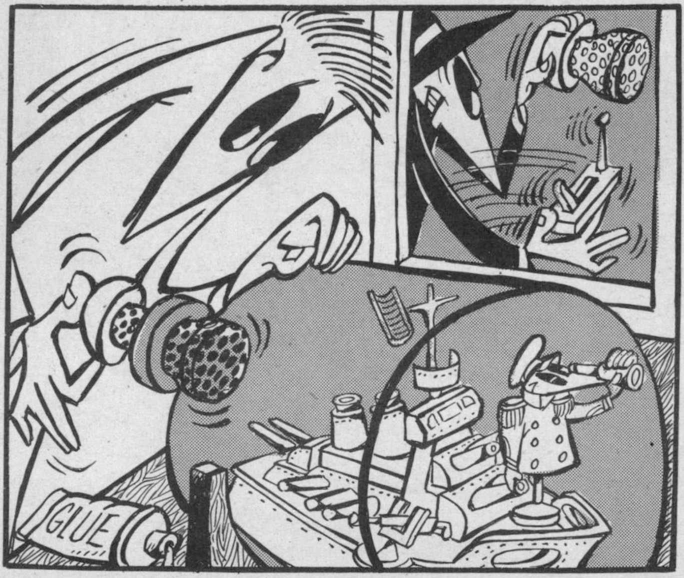
GLUE

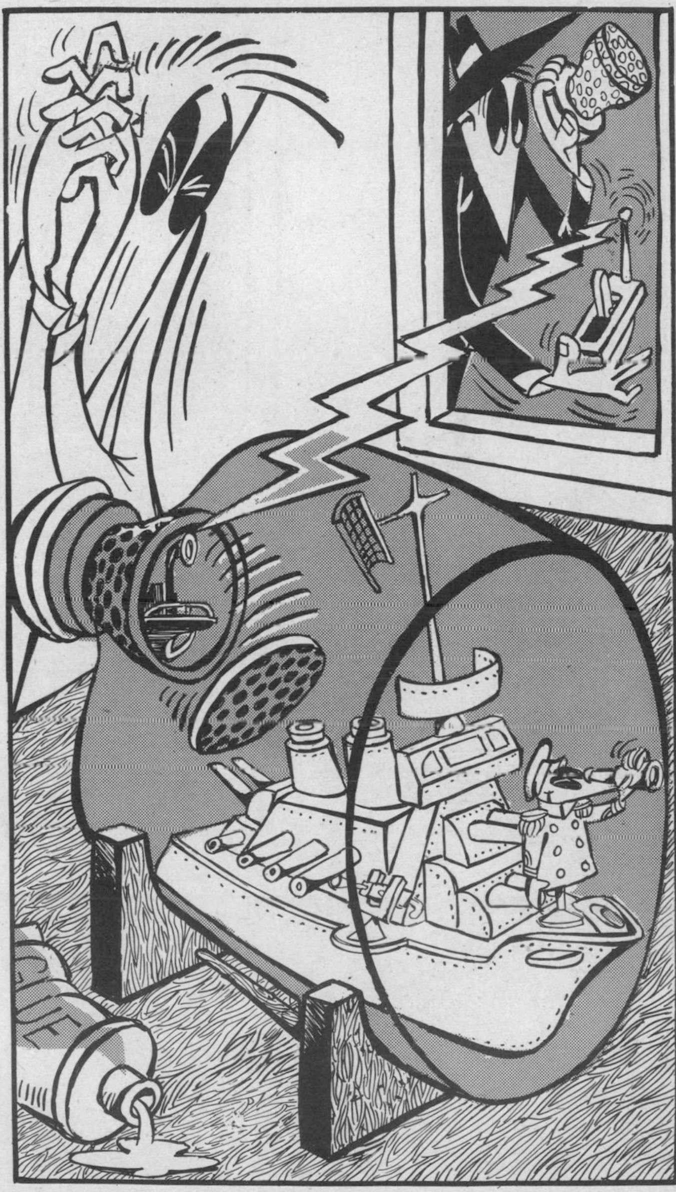

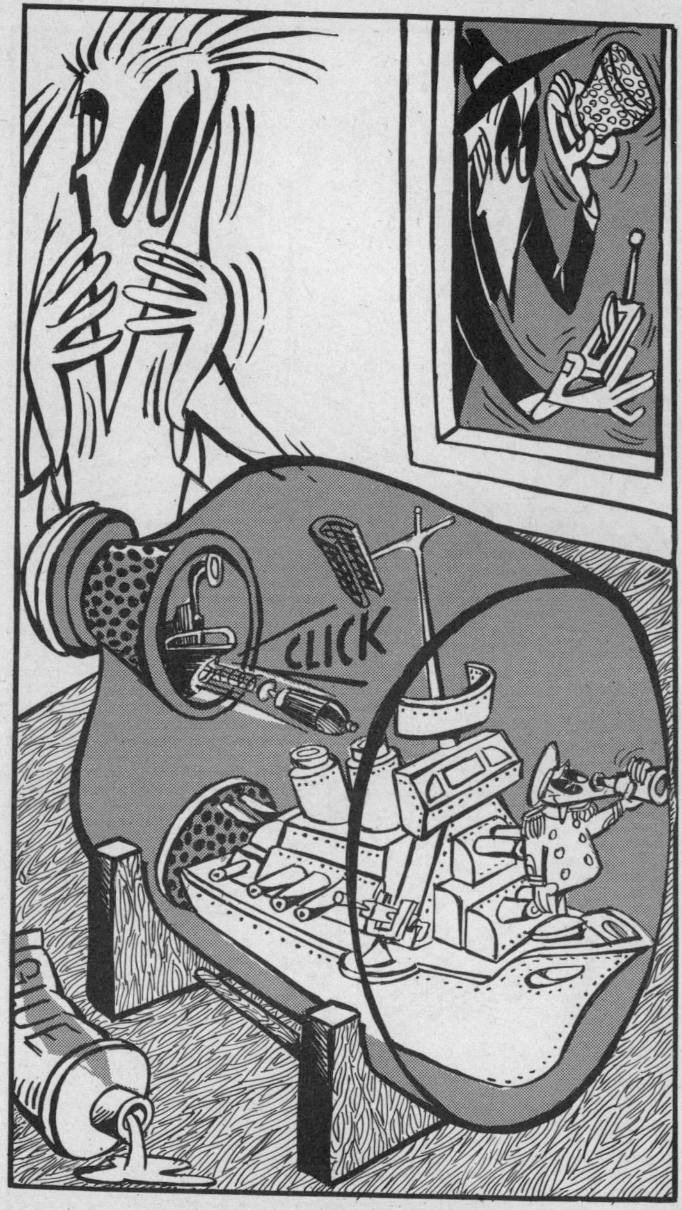
CLICK
GLUE

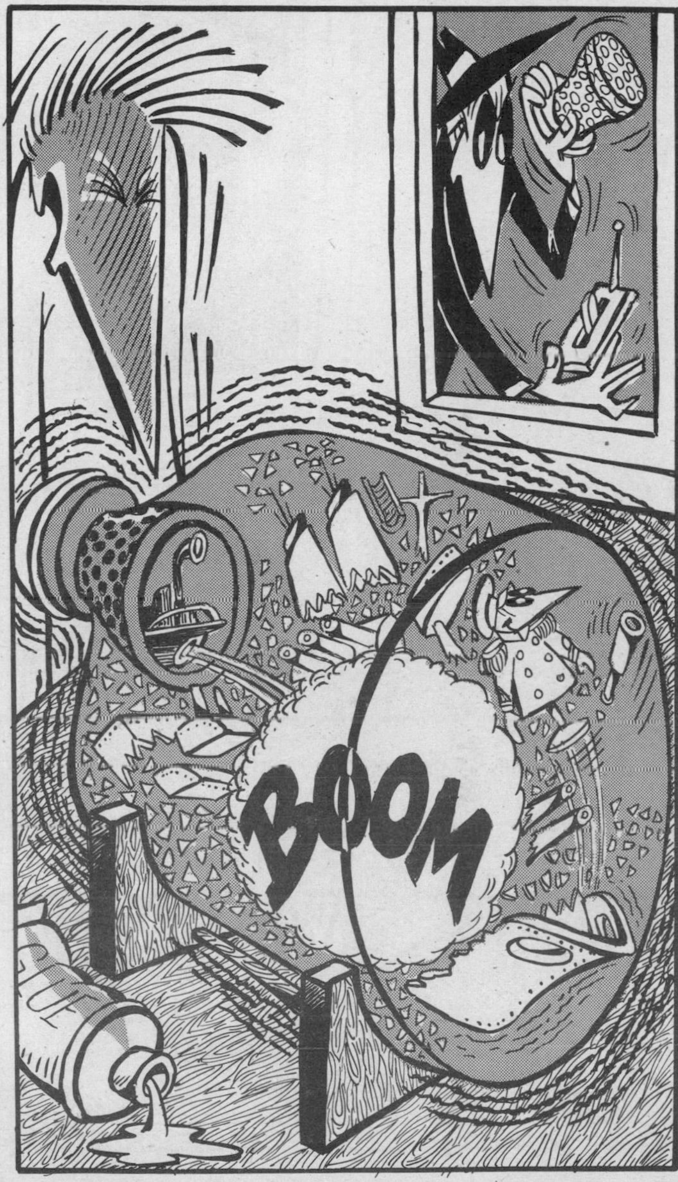
BOOM

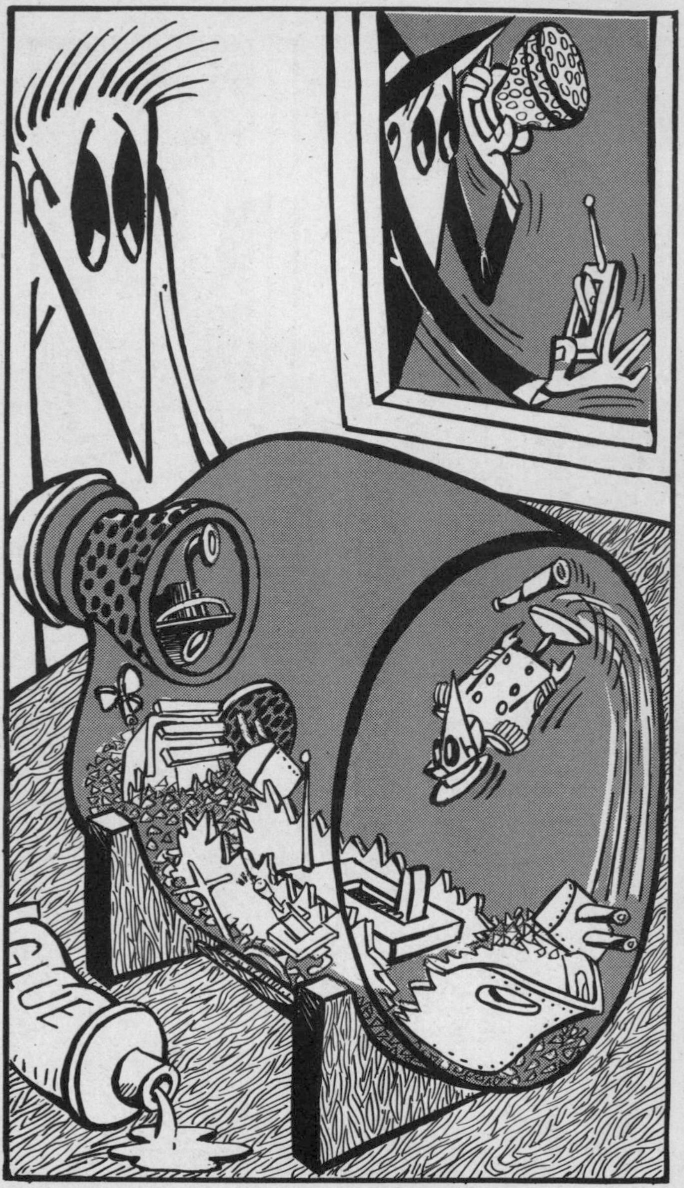
GLUE

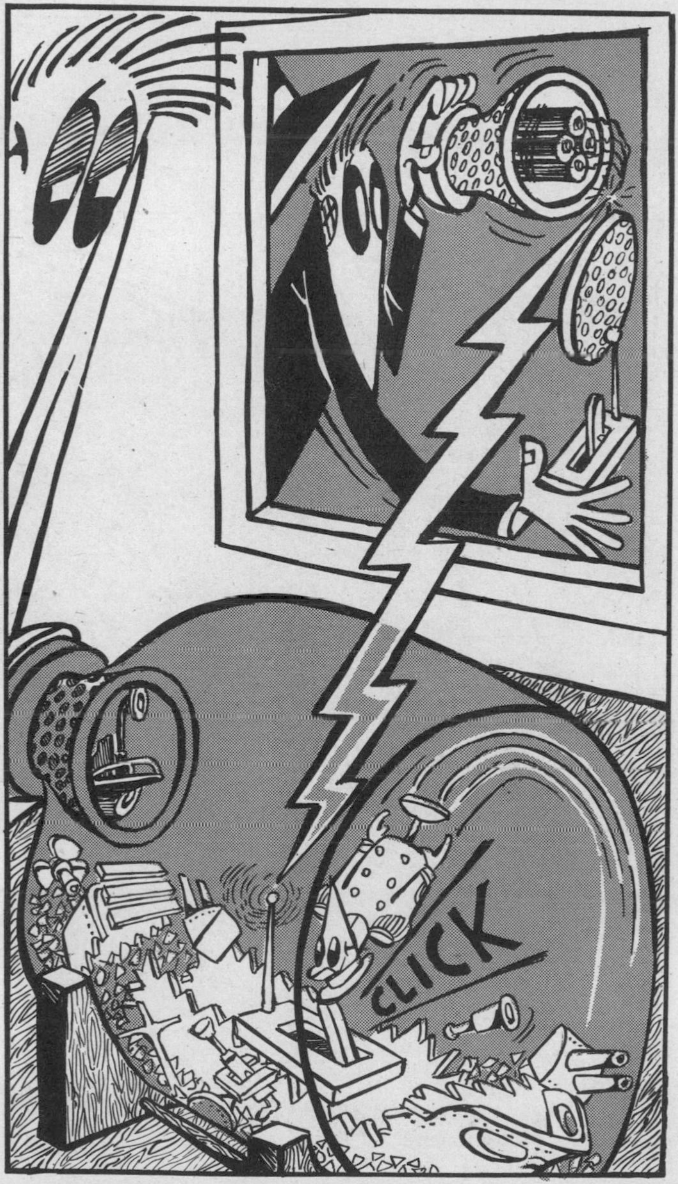
CLICK

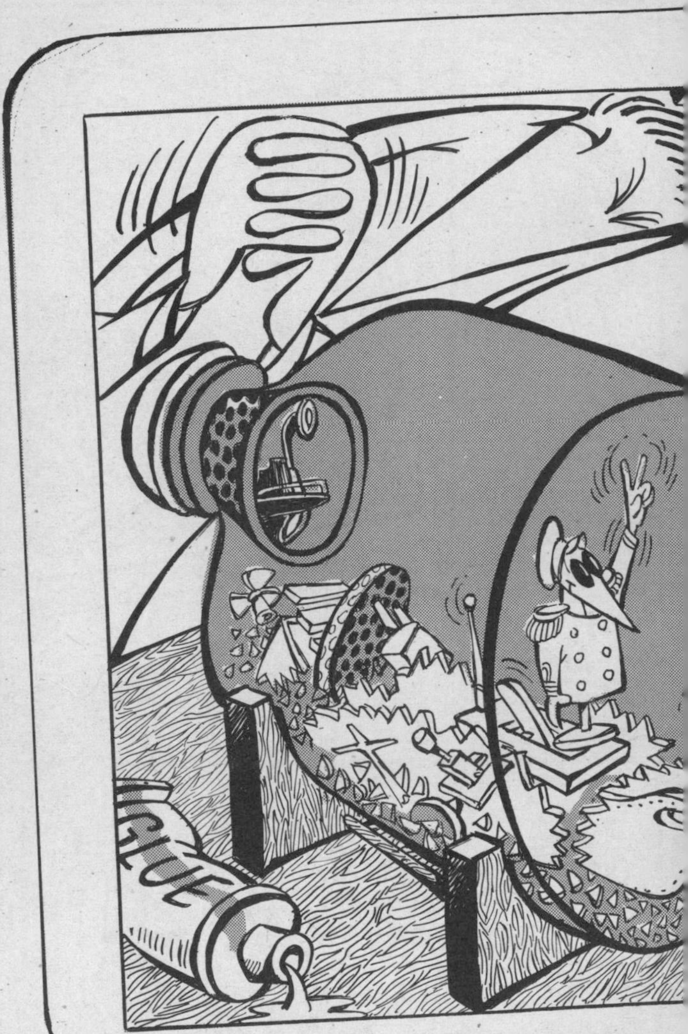
GLUE

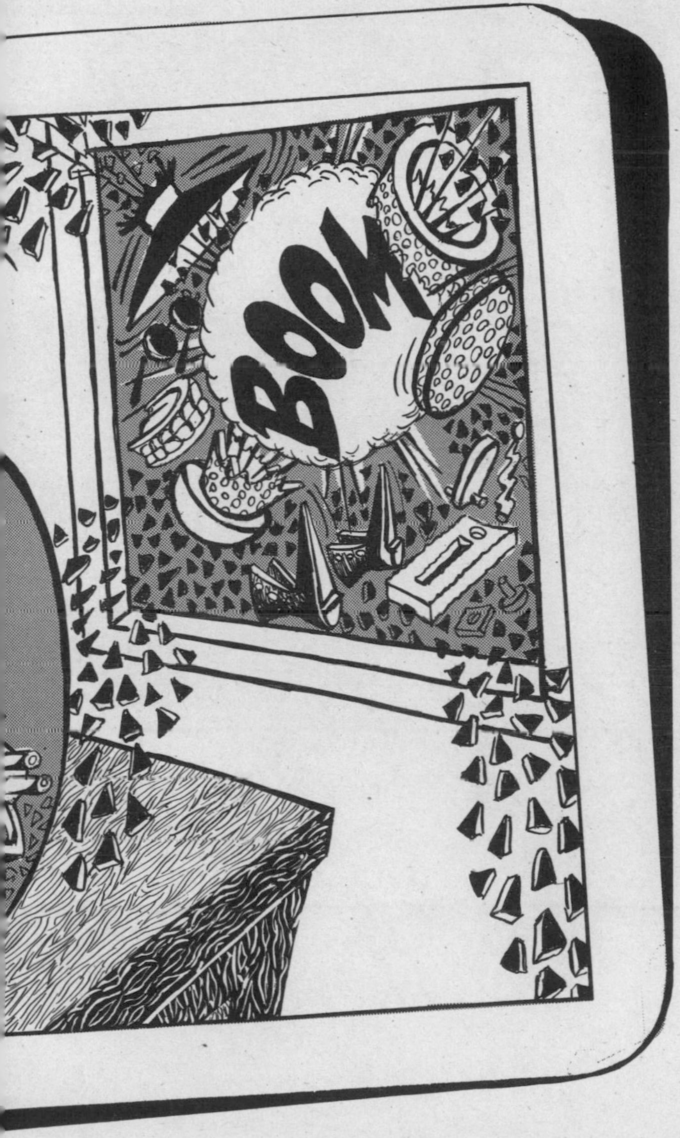
BOOM

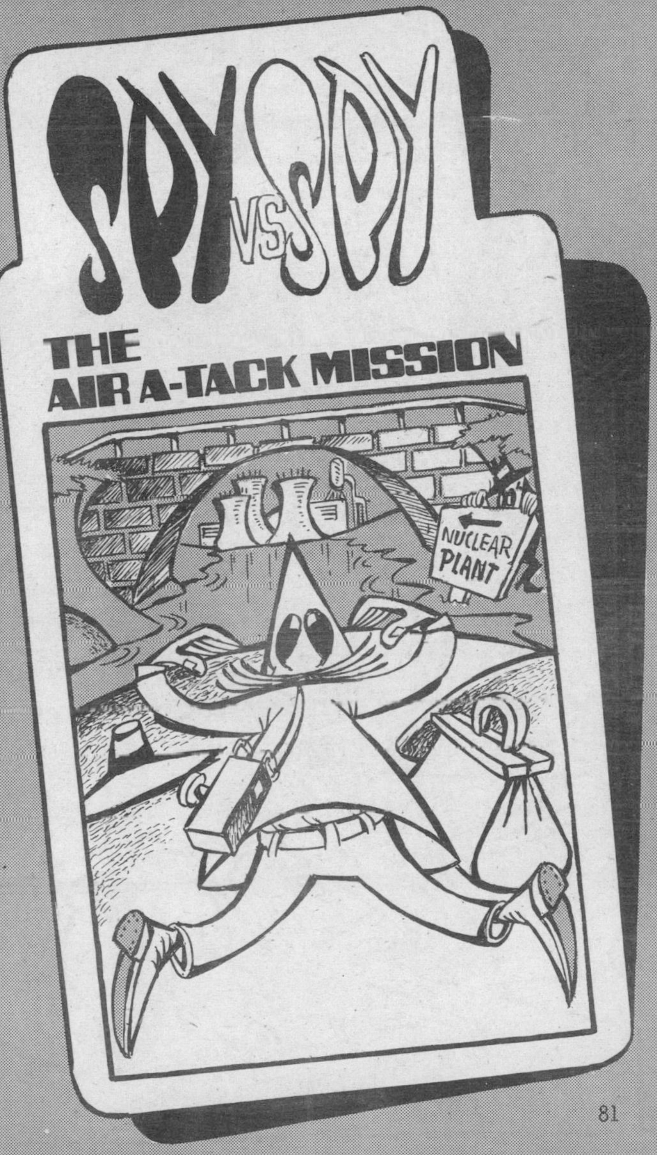
SPY VS SPY
THE AIR A-TACK MISSION
NUCLEAR PLANT

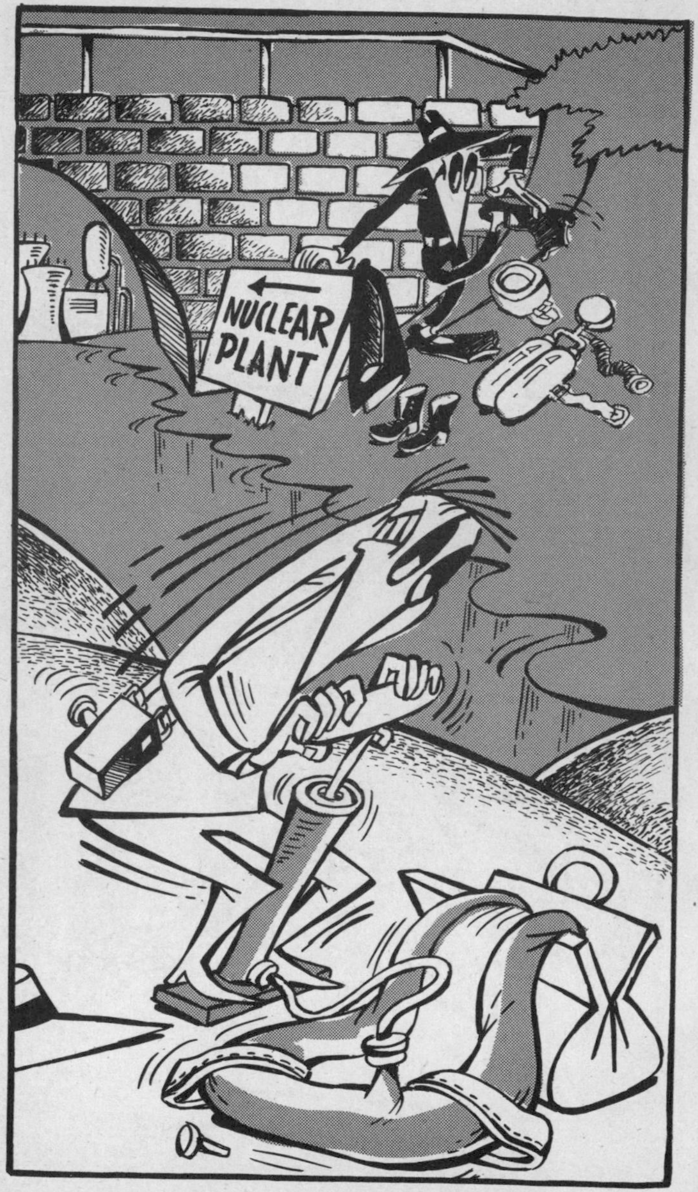
NUCLEAR
PLANT

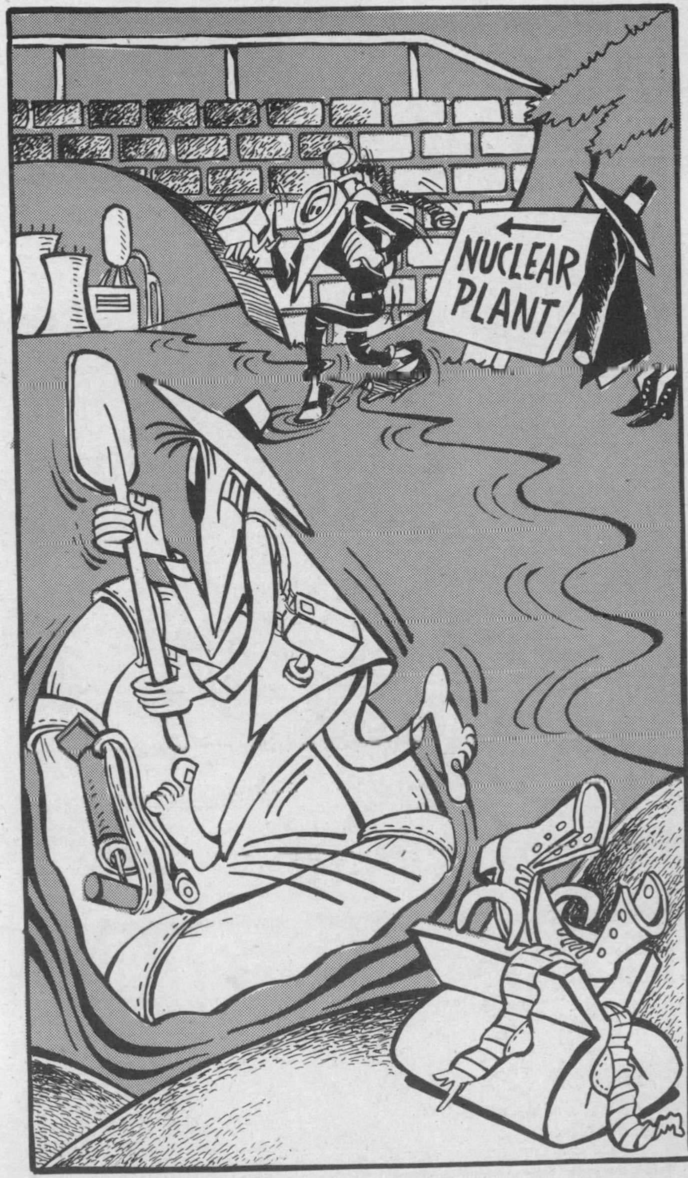

NUCLEAR PLANT

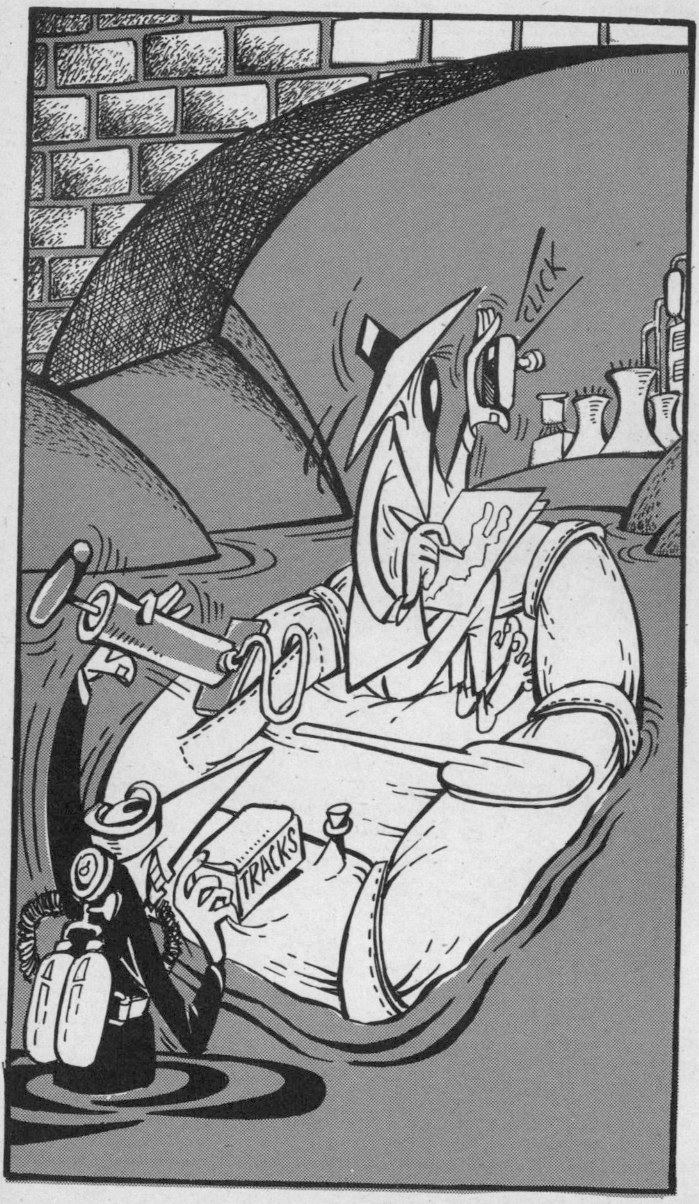
CLICK
TRACKS

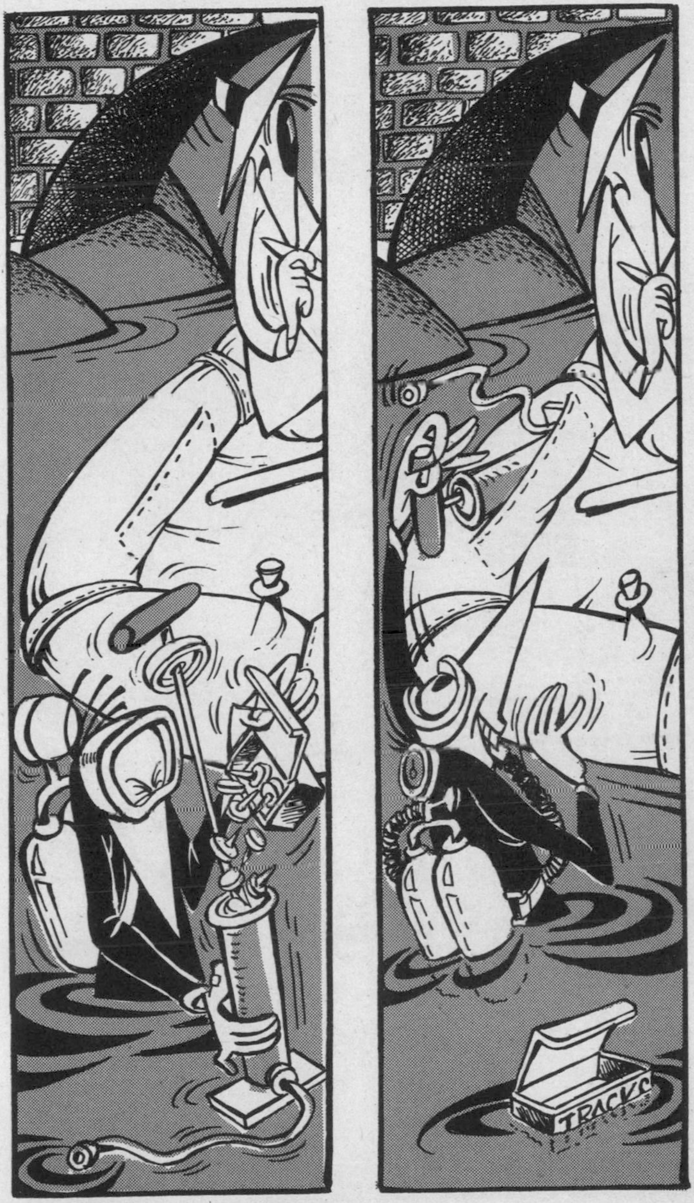
TRACKS

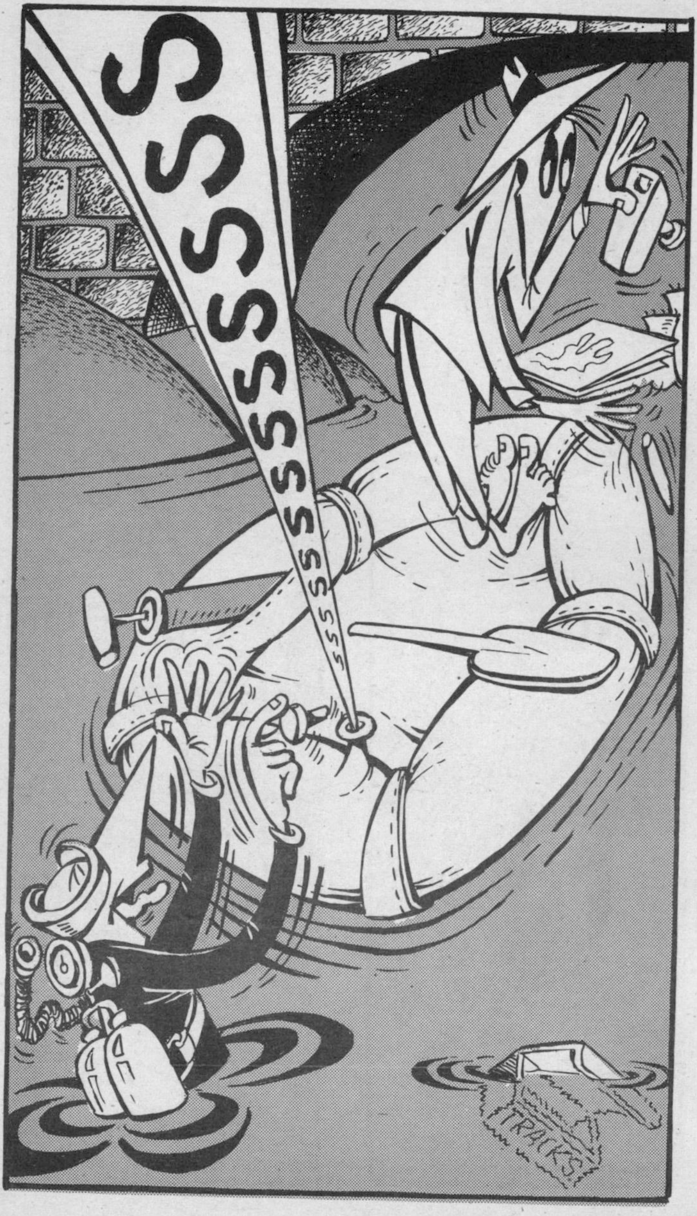
SSSSSSSSSSSSSS
TRACKS

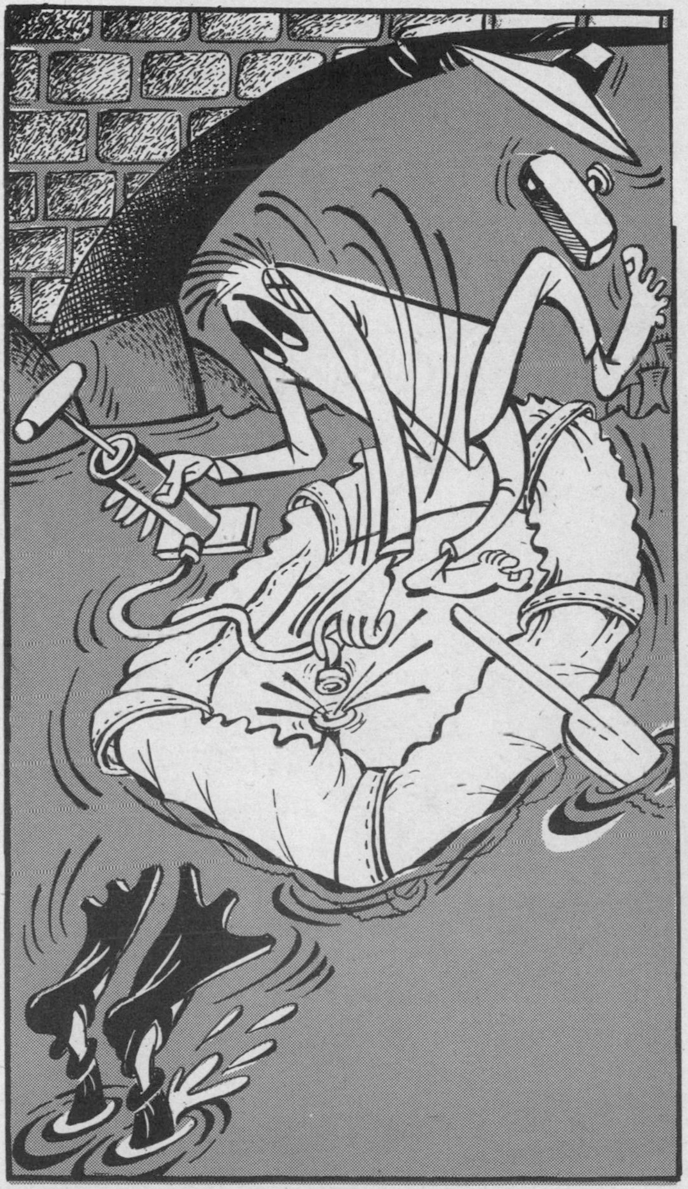

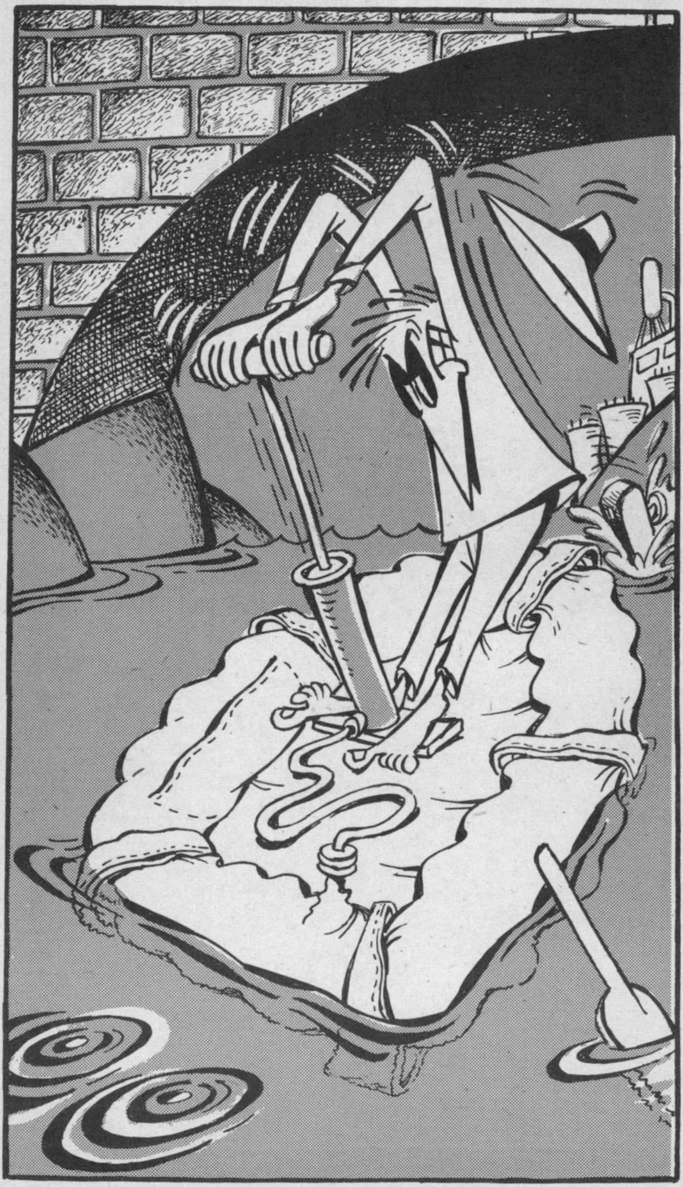

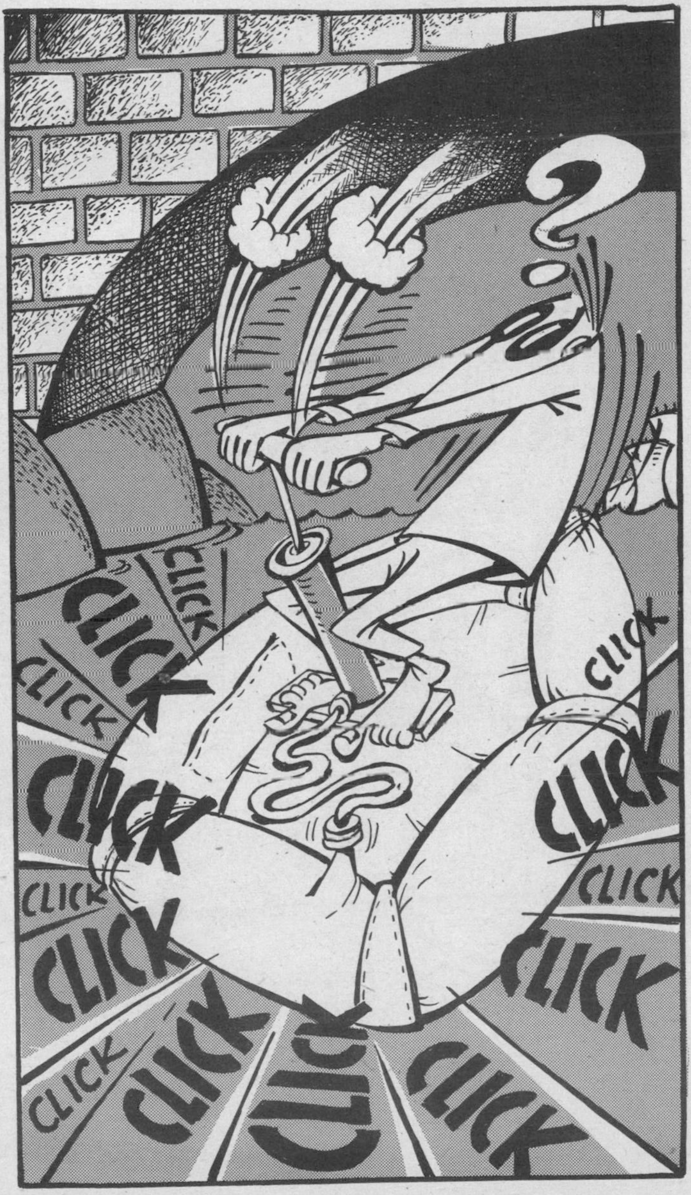
?
CLICK
CLICK
CLICK
CLICK
CLICK
CLICK
CLICK
CLICK
CLICK
CLICK
CLICK
CLICK
CLICK
CLICK

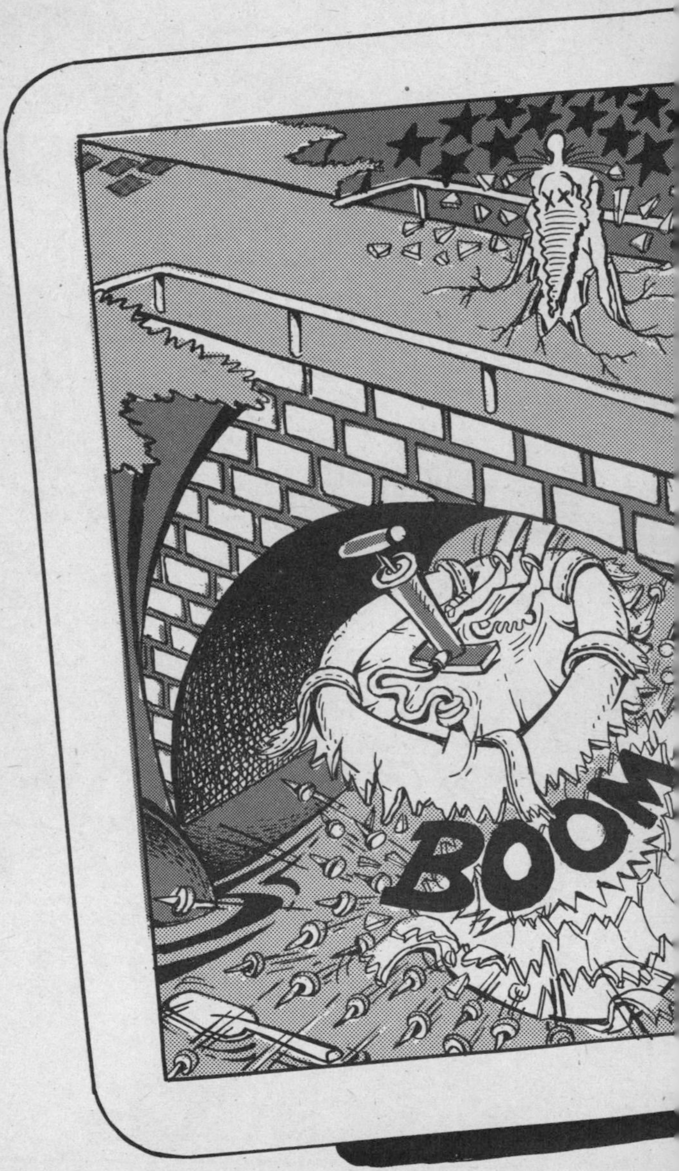
BOO

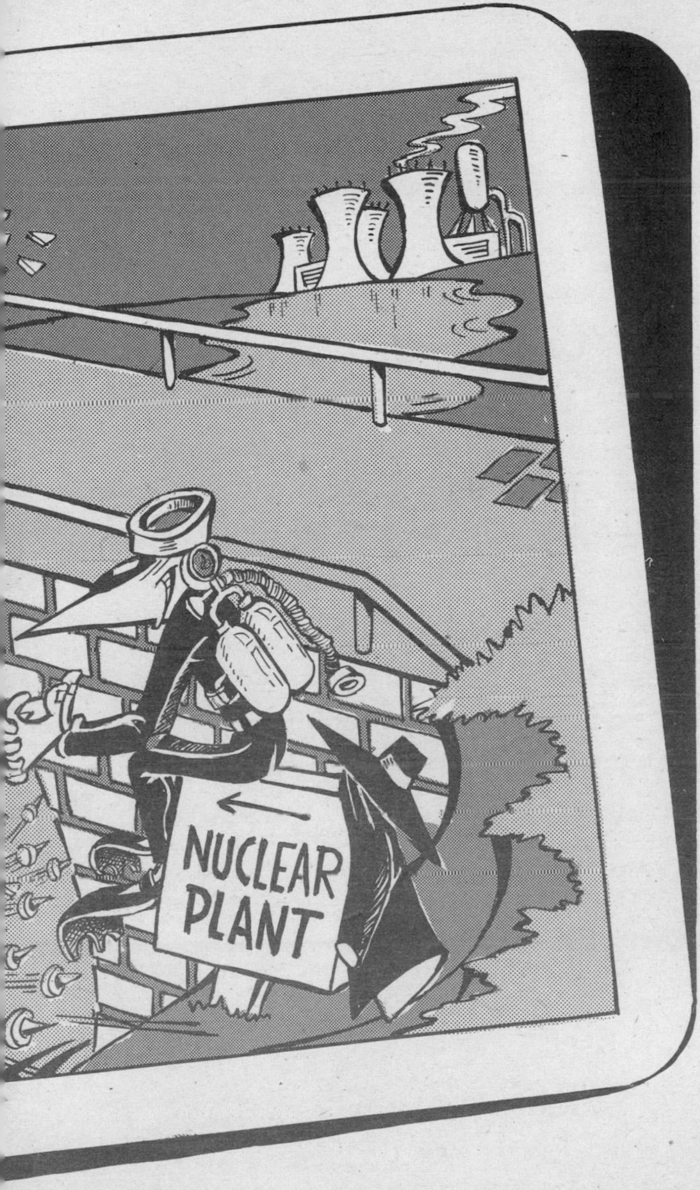
NUCLEAR
PLANT

SPY vs SPY

the POOL SHARK PORTFOLIO

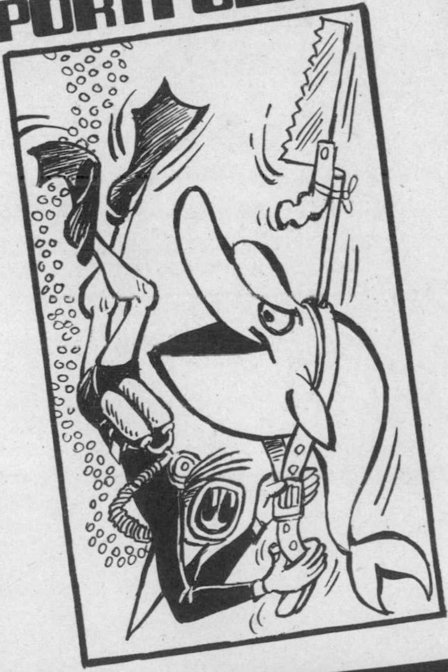

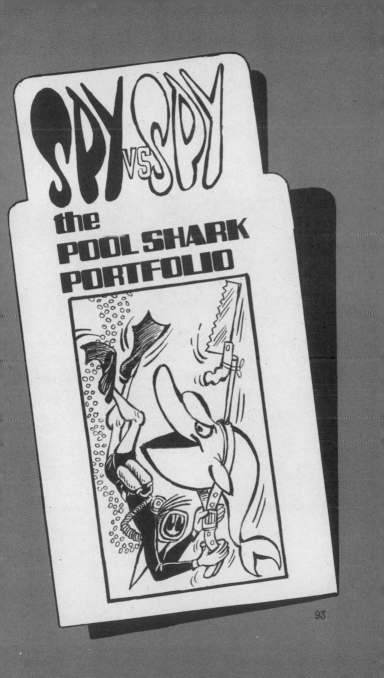

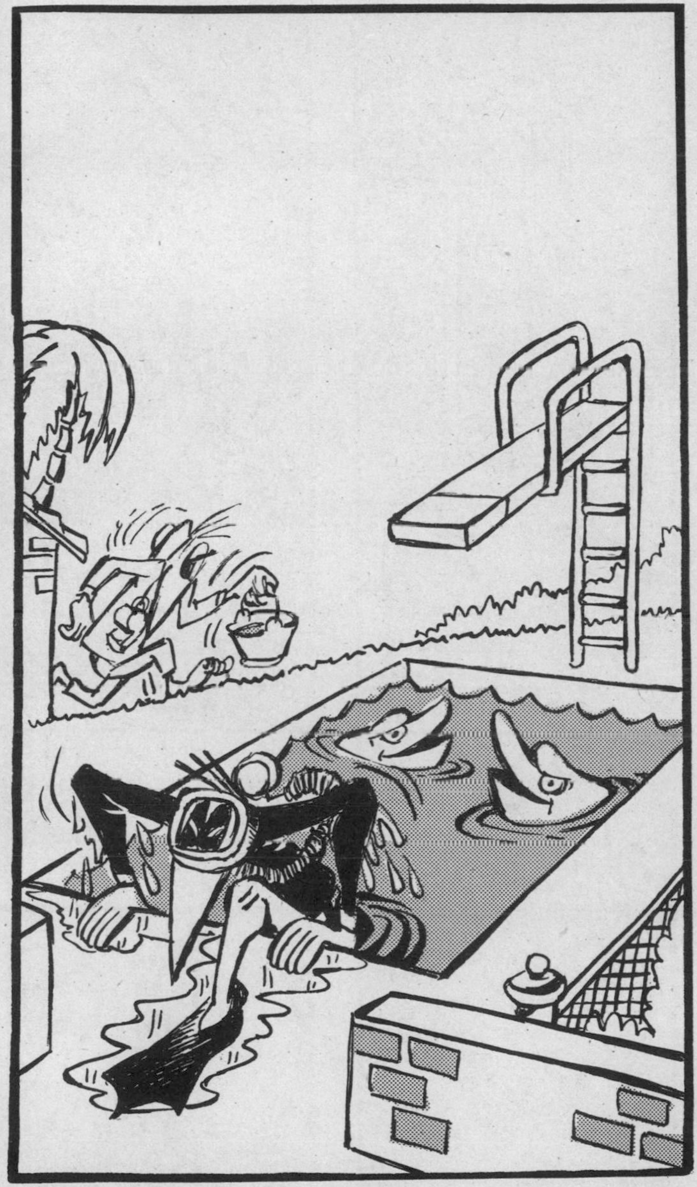

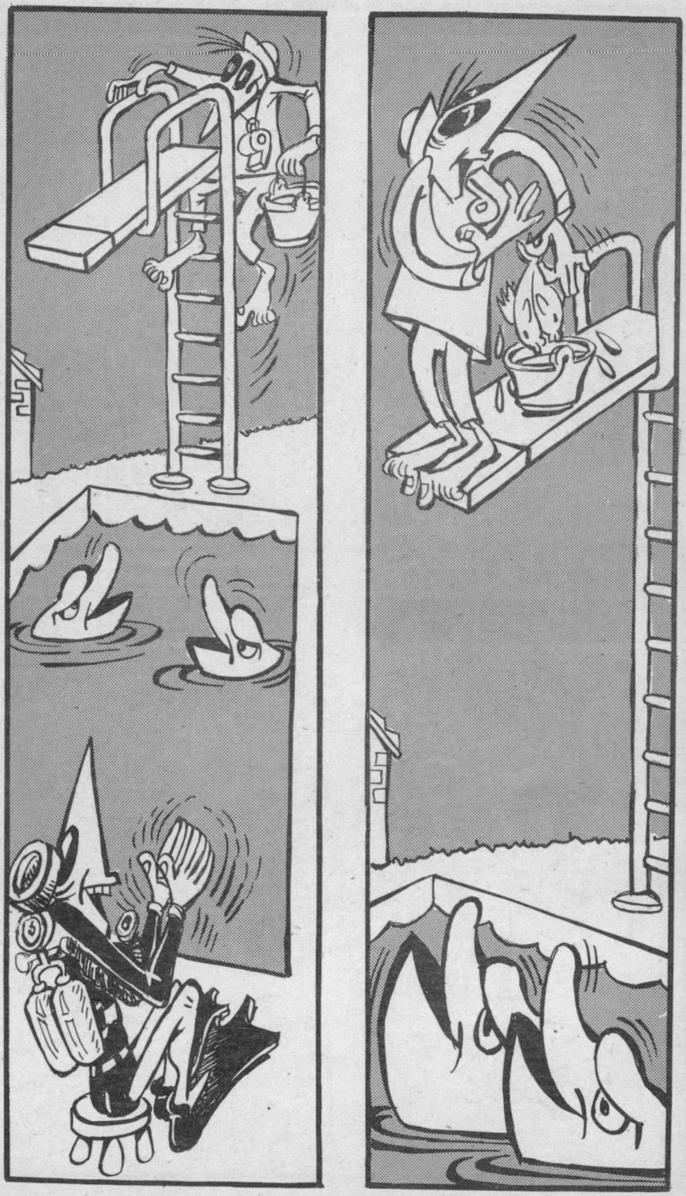

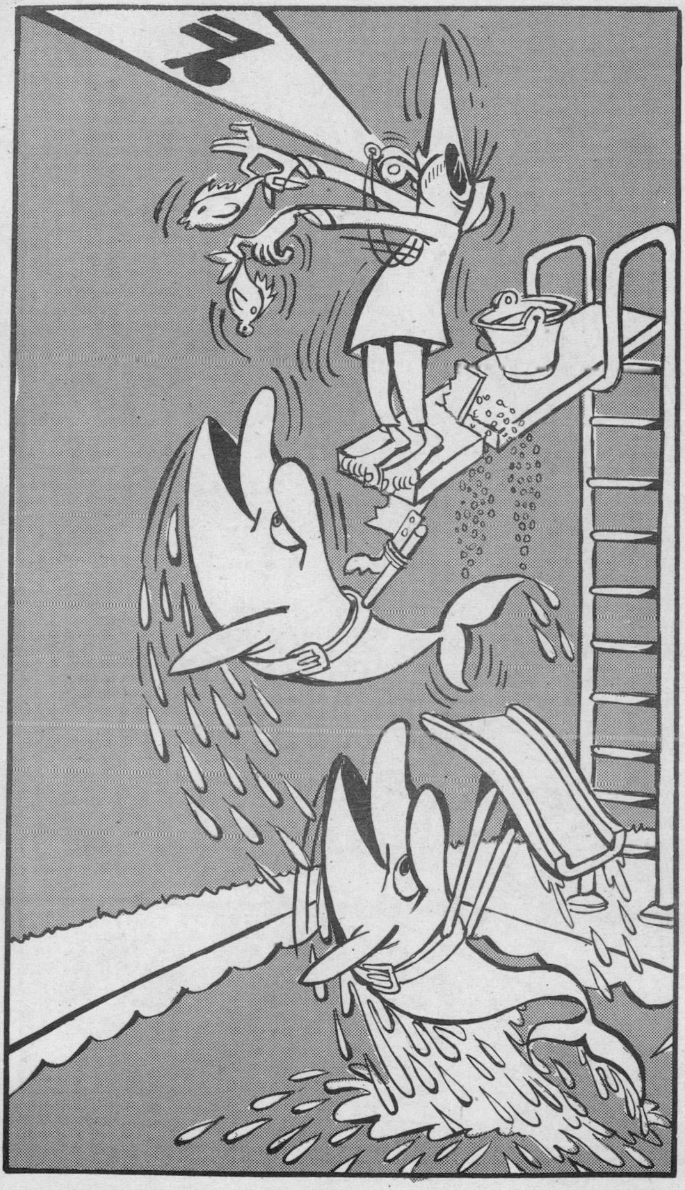
7

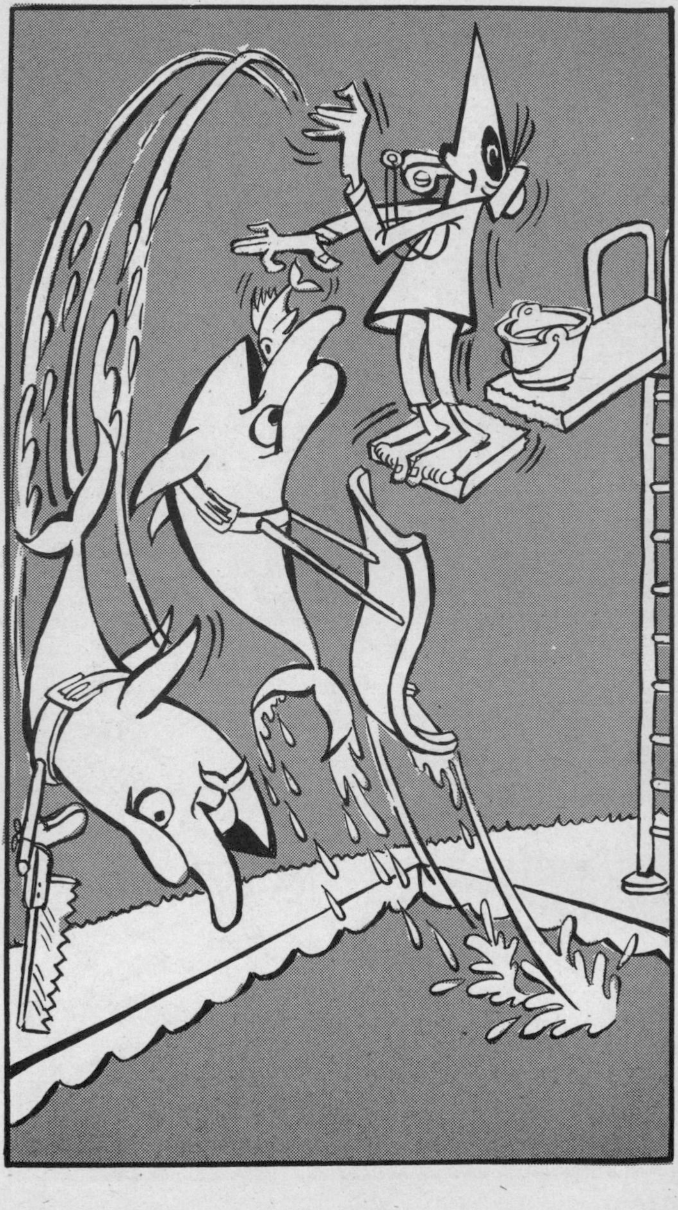

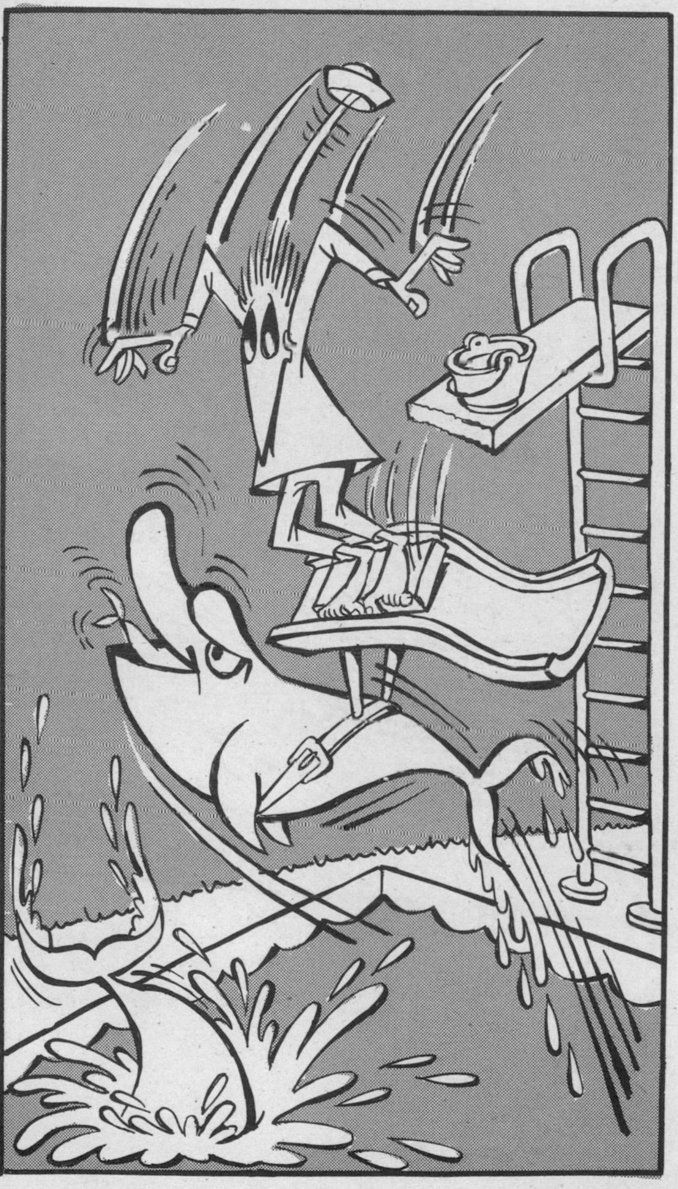

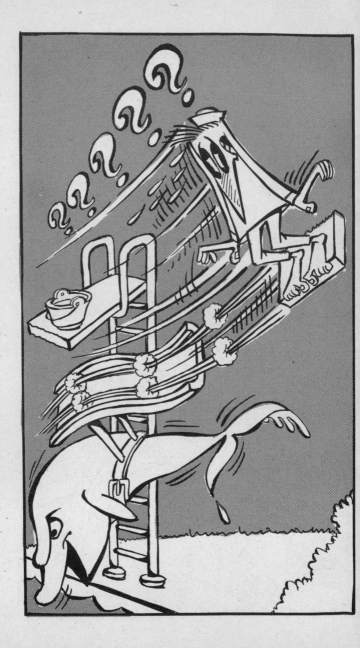

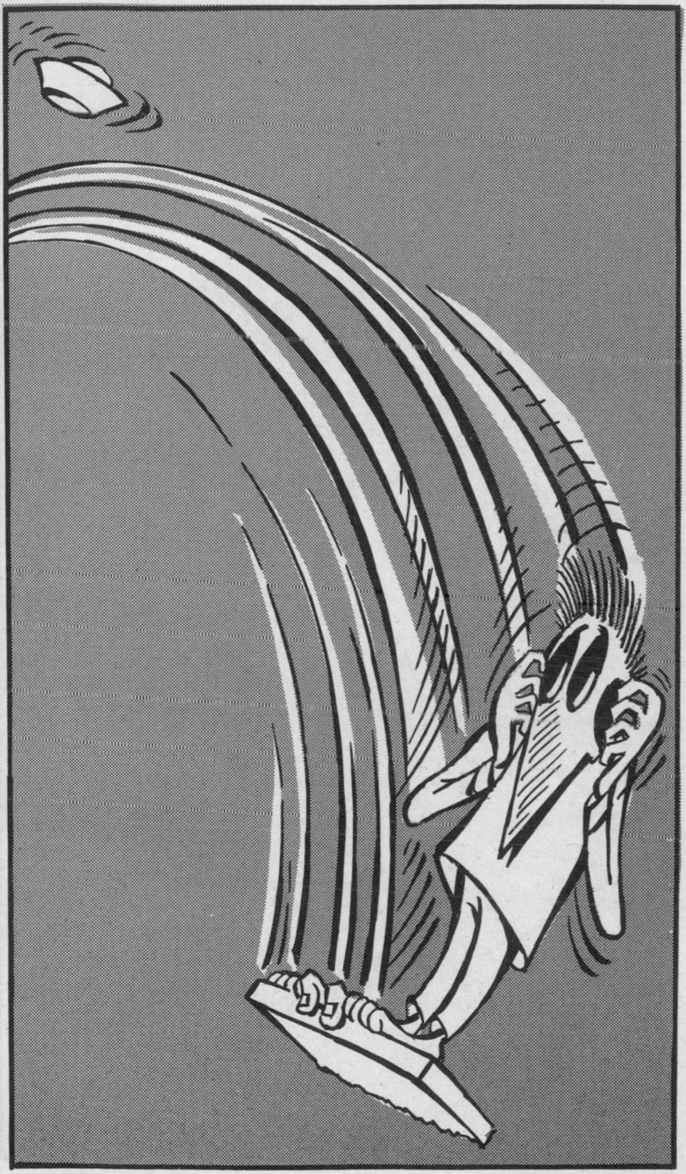

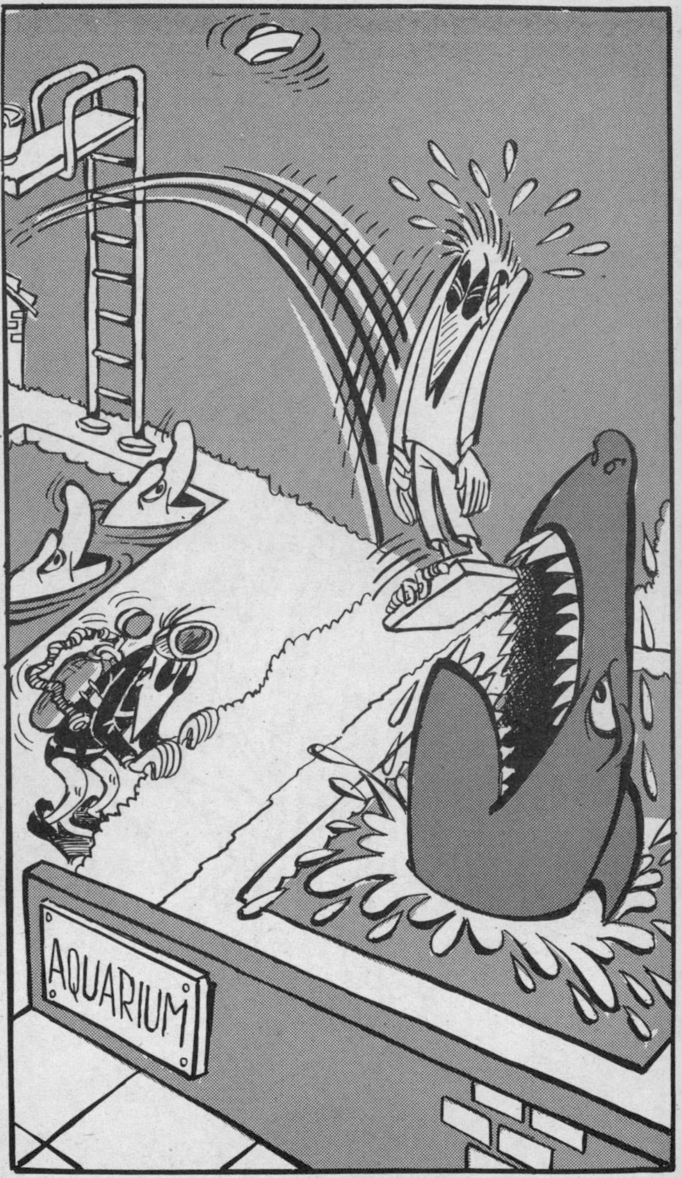
AQUARIUM

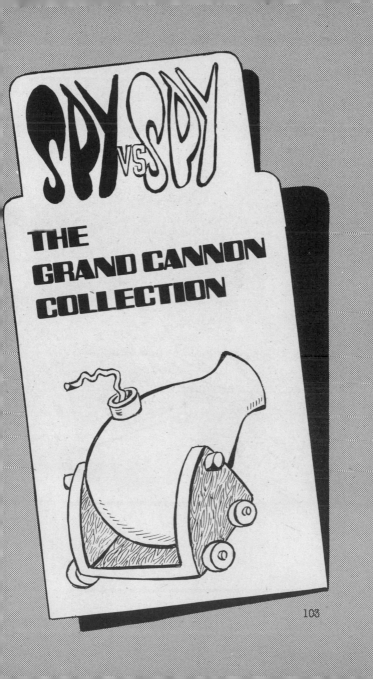

SPY vs SPY

THE GRAND CANNON COLLECTION

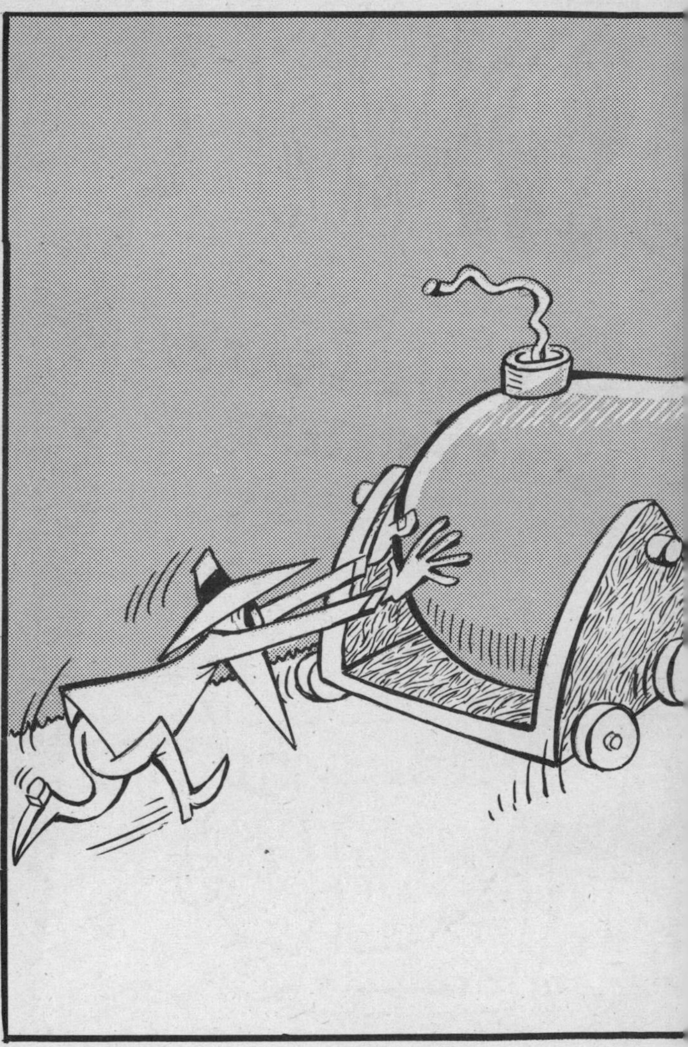

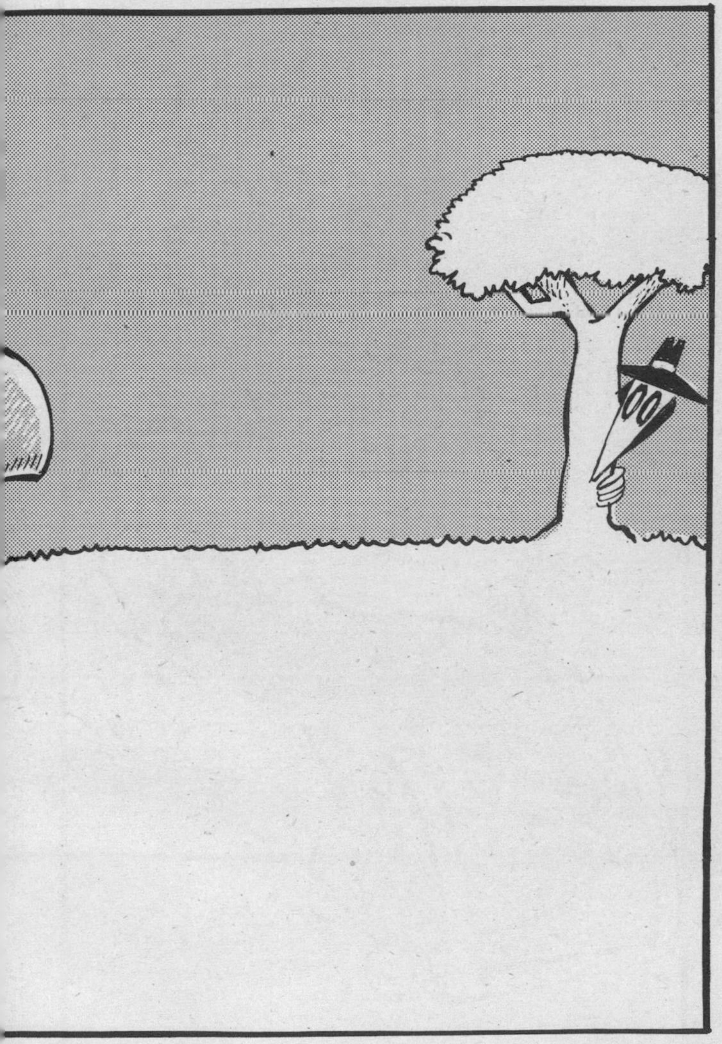

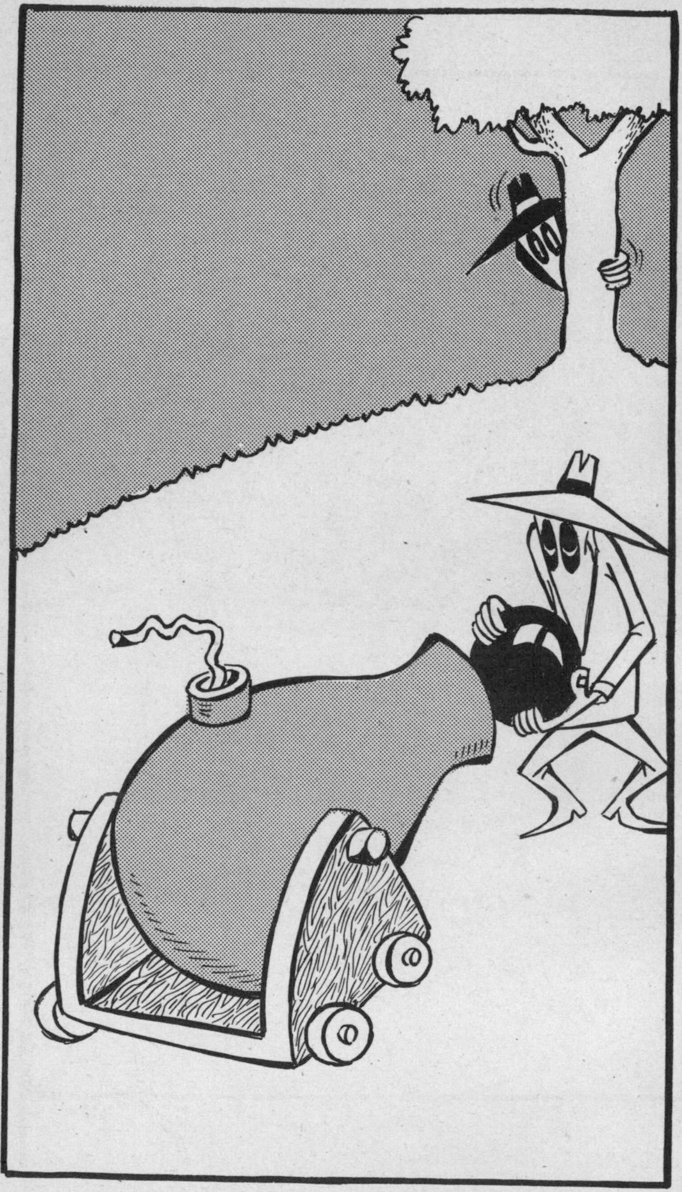

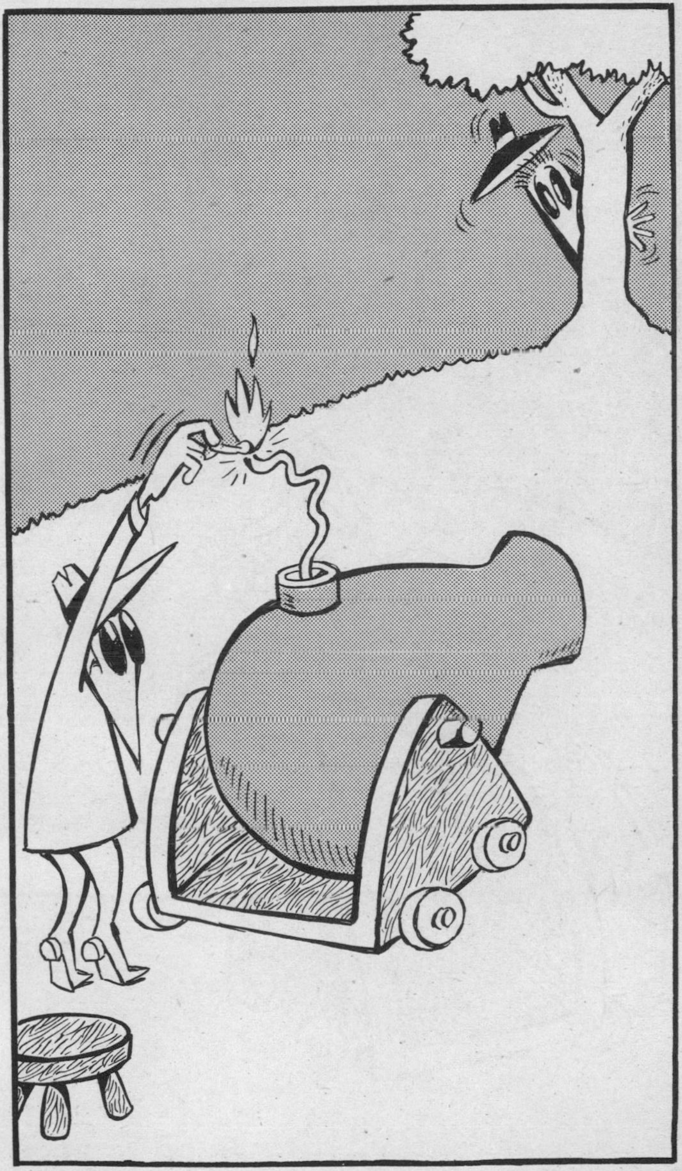

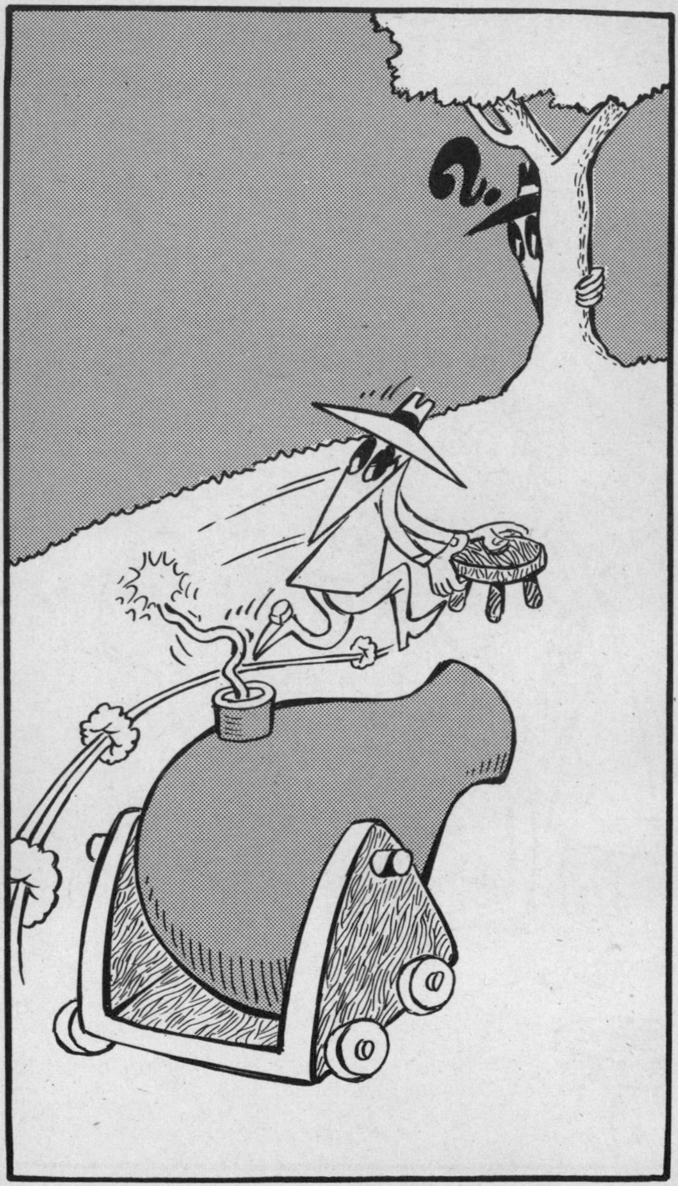

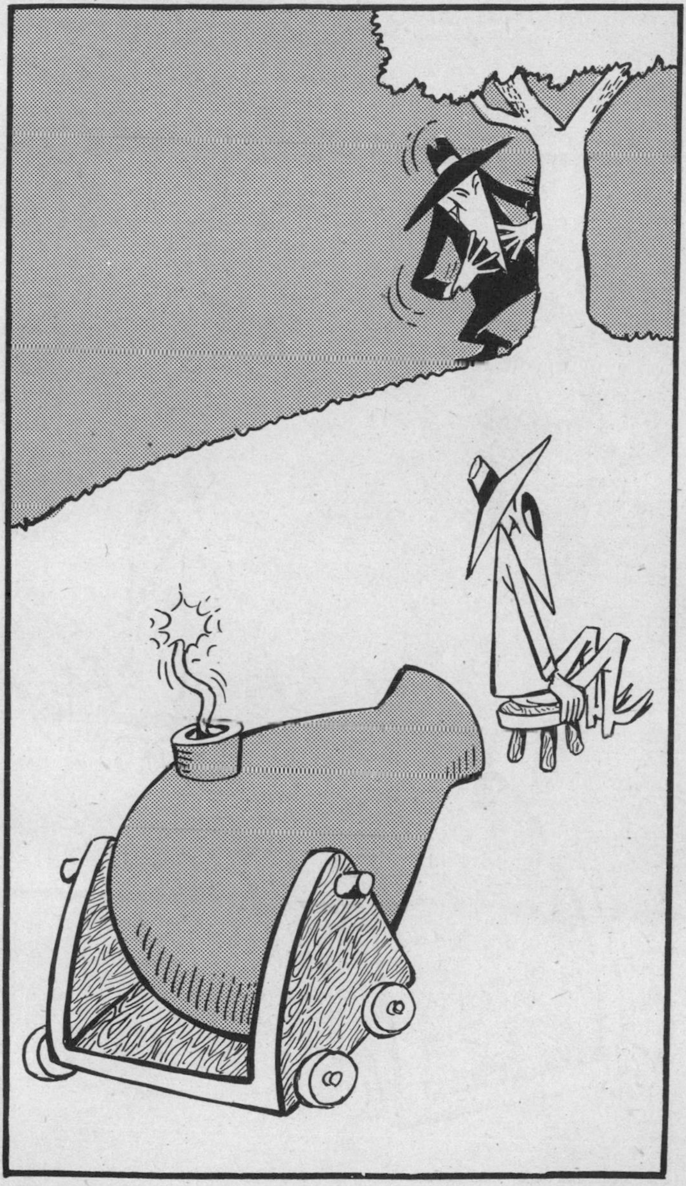

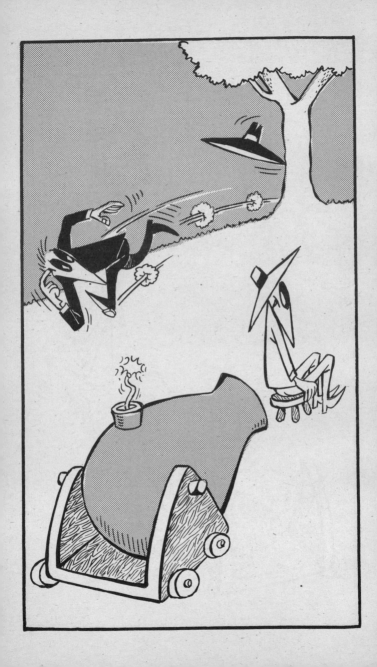

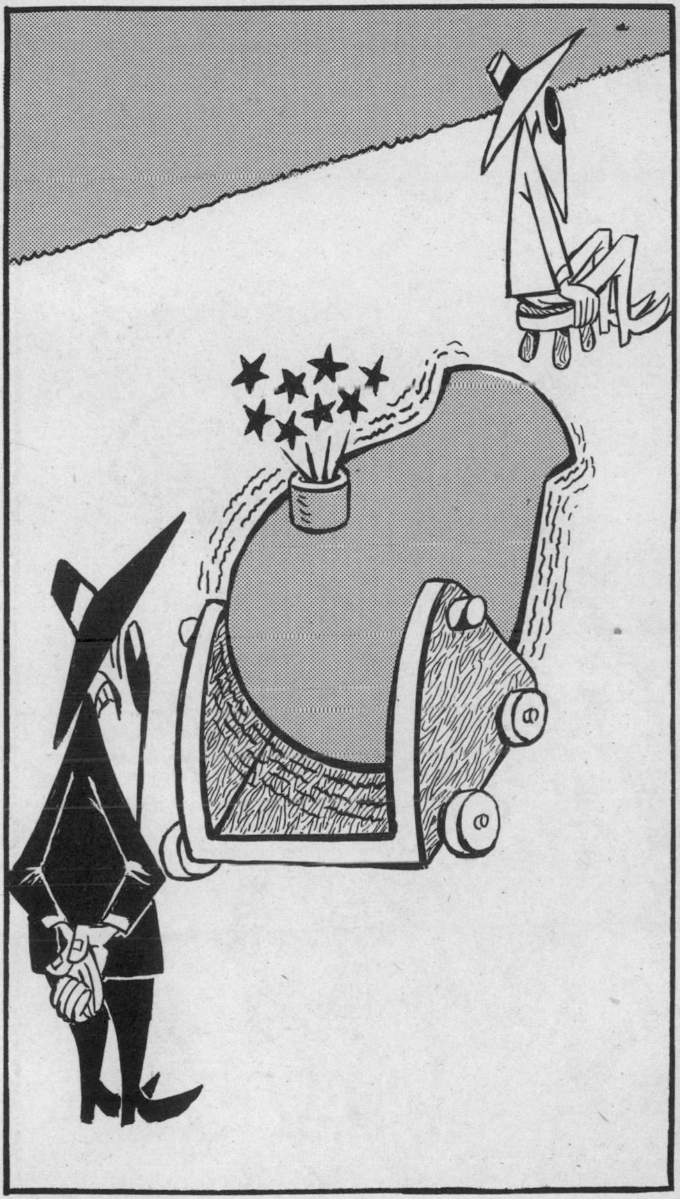

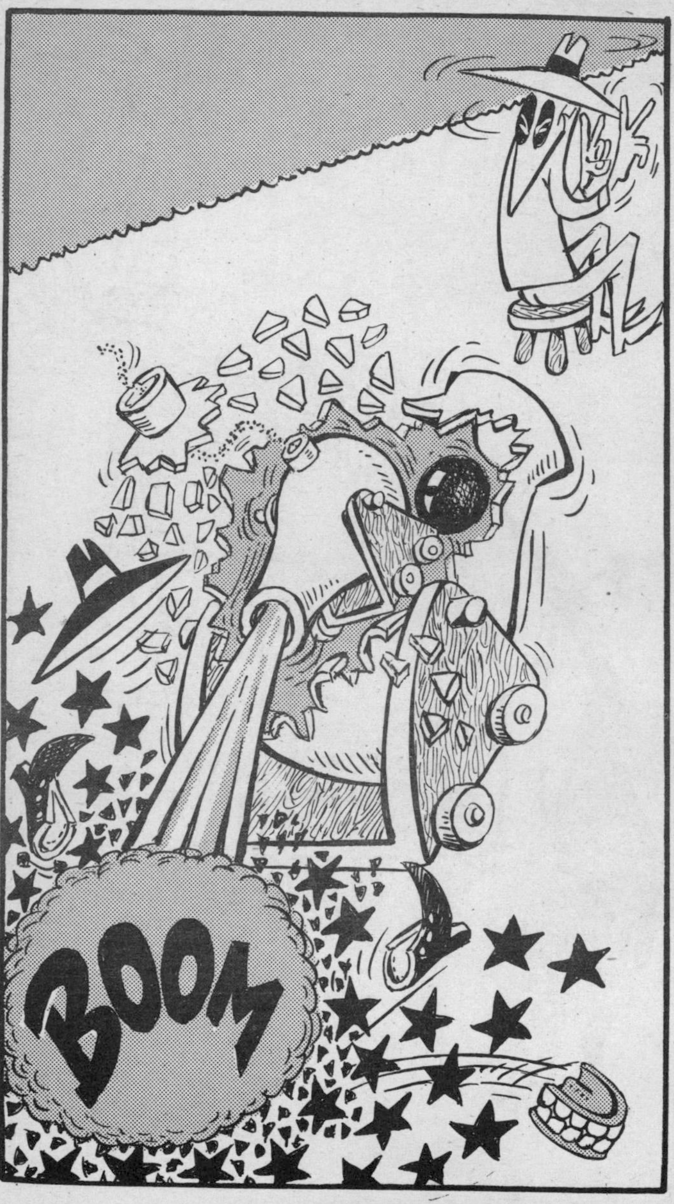
BOOM

SPY vs SPY

the SHELL GAME REPORT

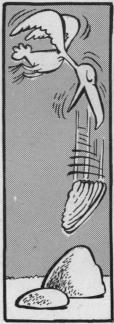

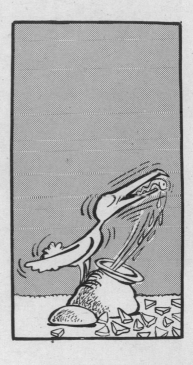

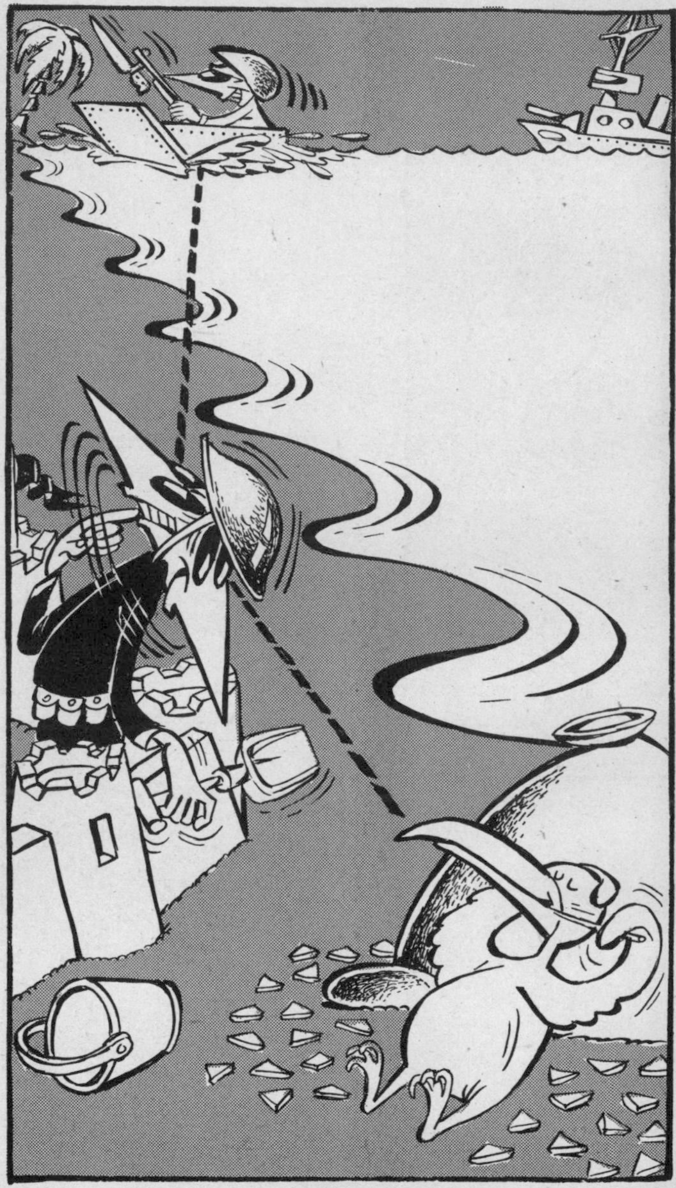

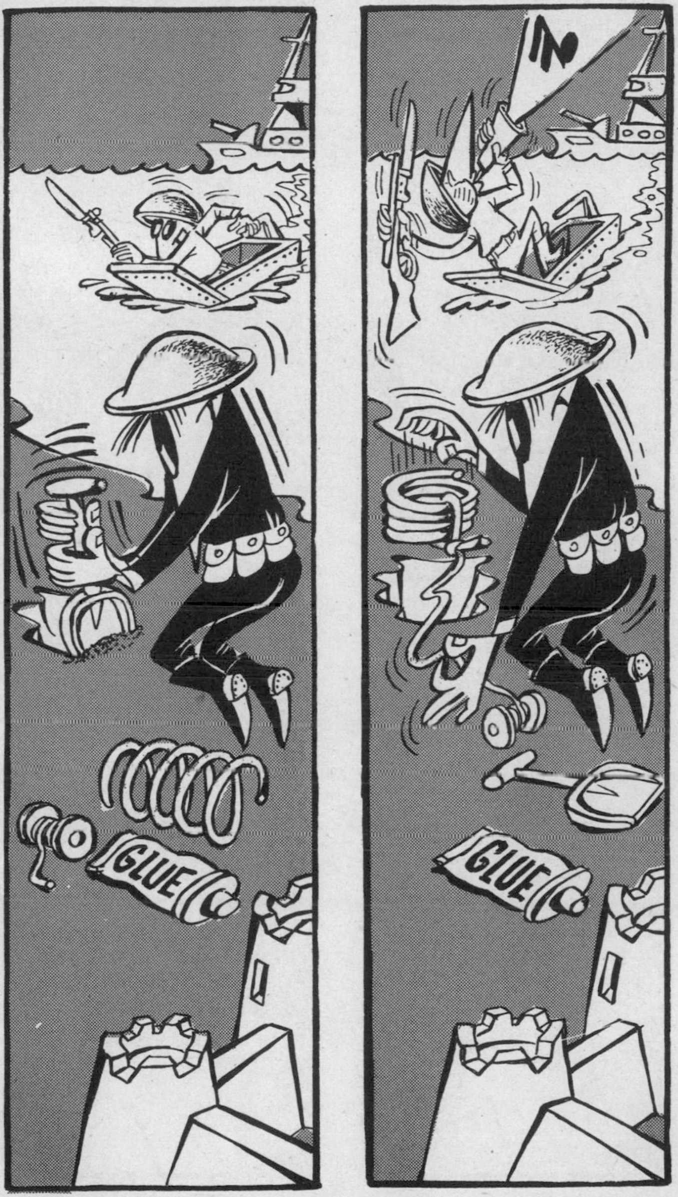
GLUE
GLUE

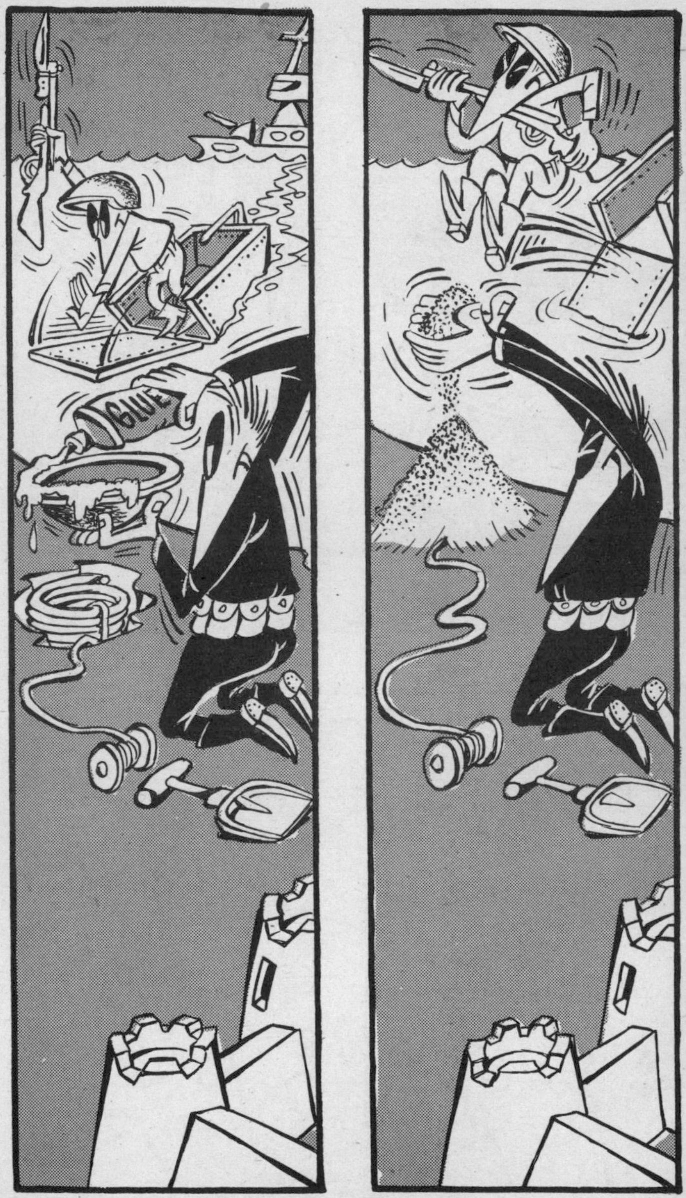
GLUE

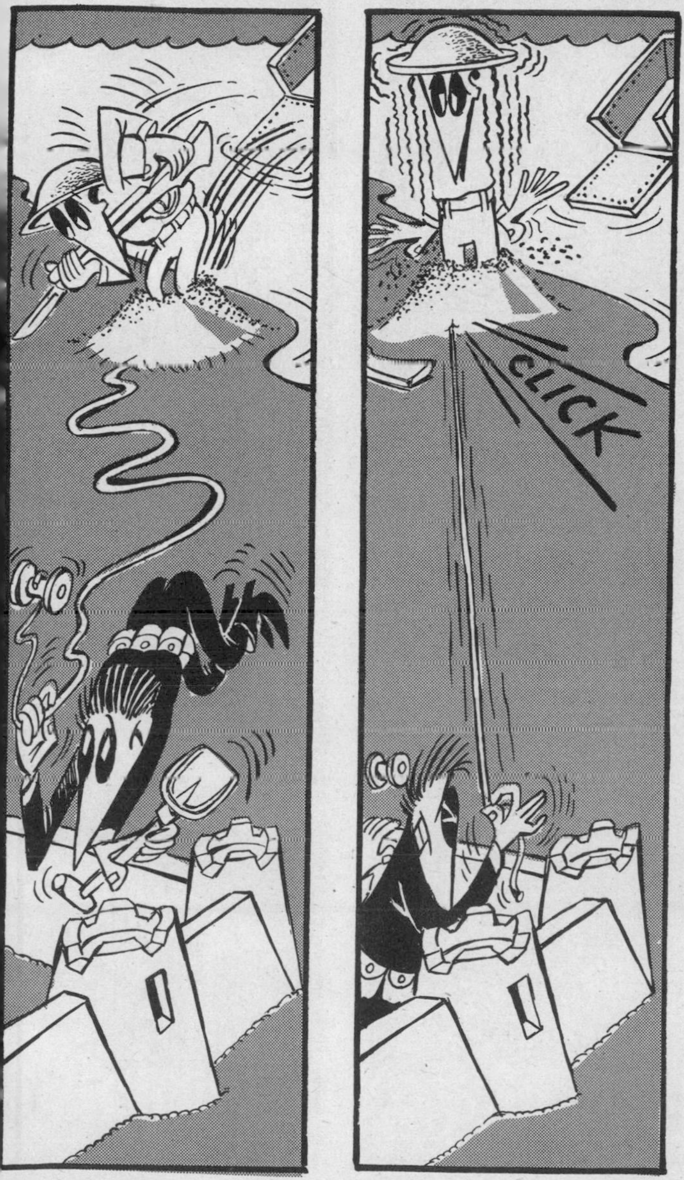
CLICK

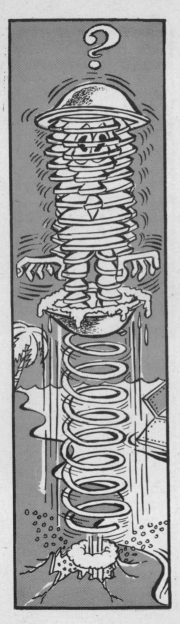

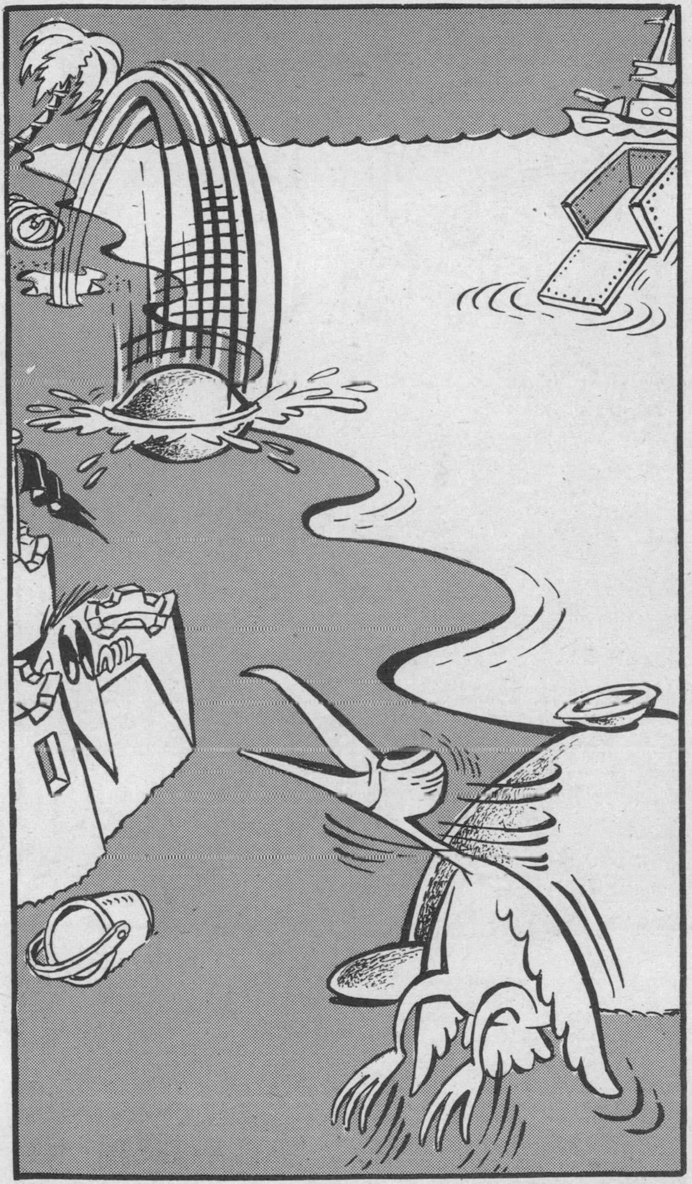

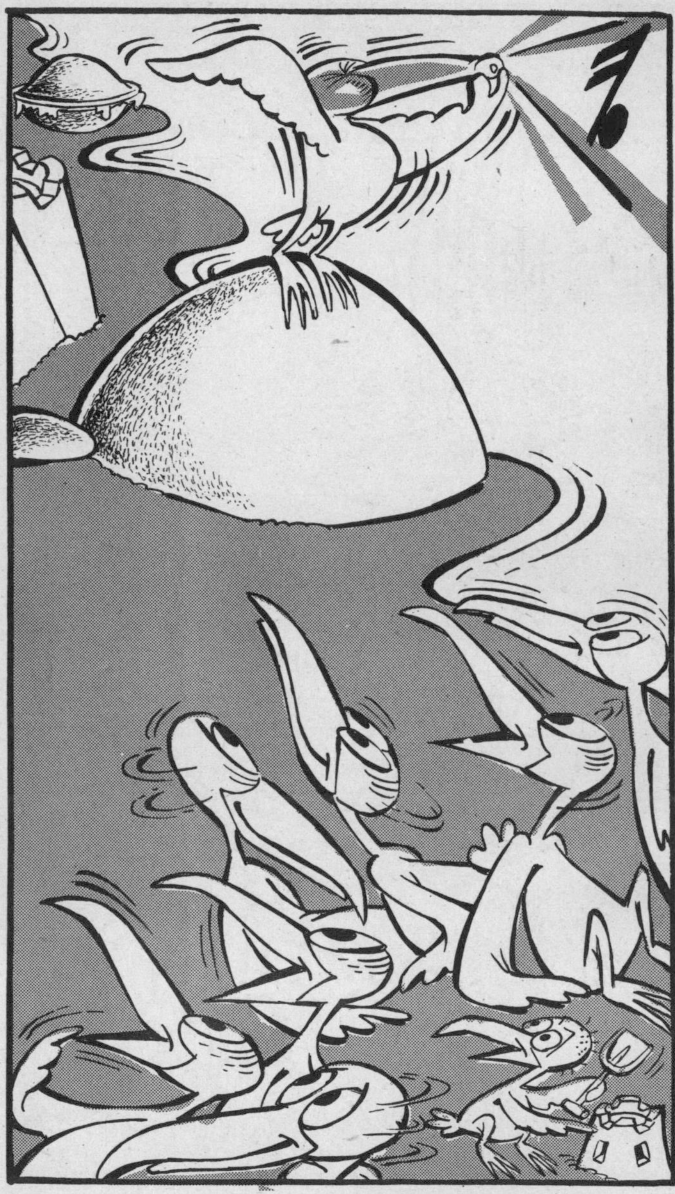

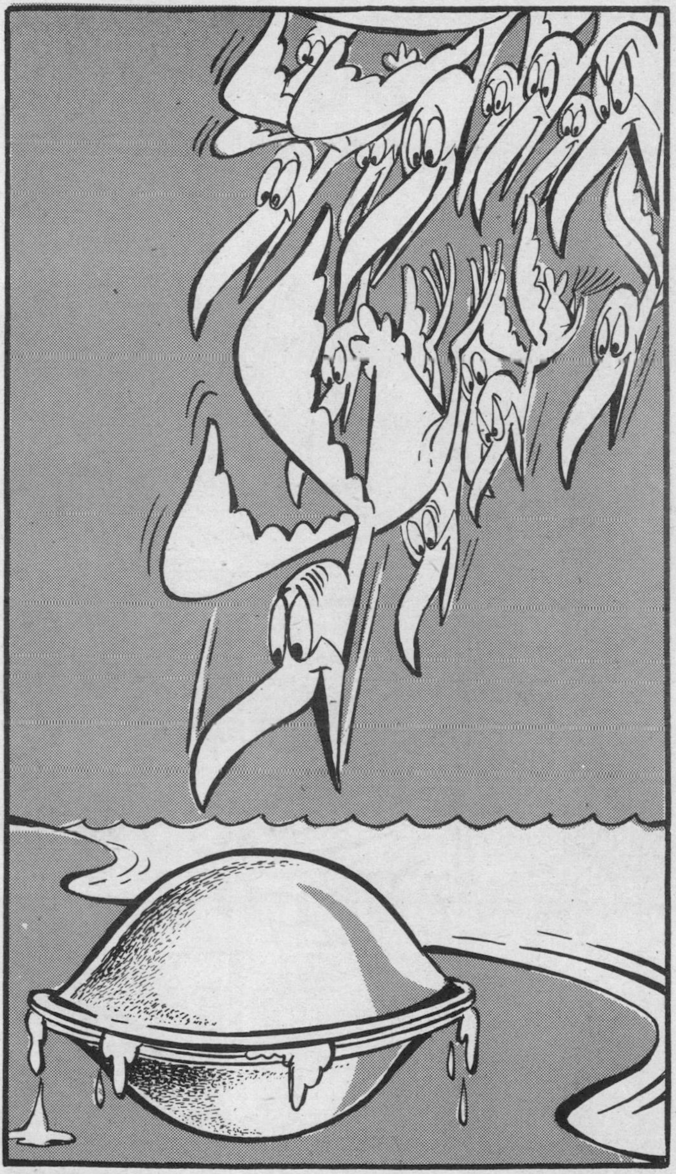

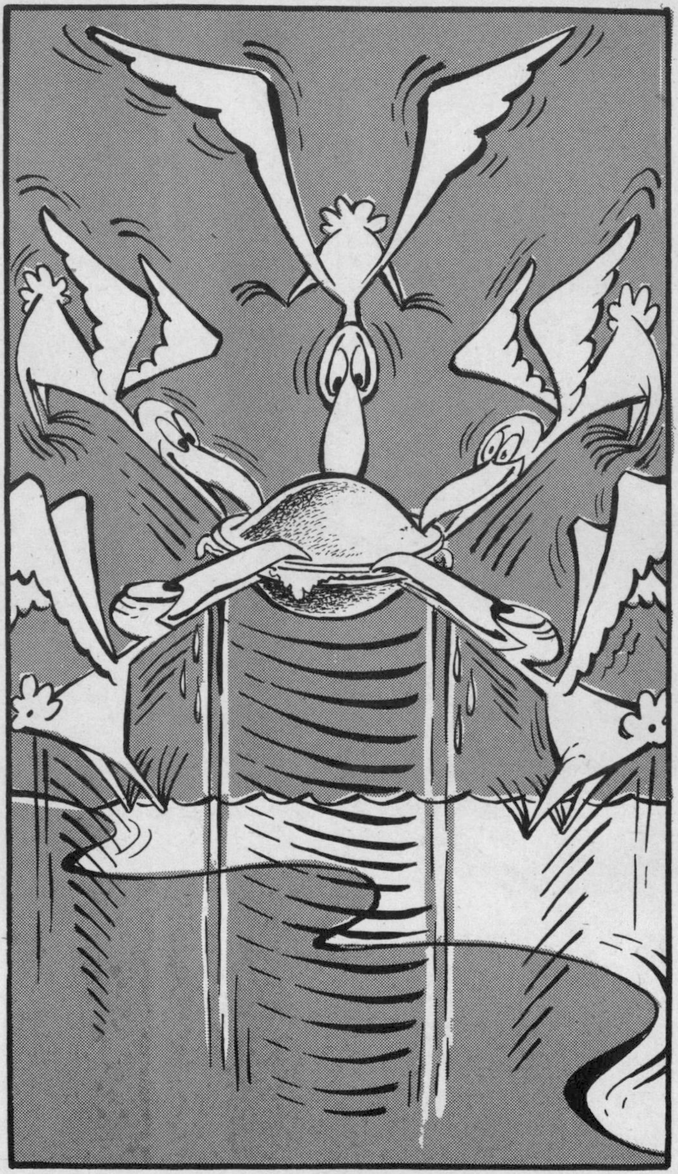

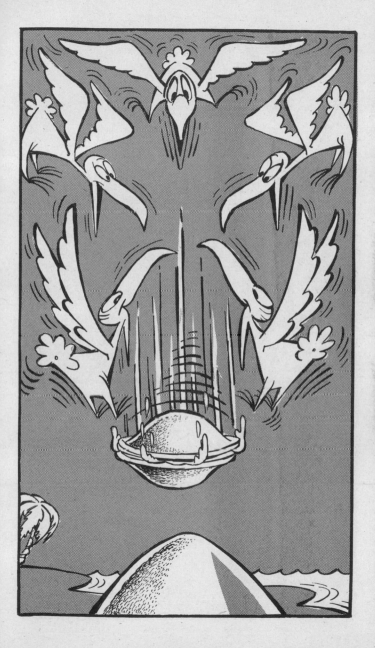

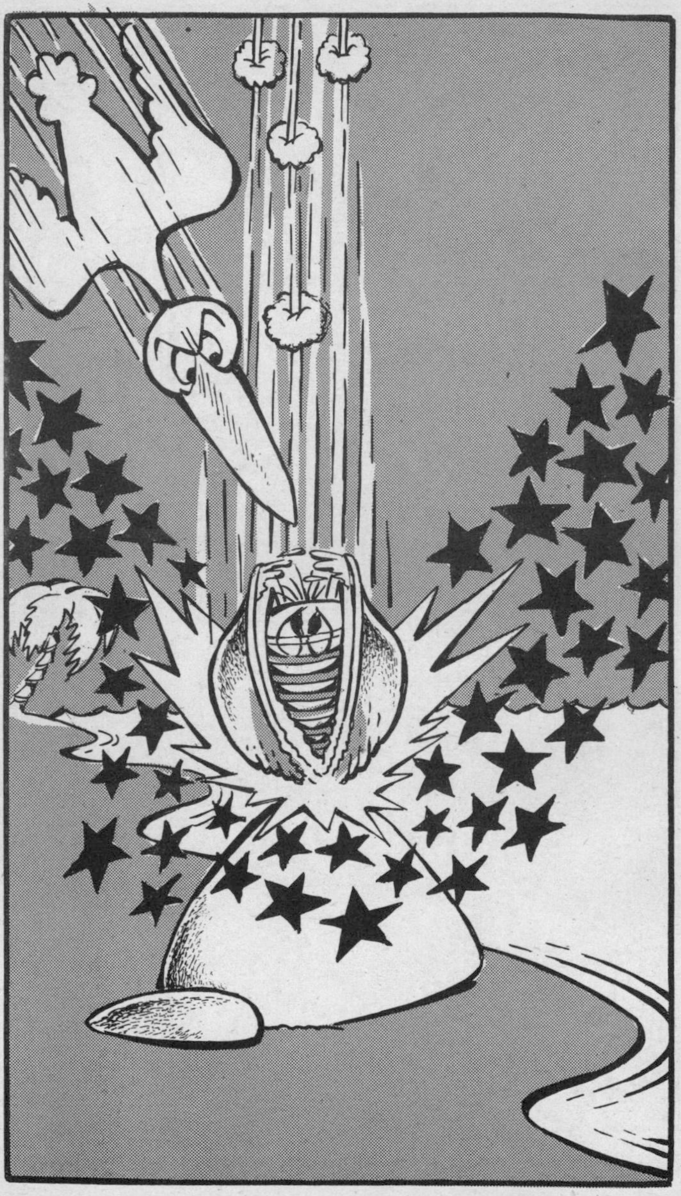

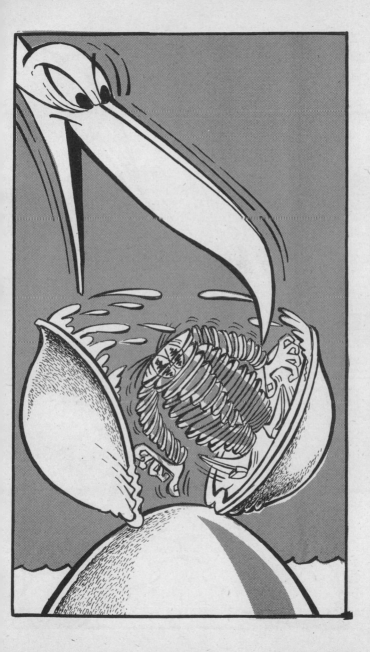

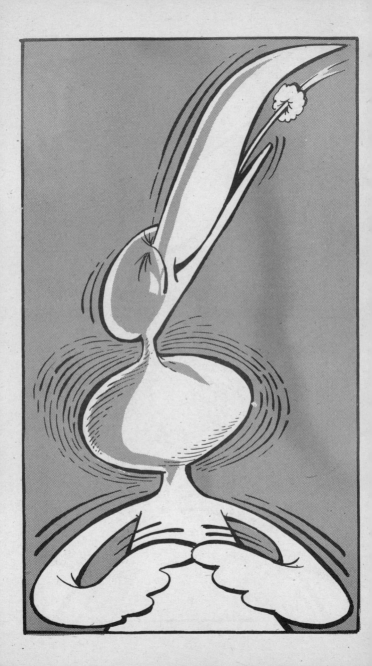

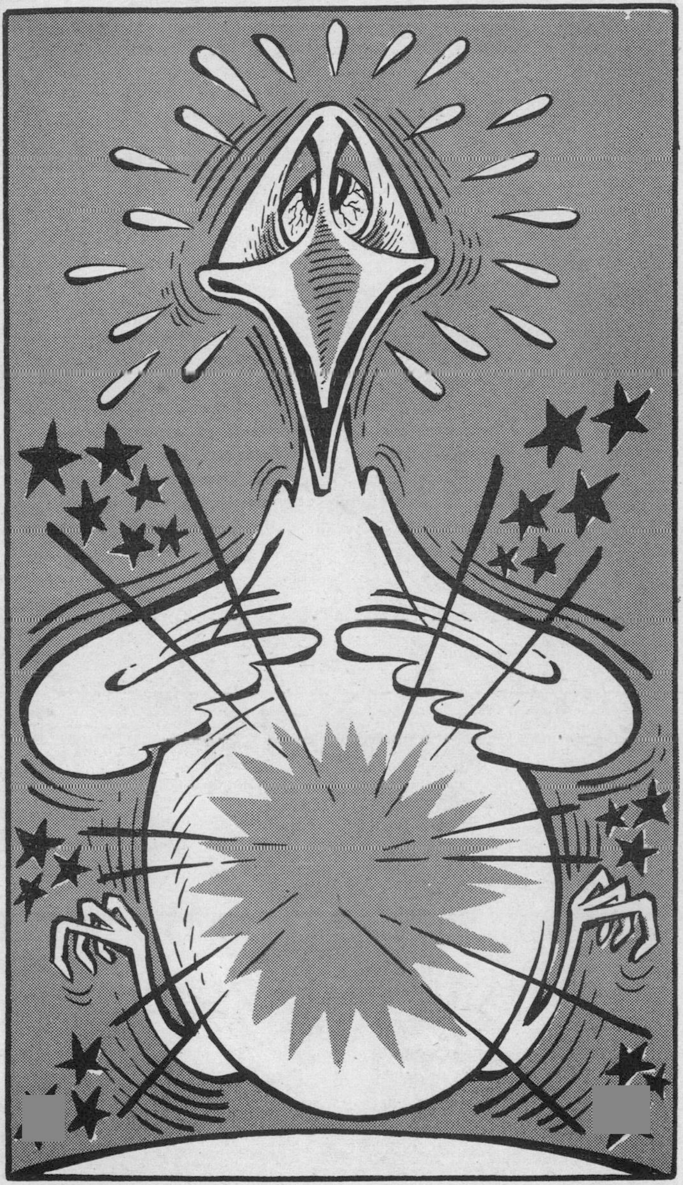

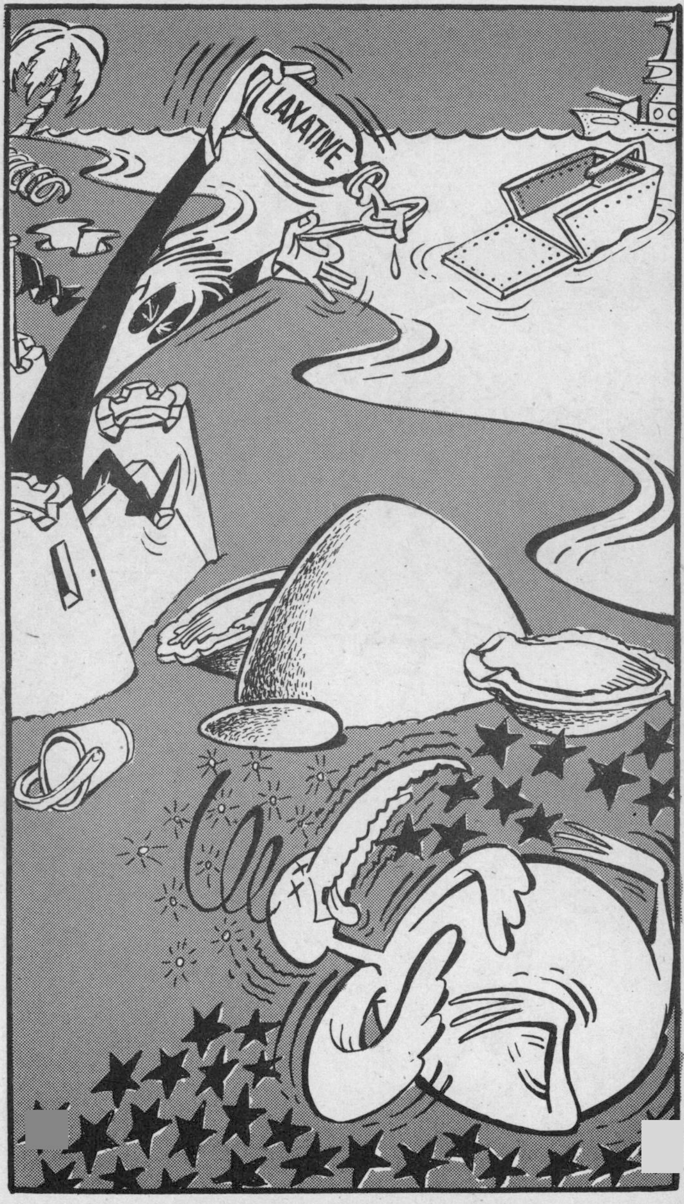
LAXATIVE

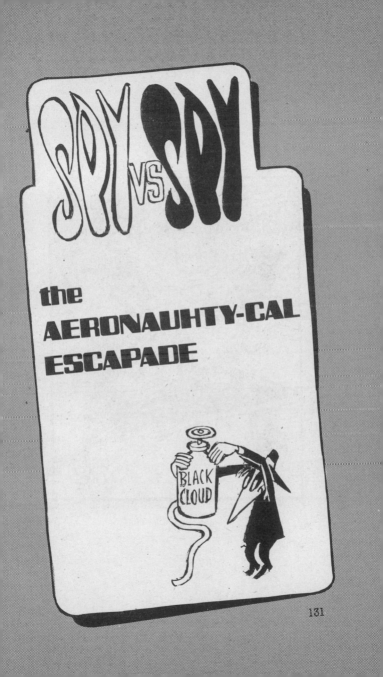

SPY vs SPY

the AERONAUHTY-CAL ESCAPADE

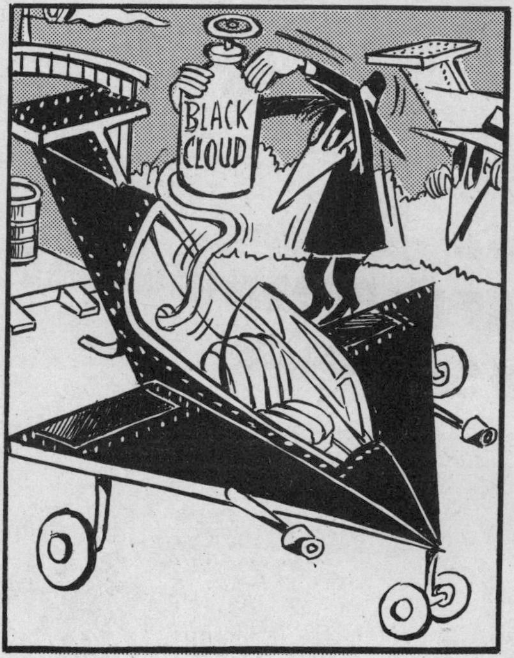
BLACK
CLOUD

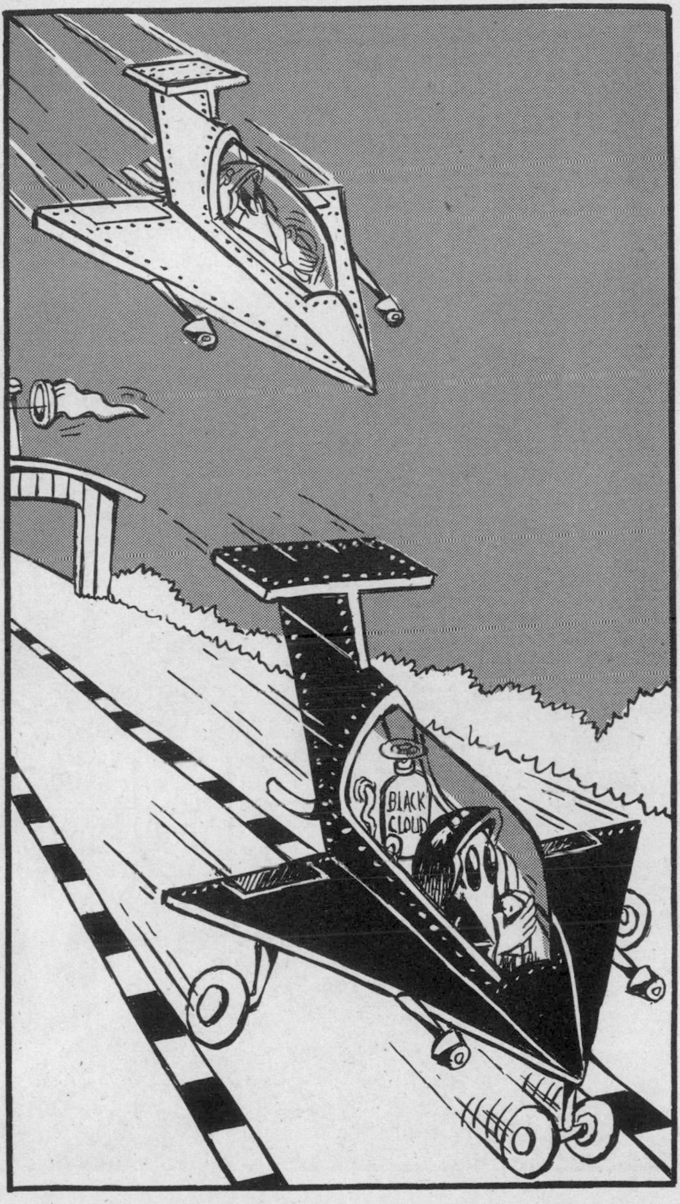
BLACK
CLOUD

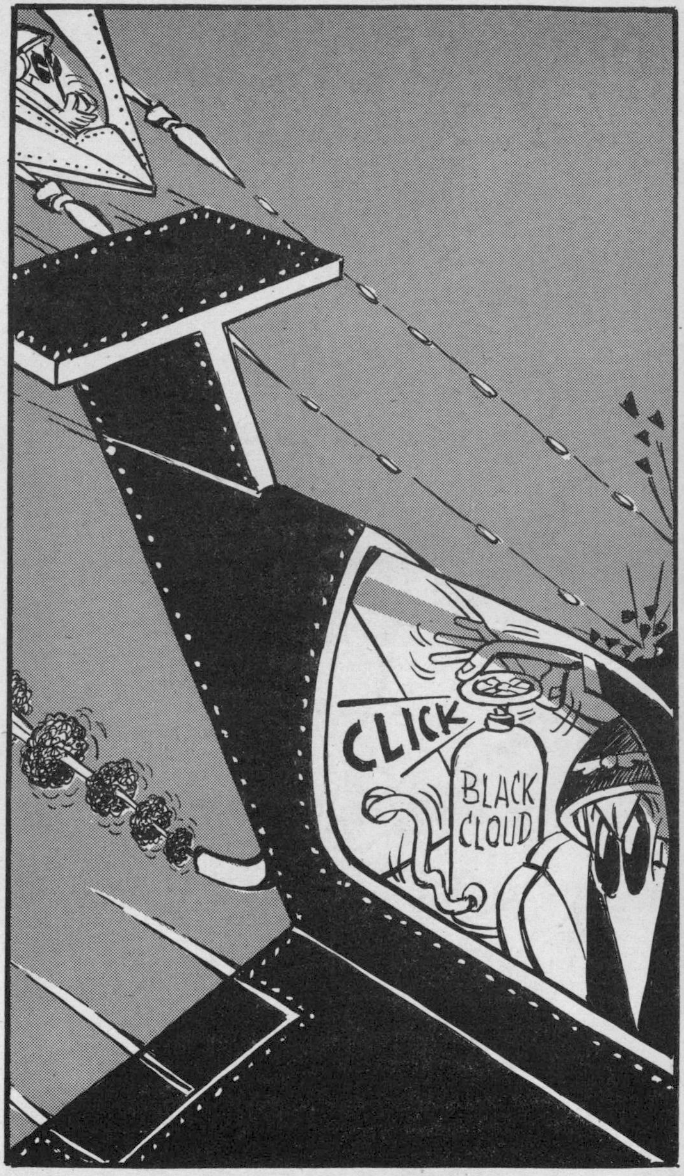
CLICK
BLACK CLOUD

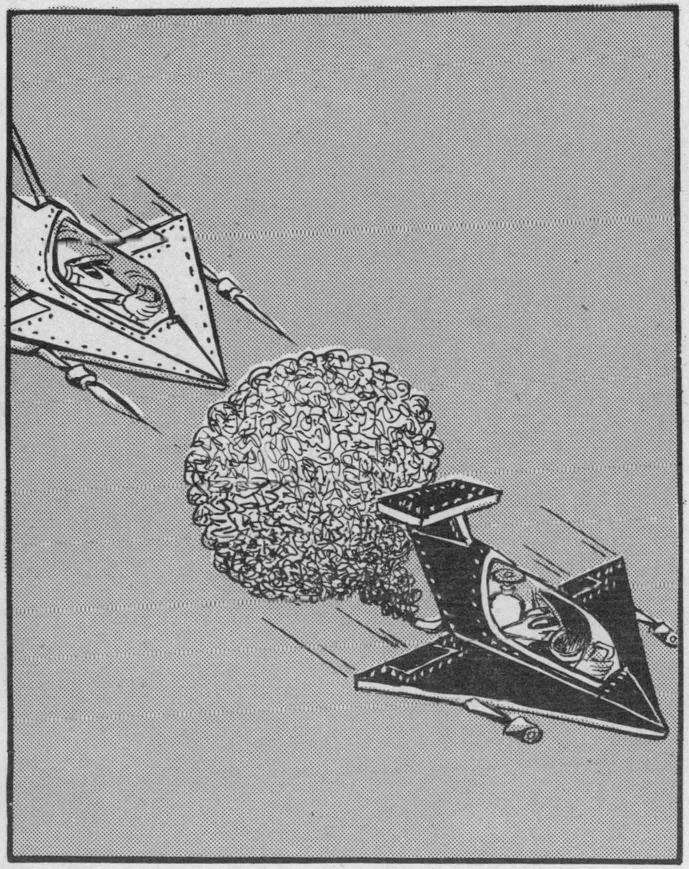

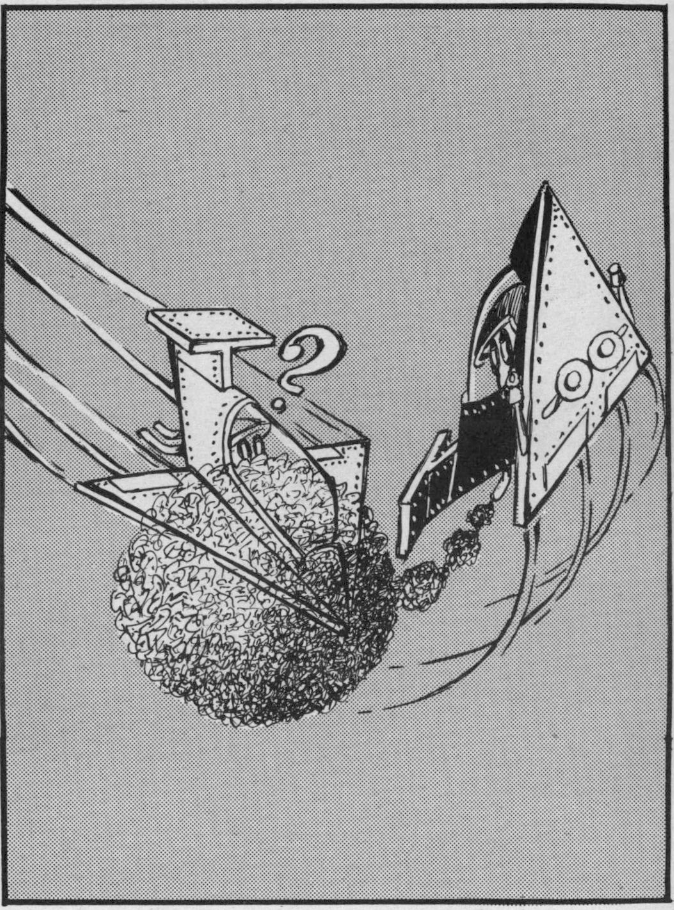
?

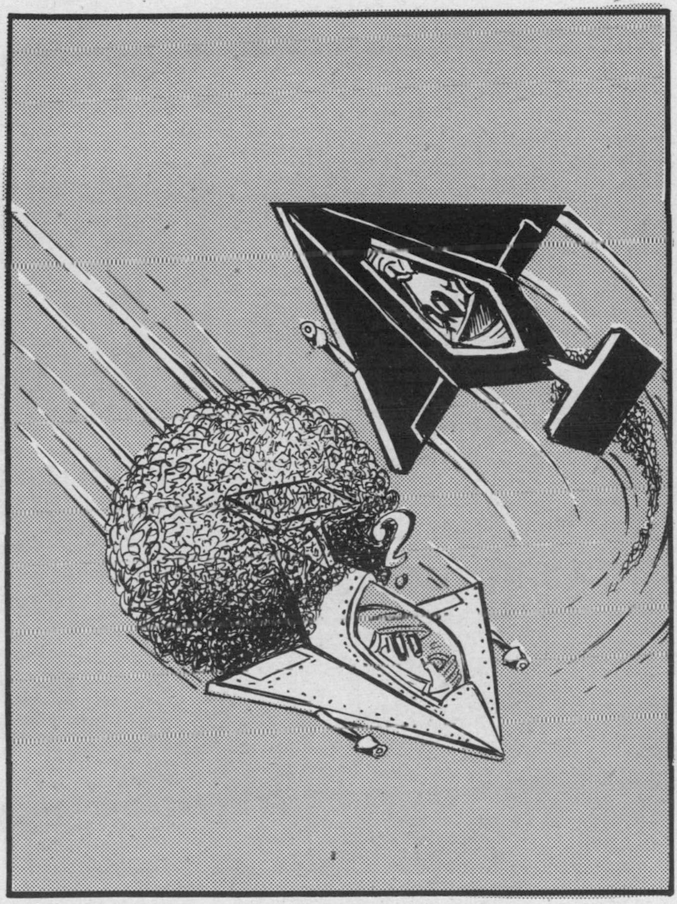

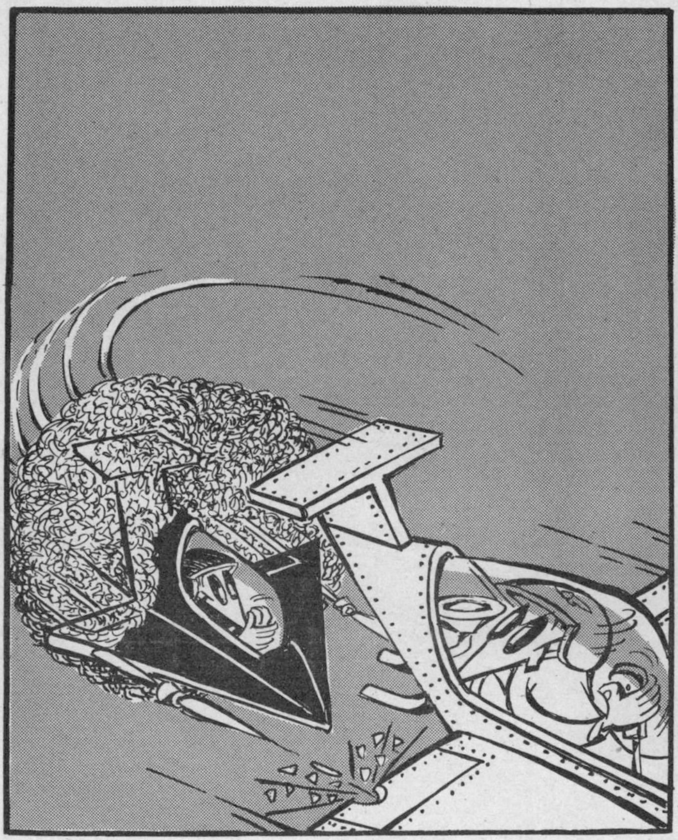

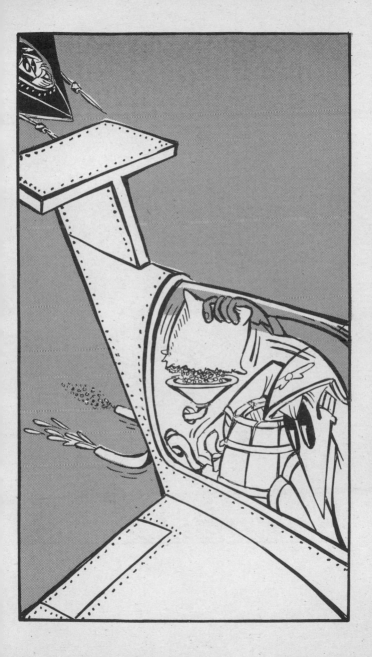

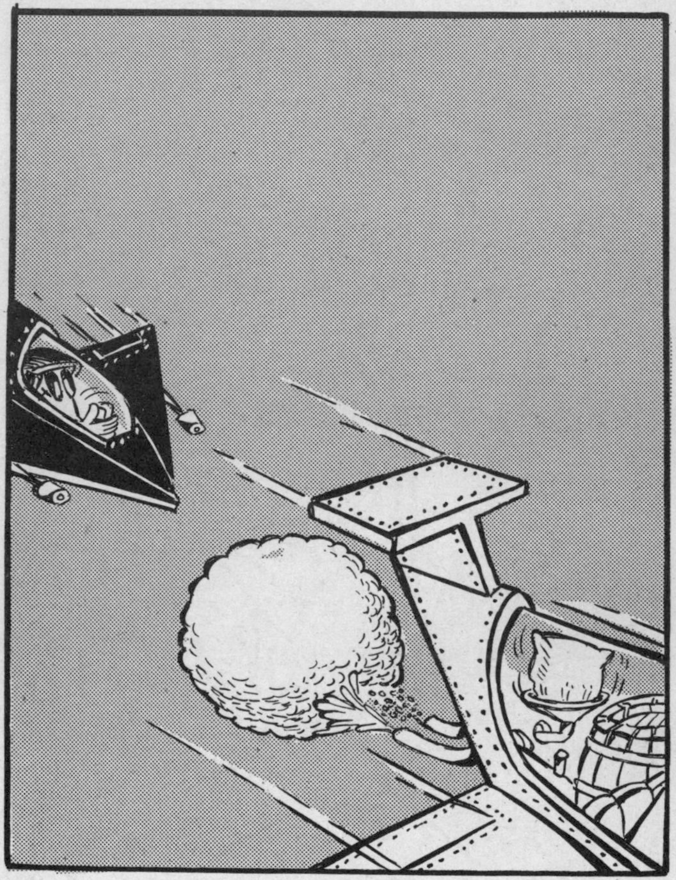

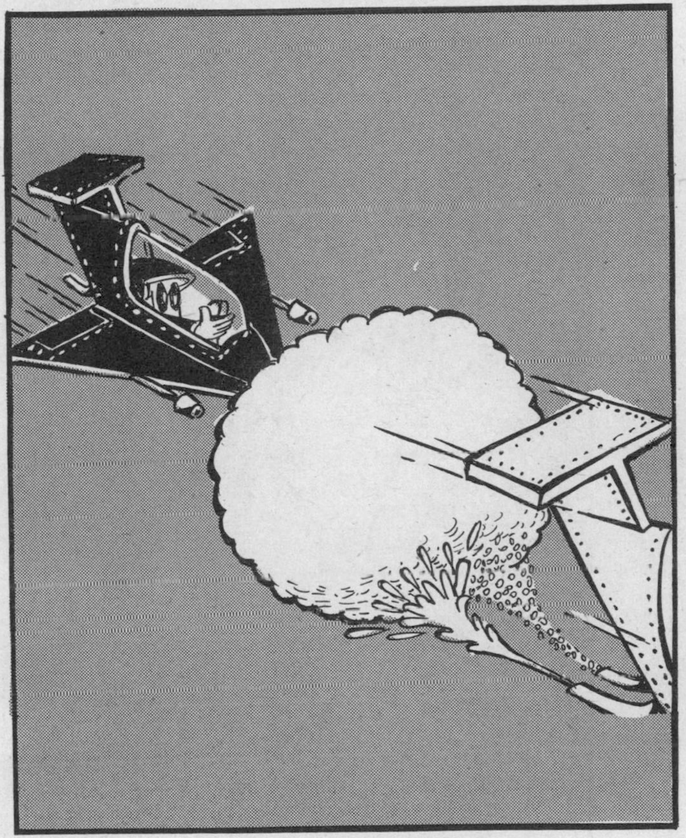

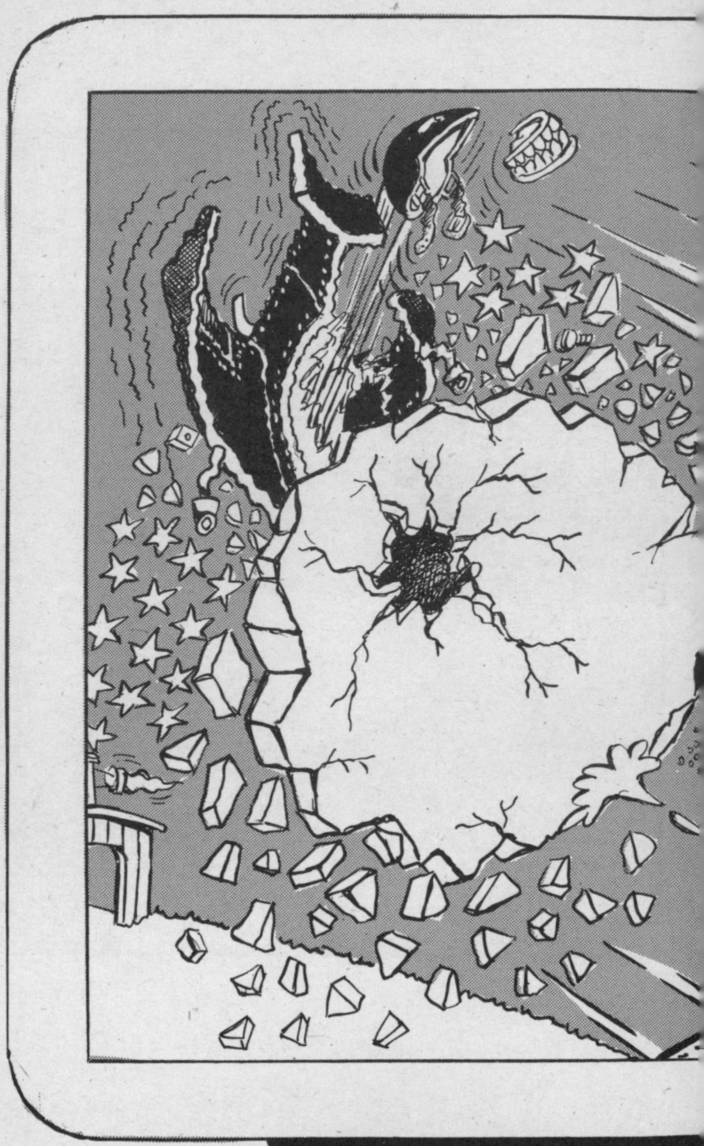

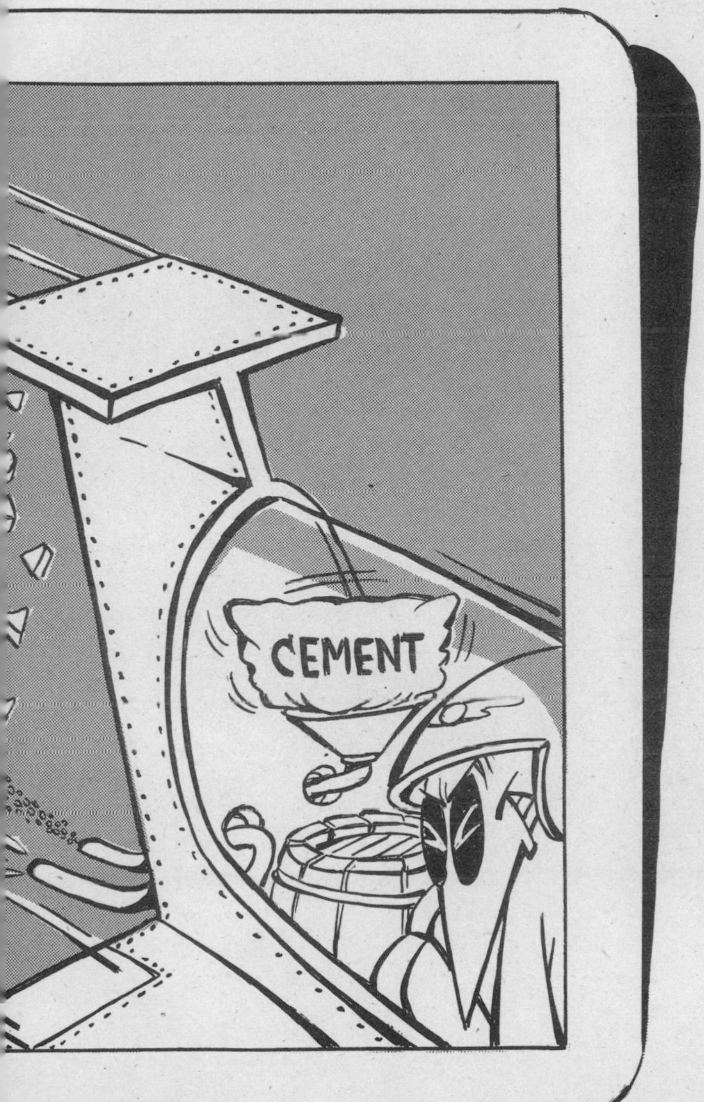
CEMENT

SPY vs SPY

THE ONE THAT GOT AWAY AFFAIR

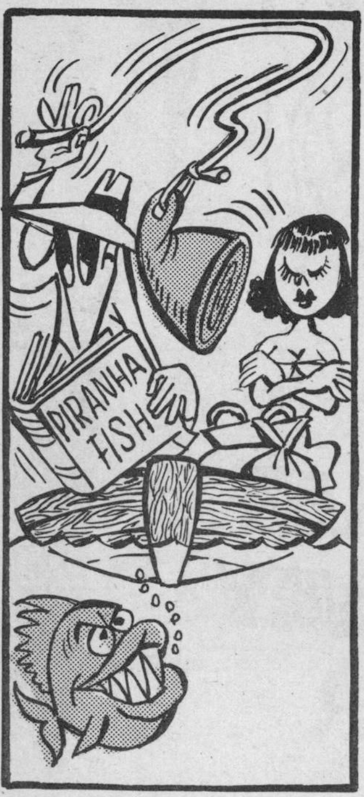
PIRANHA FISH

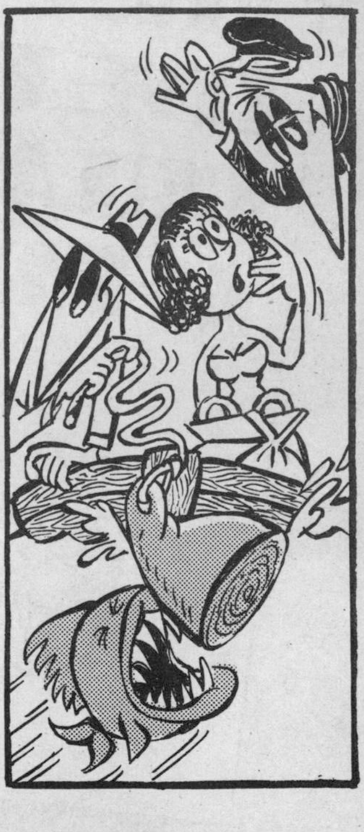

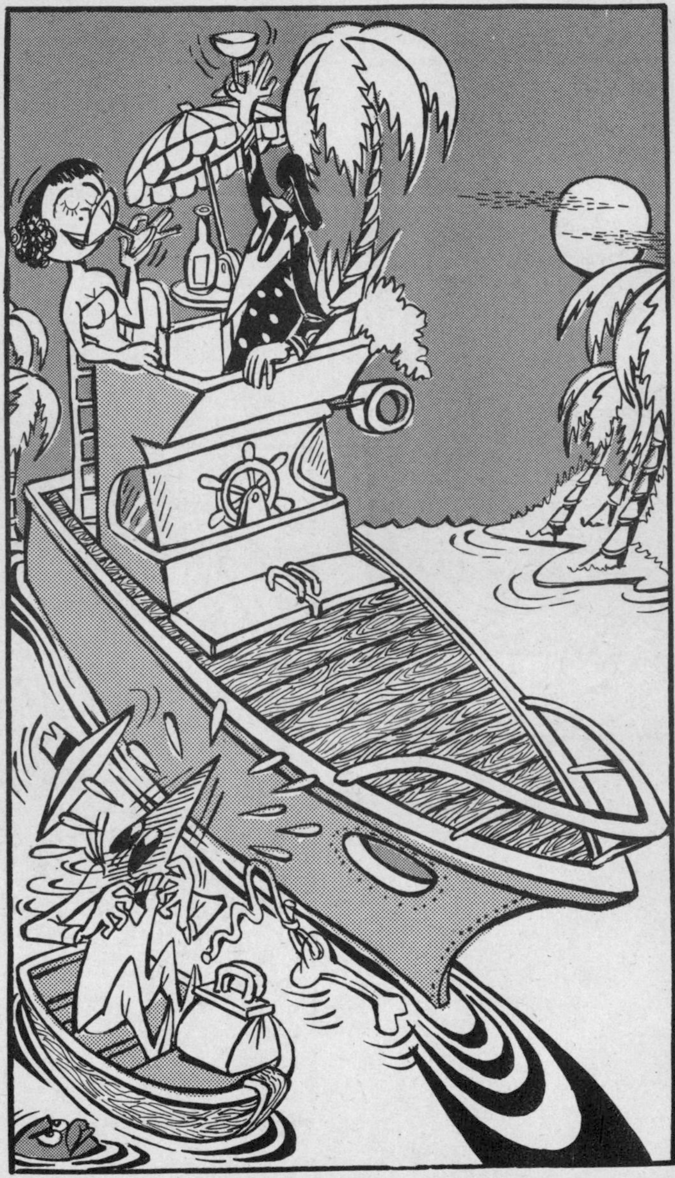

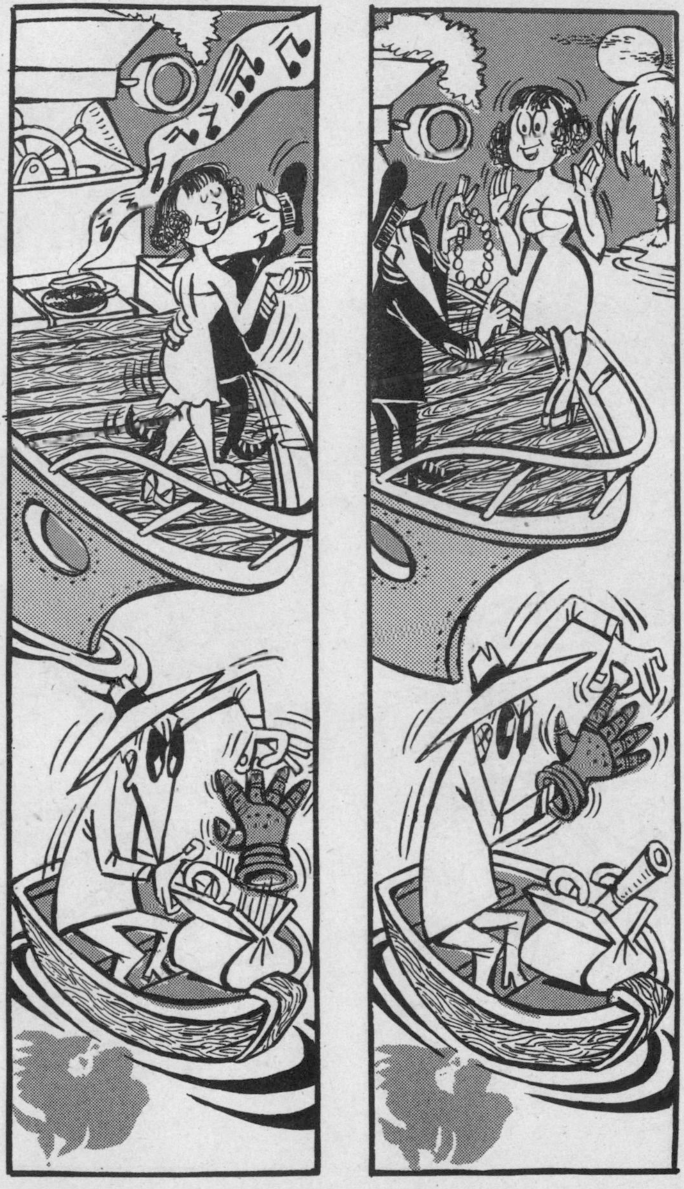

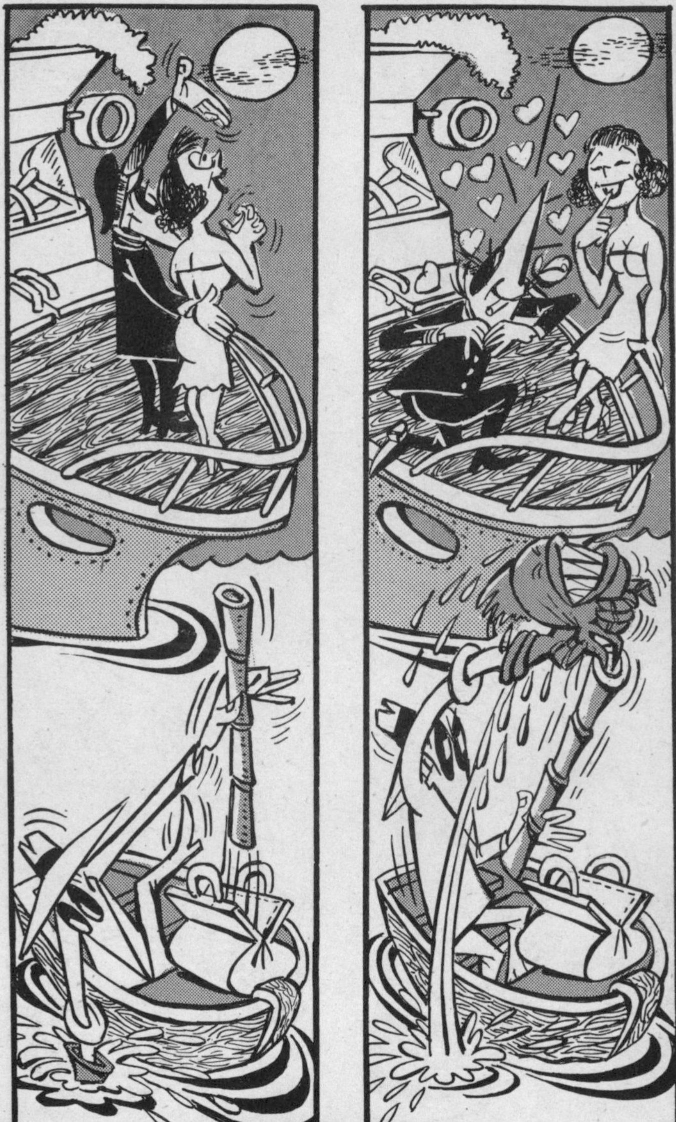

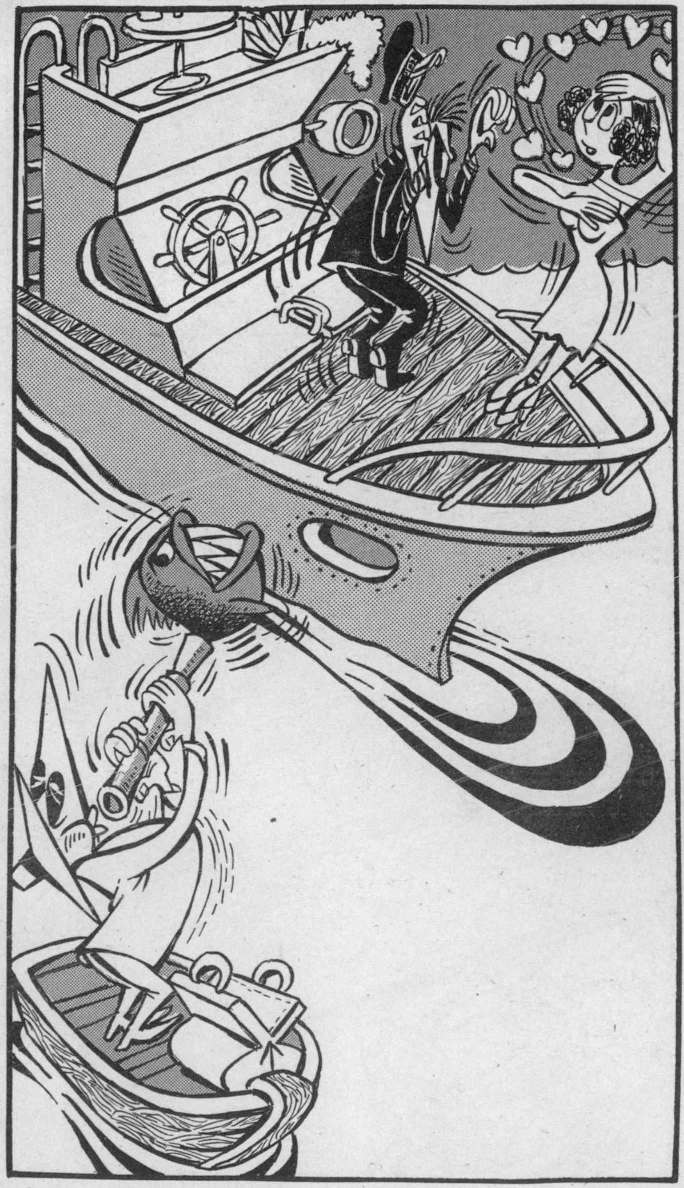

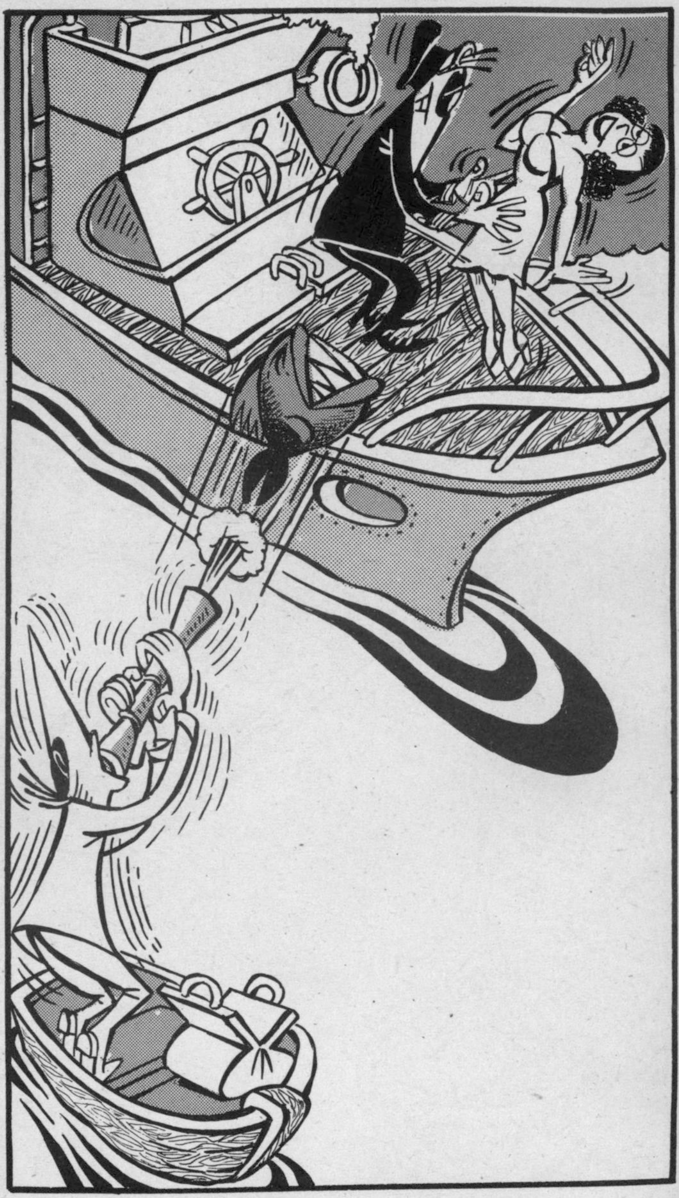

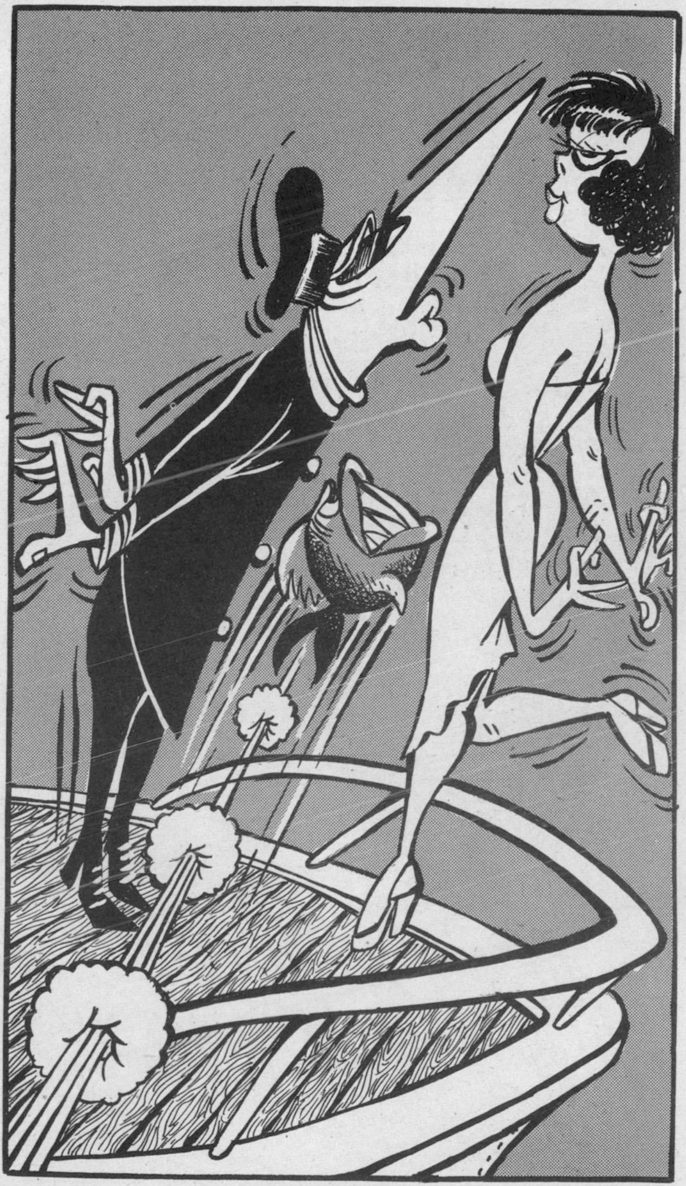

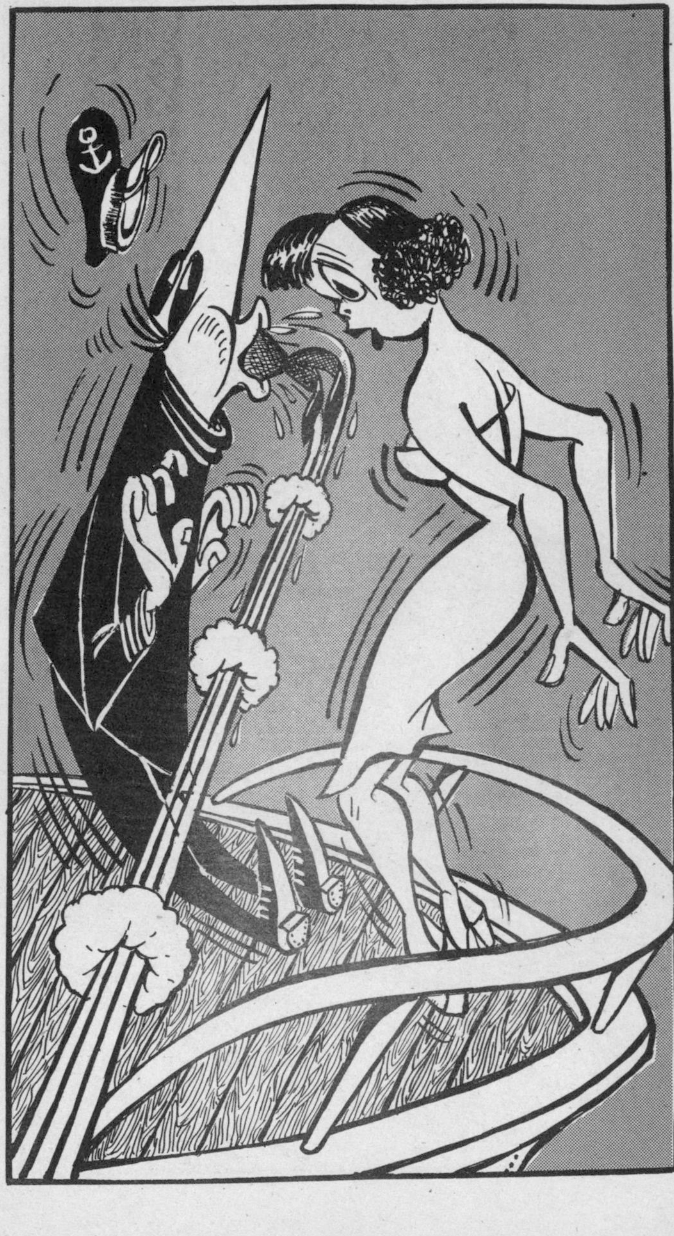

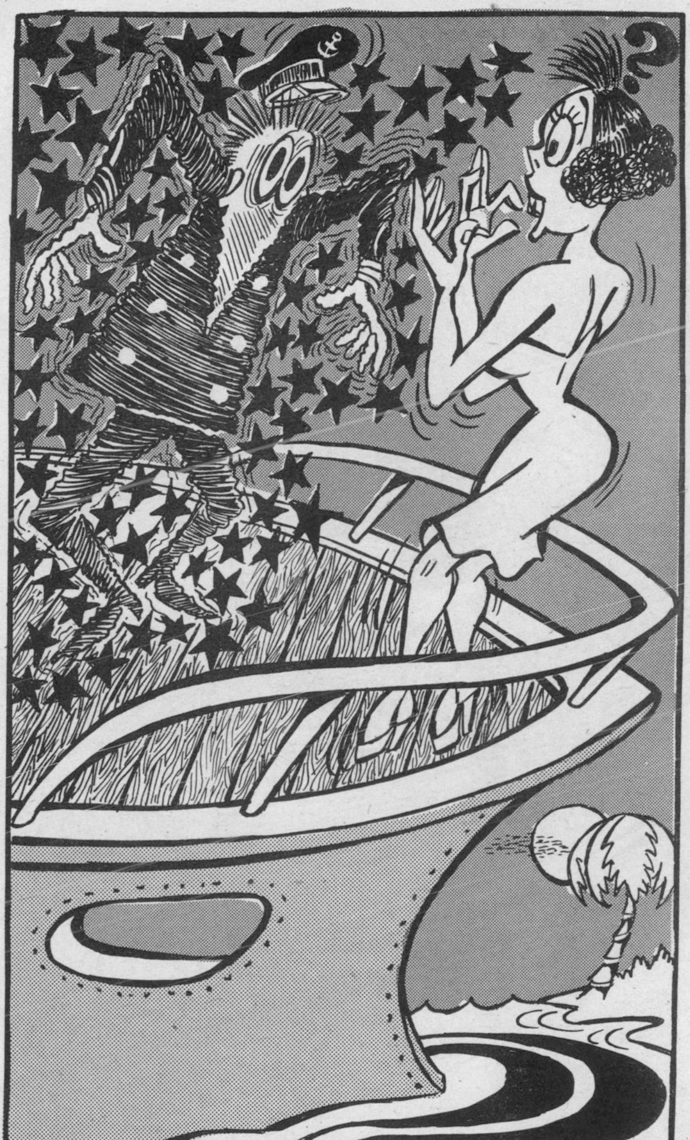

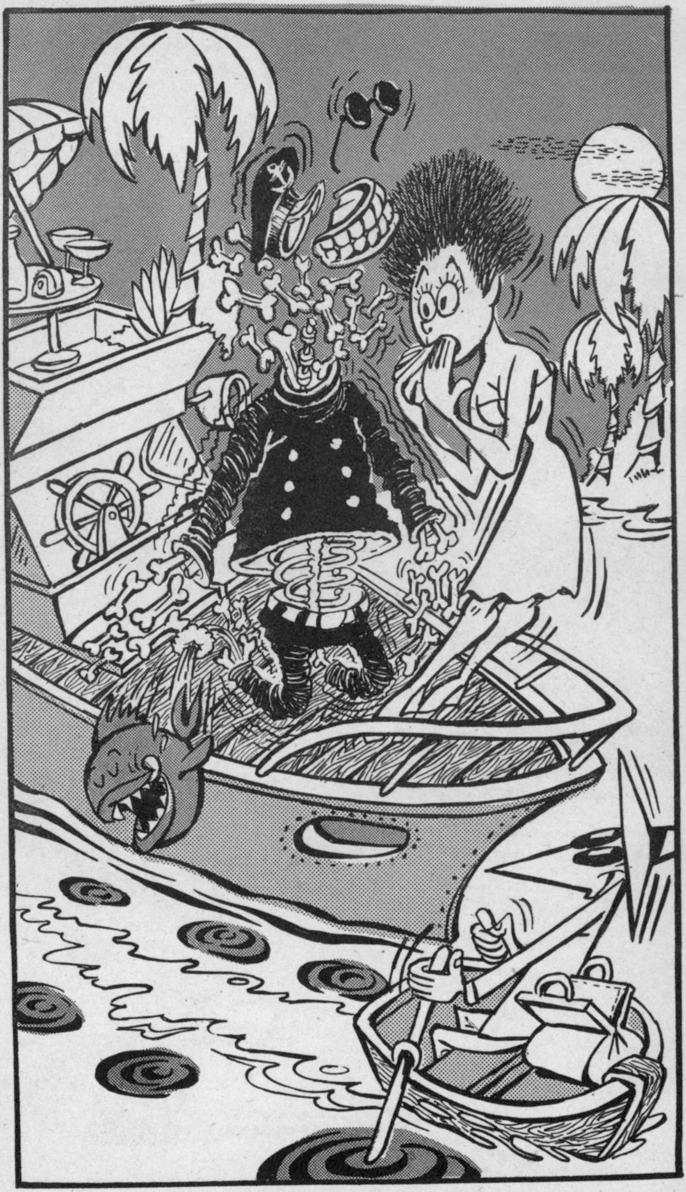

SPY vs SPY

THE SUCKER-PLAY CAPER

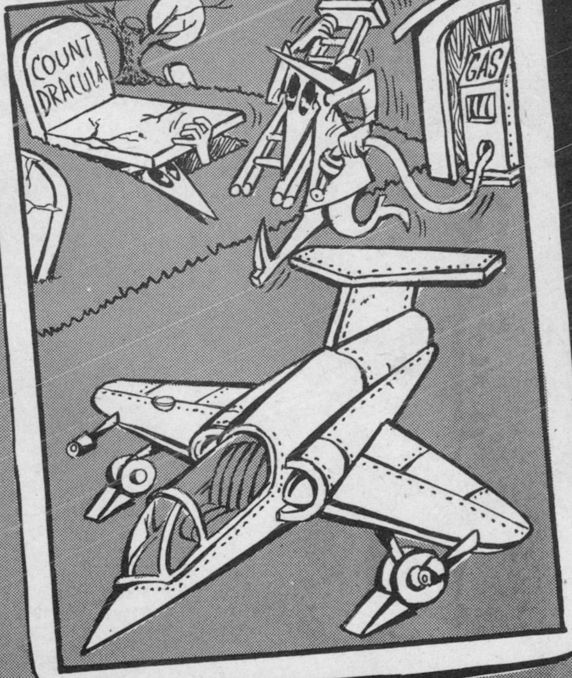
COUNT DRACULA
GAS

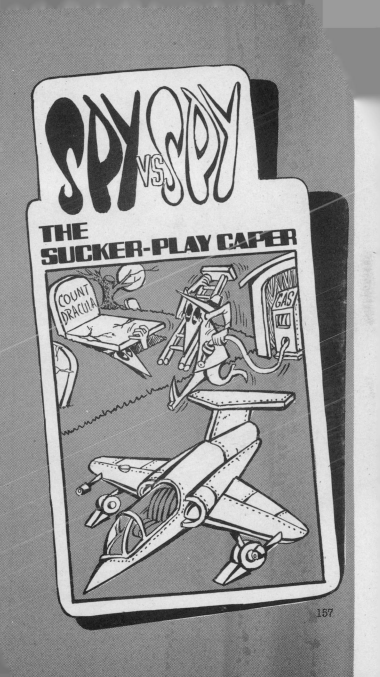

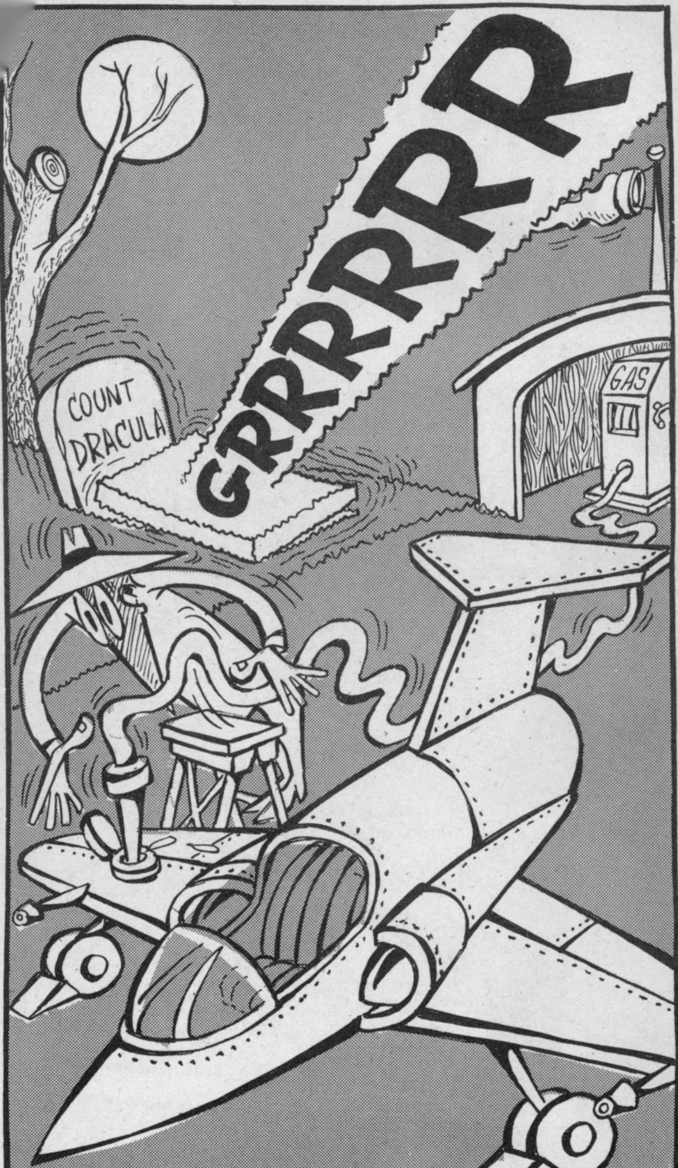
GRRRRRR
COUNT DRACULA
GAS

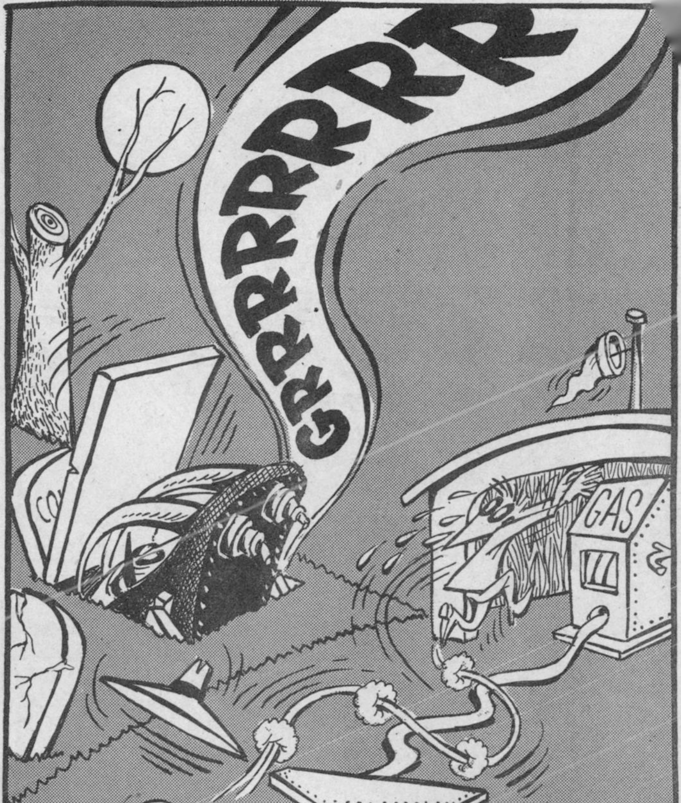
GRRRRRRRR
GAS

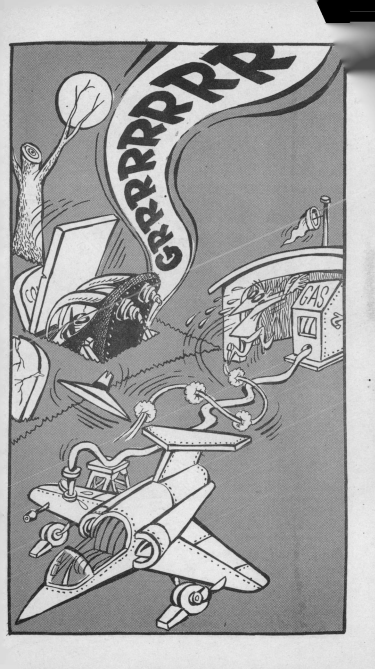

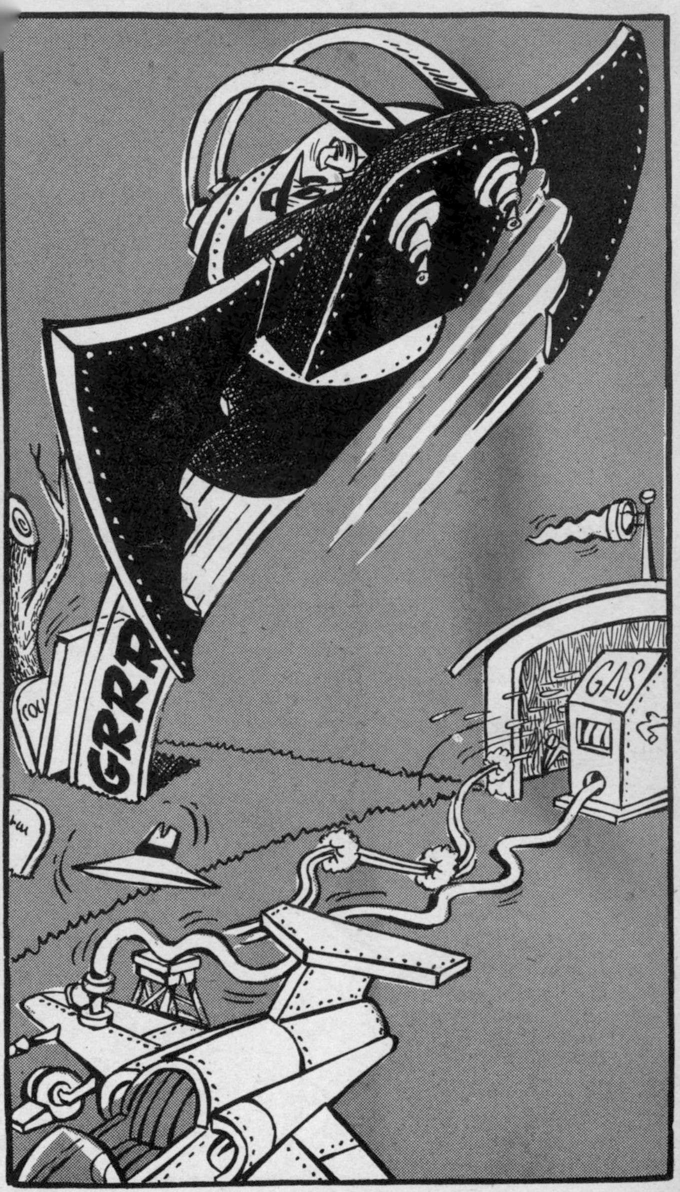
GRRR
GAS

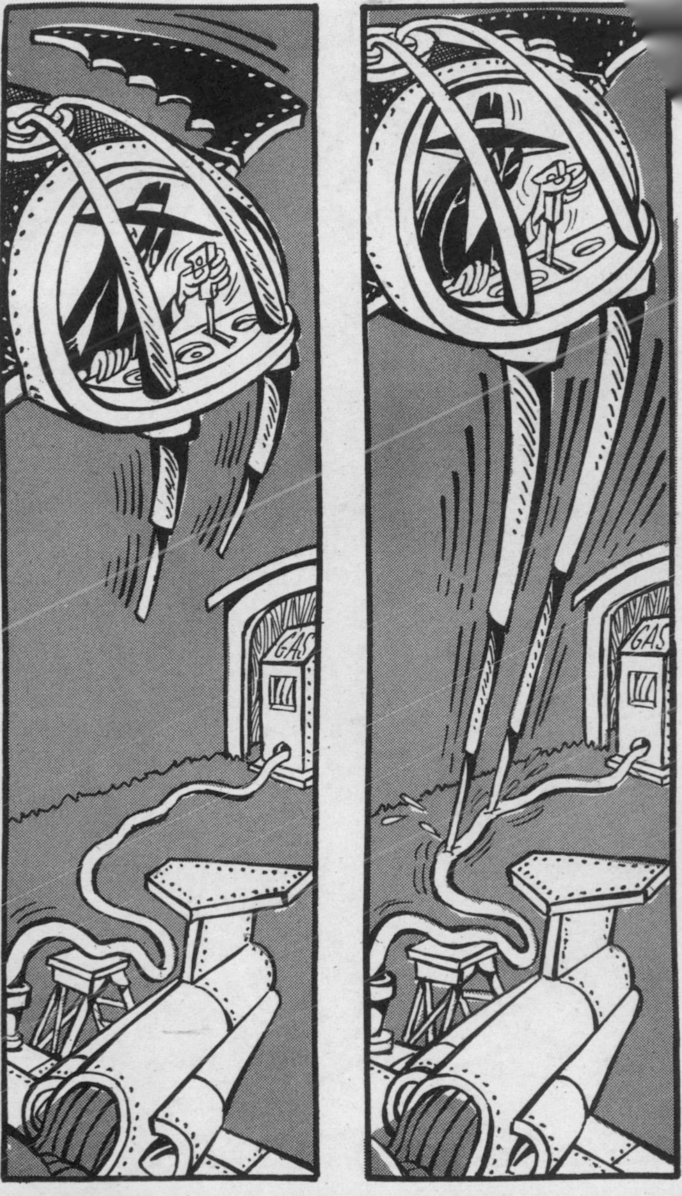
GAS
GAS

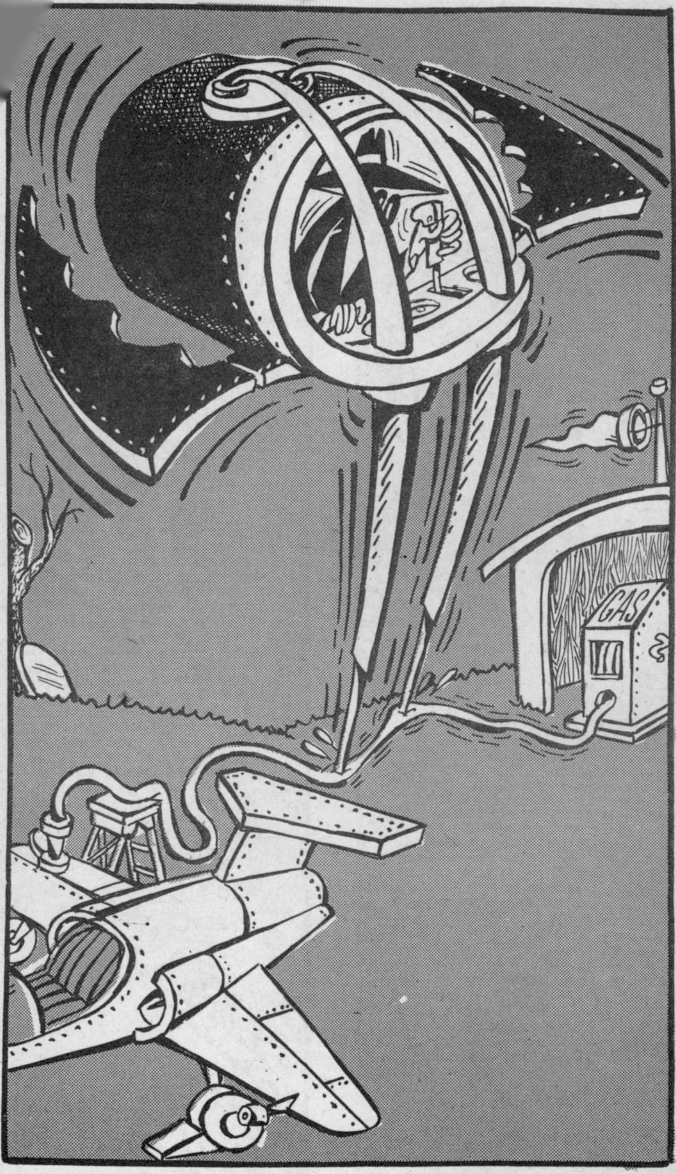
GAS

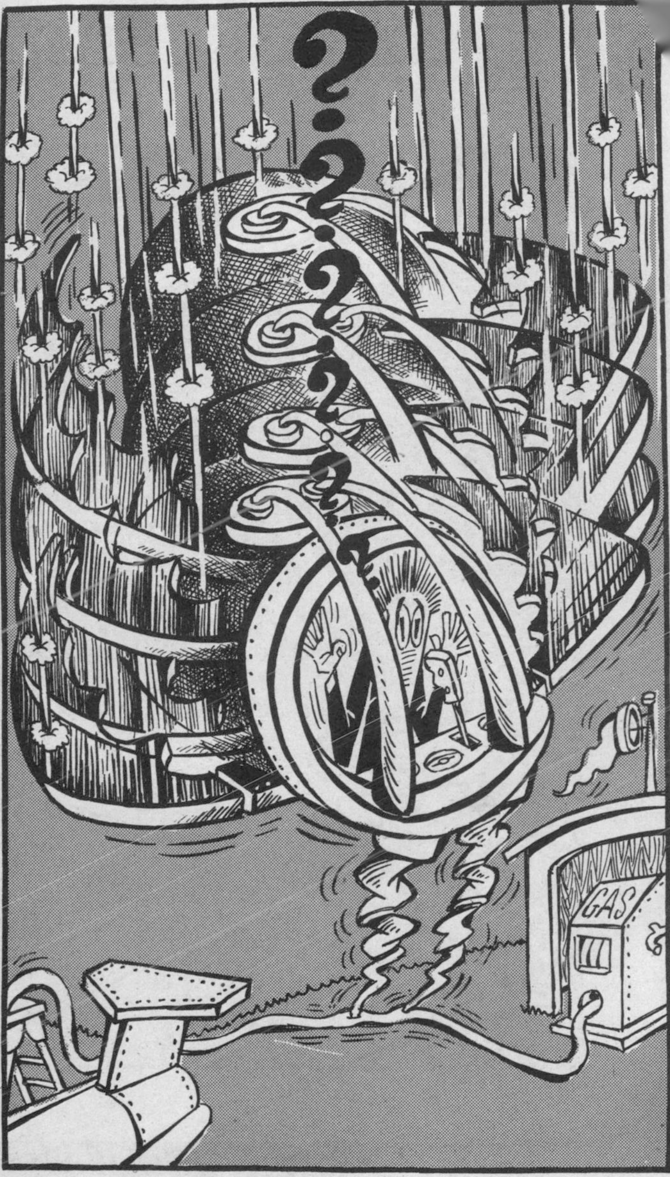
GAS

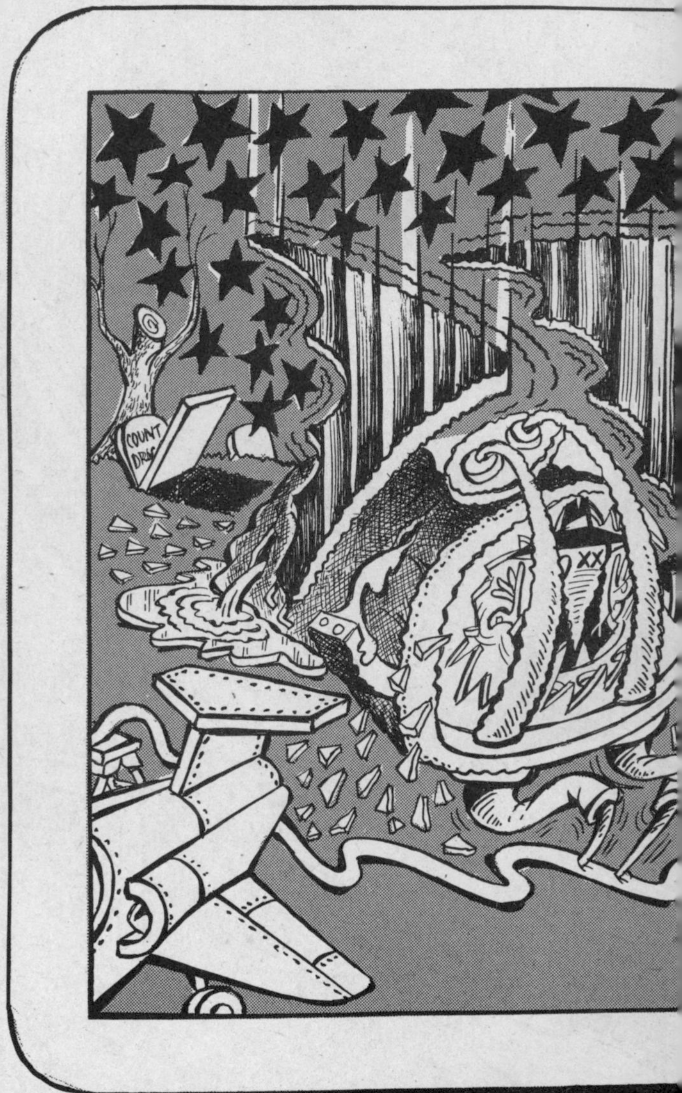
COUNT
DRAC
XX

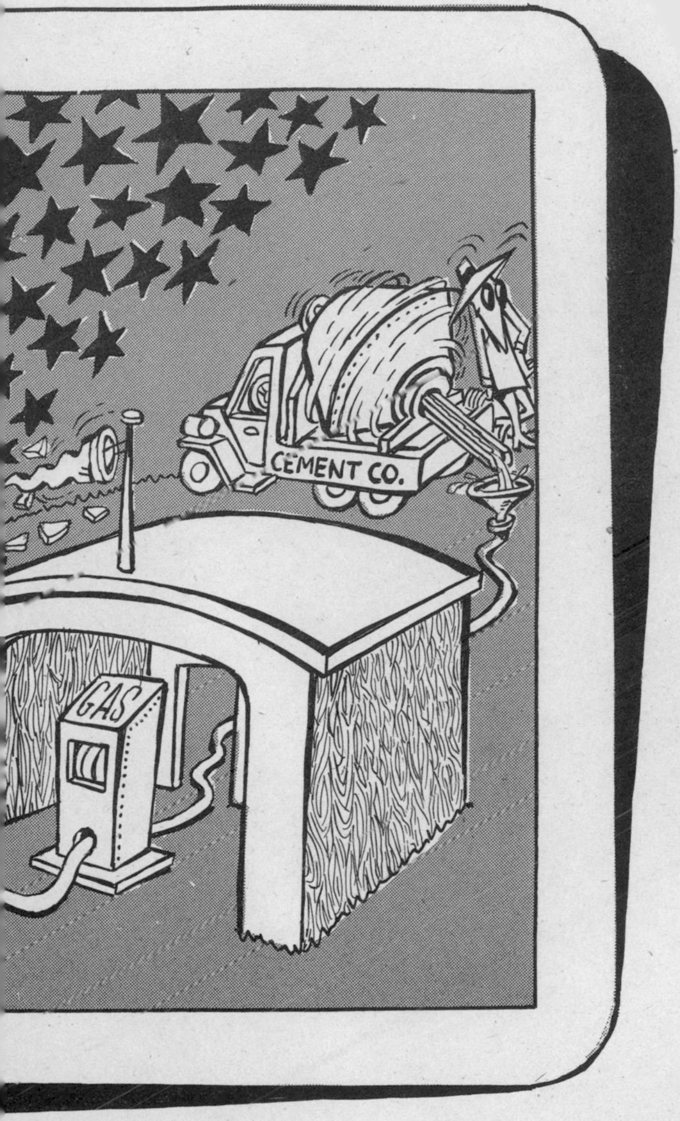
CEMENT CO.
GAS

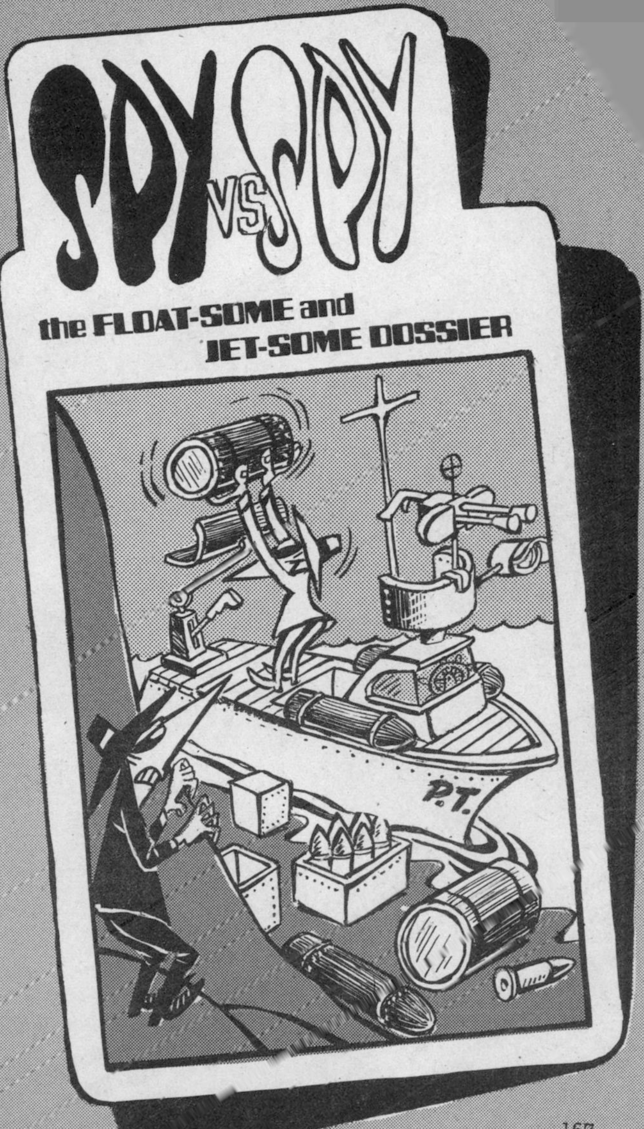
SPY vs SPY
the FLOAT-SOME and
JET-SOME DOSSIER
P.T.

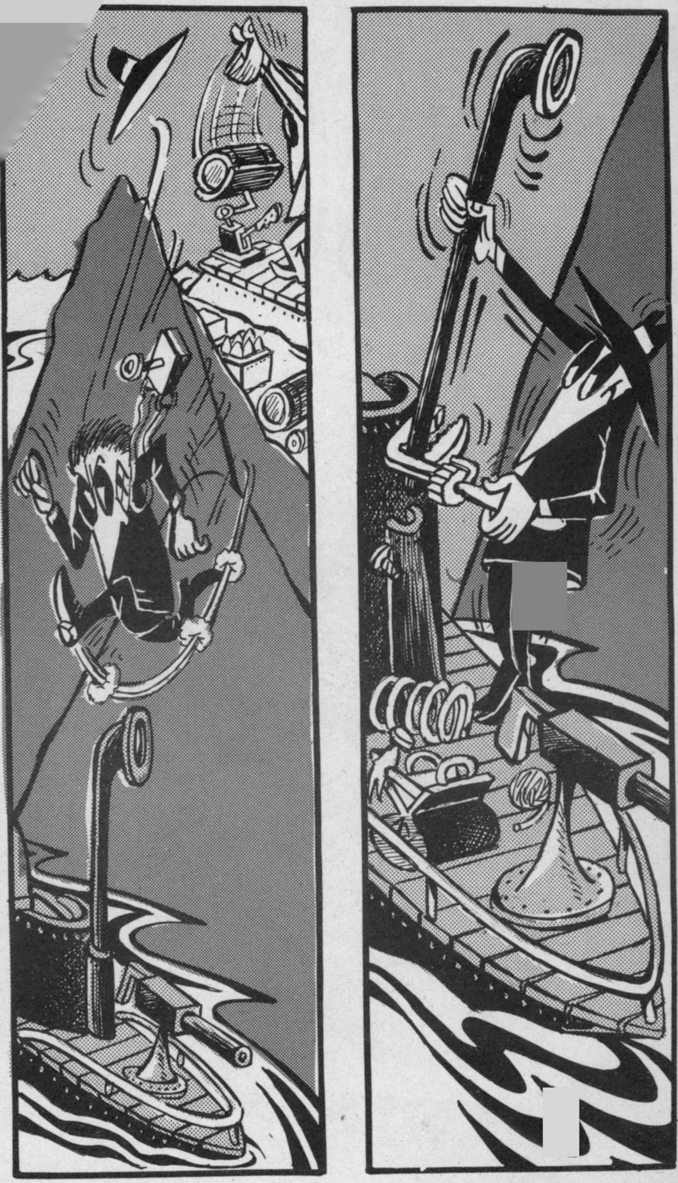

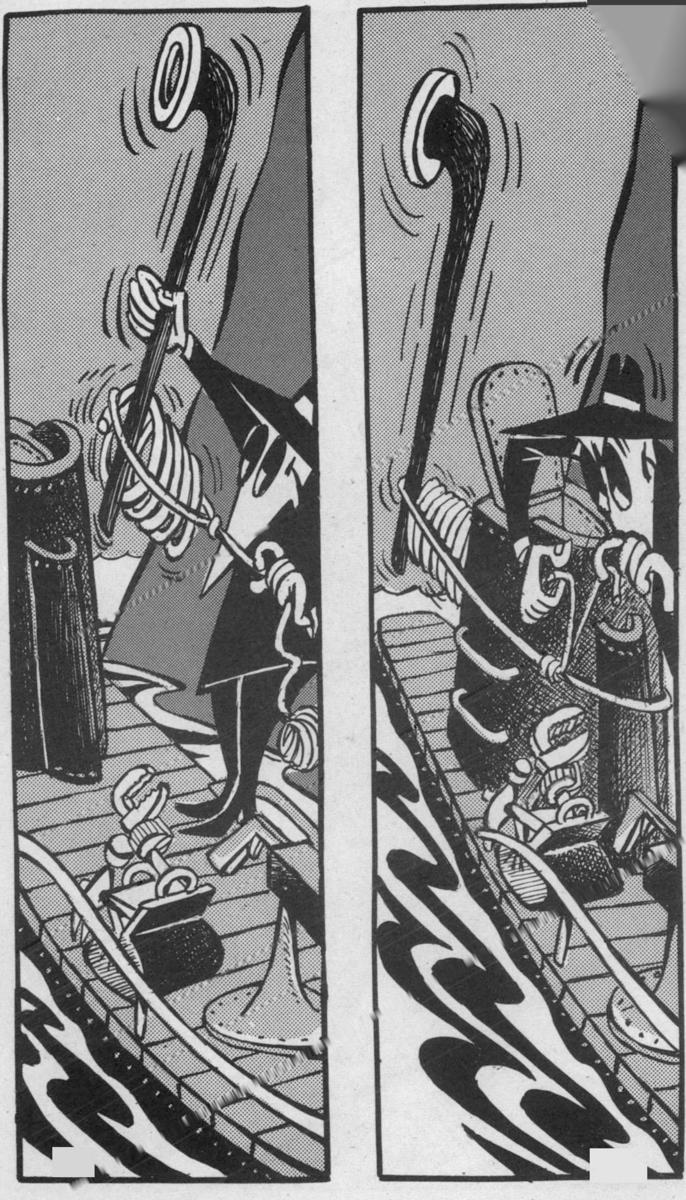

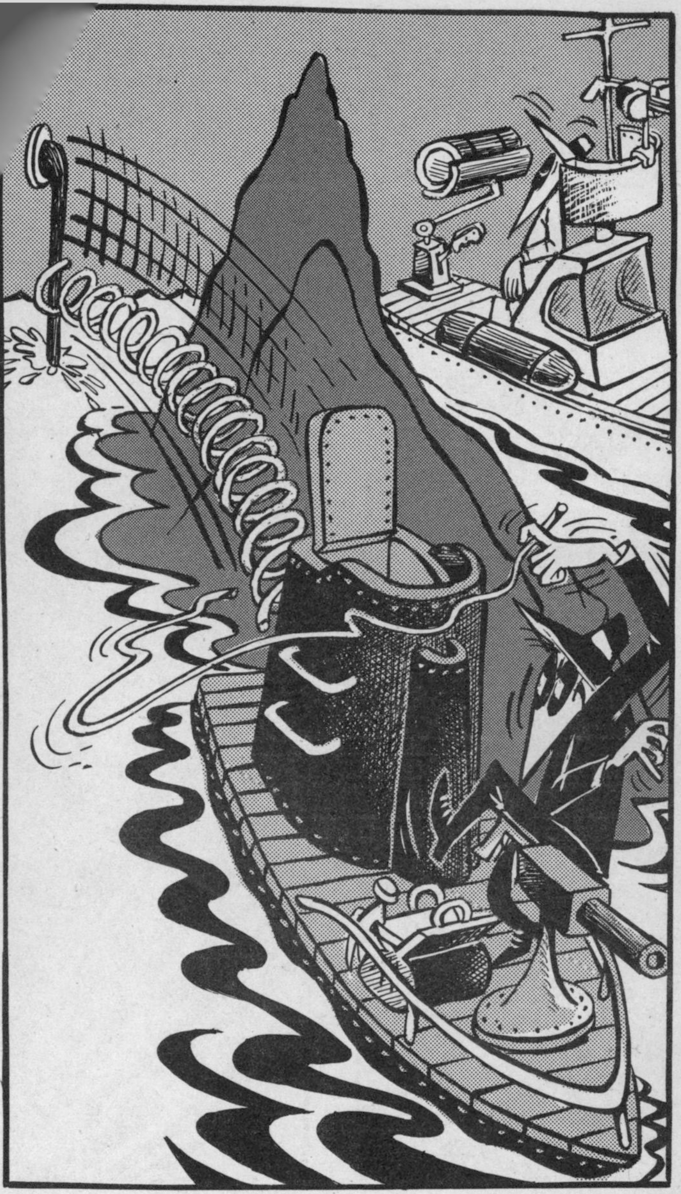

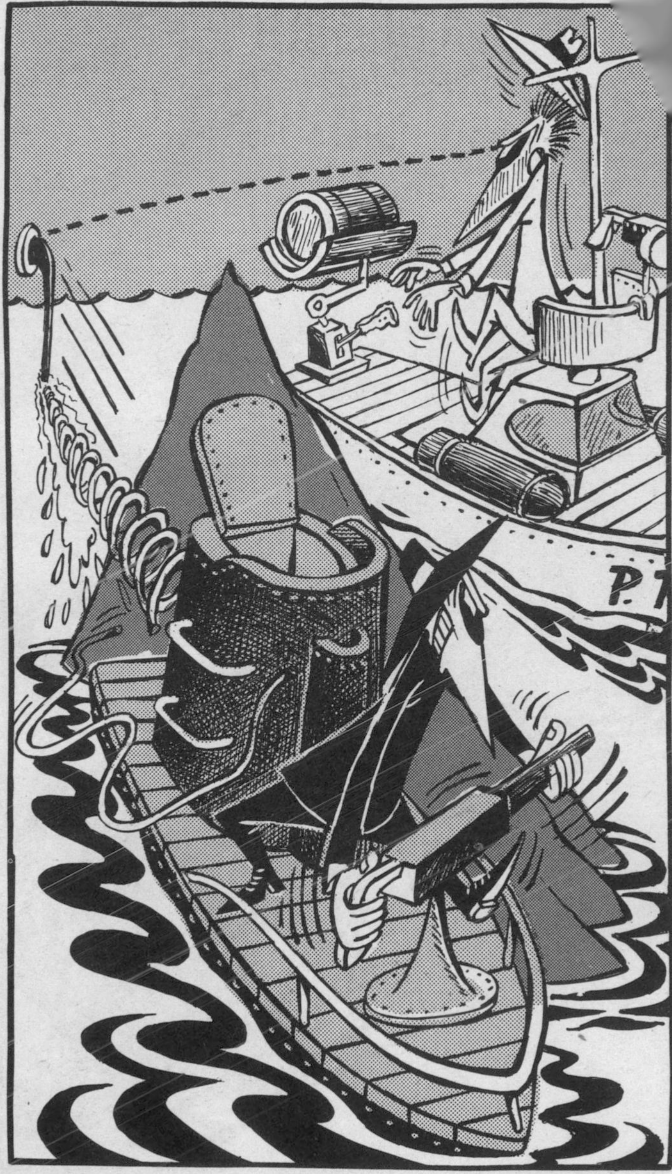
P.T

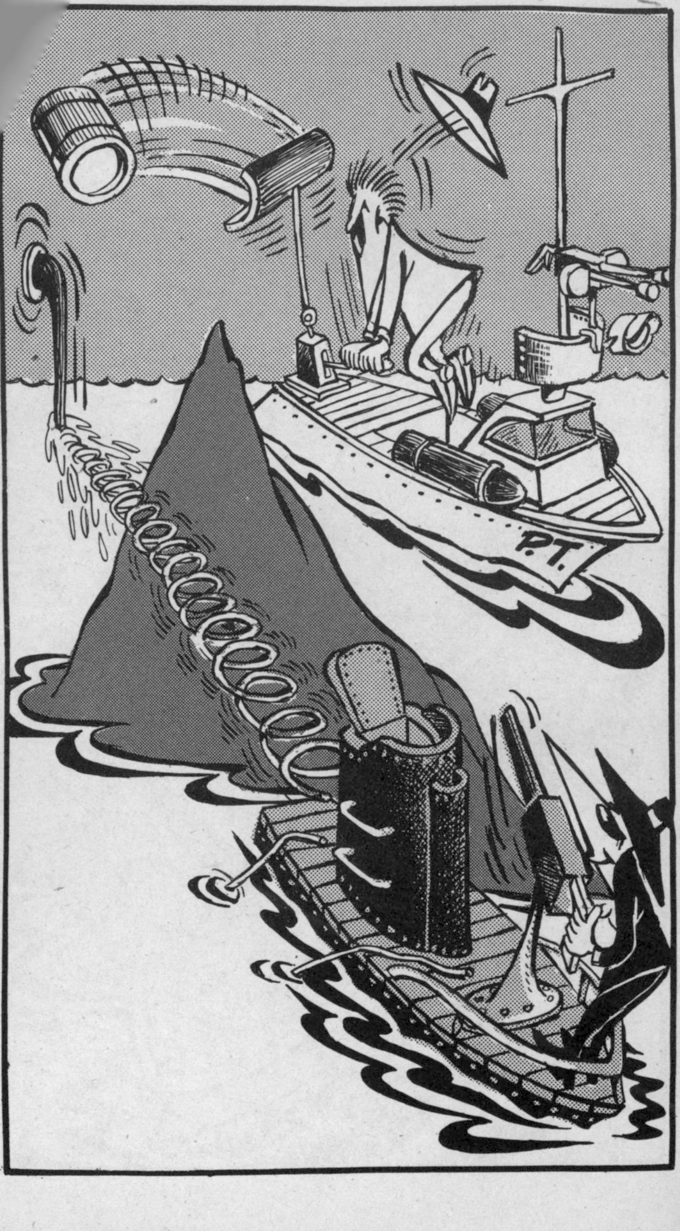
P.T.

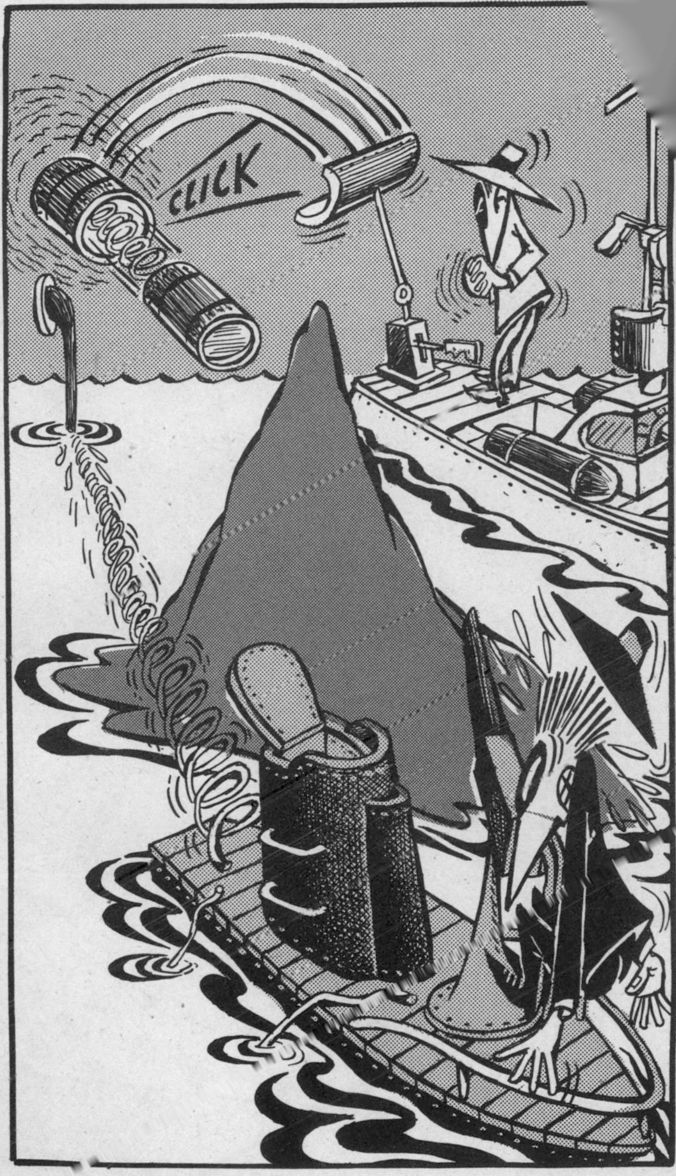
CLICK

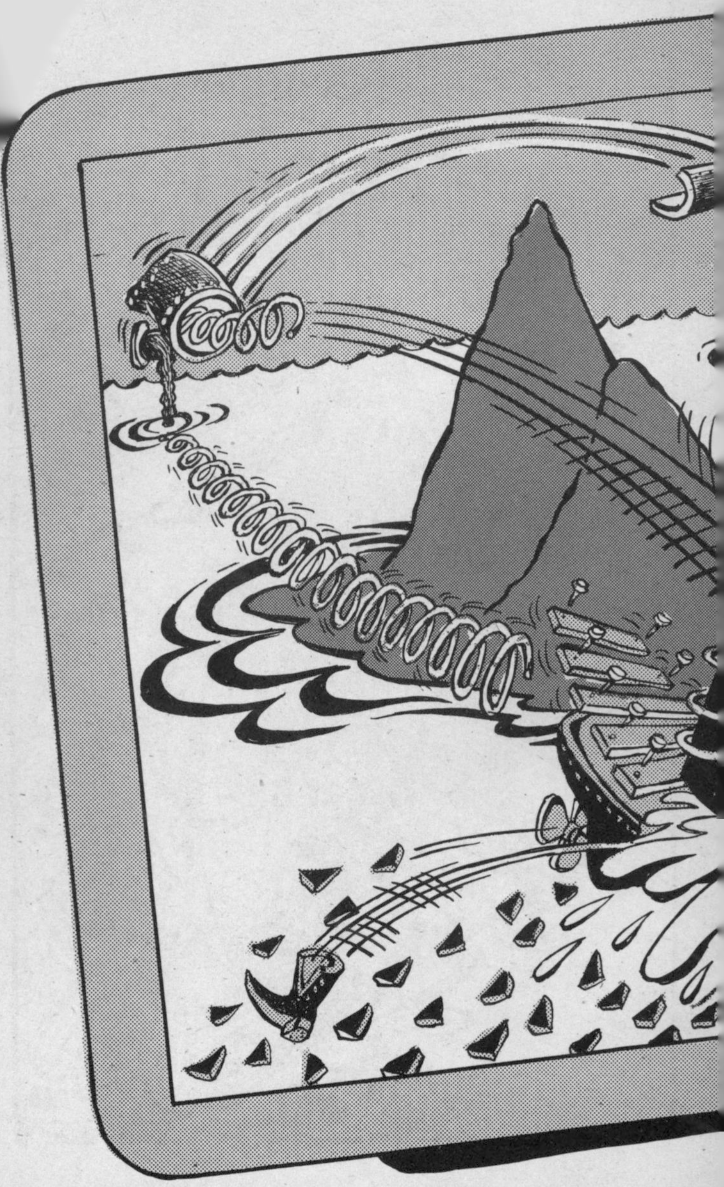

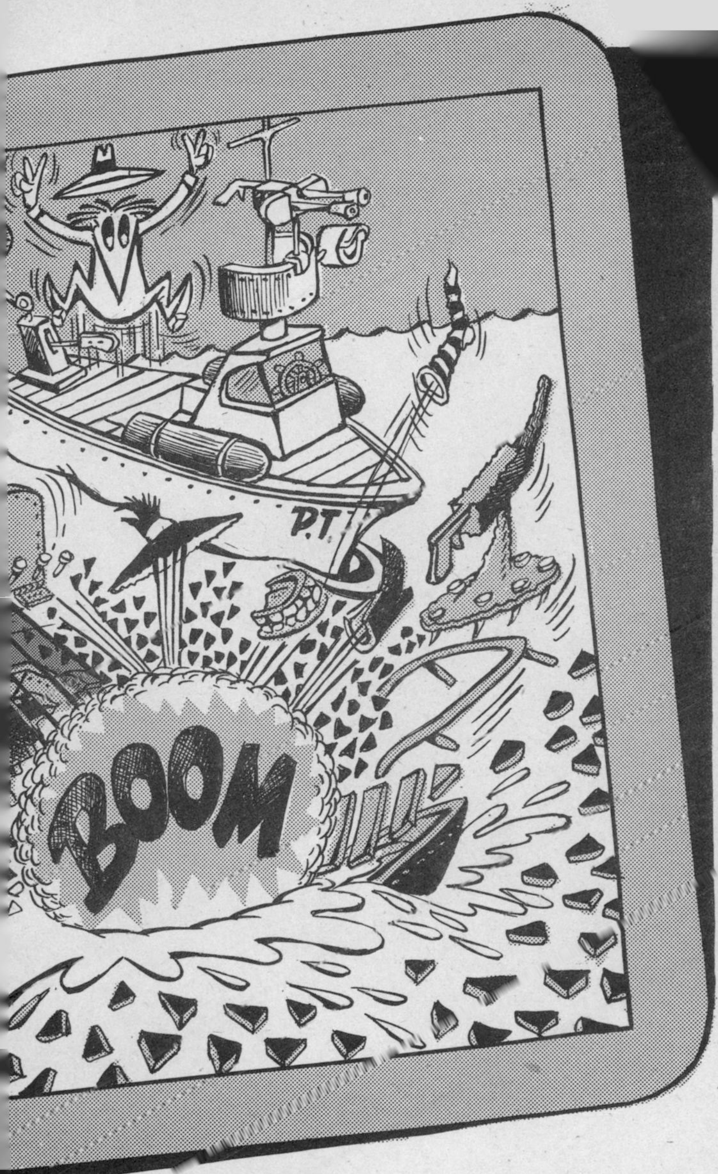
P.T.
BOOM

SPY vs SPY

the PLANE NONSENSE ACCOUNT

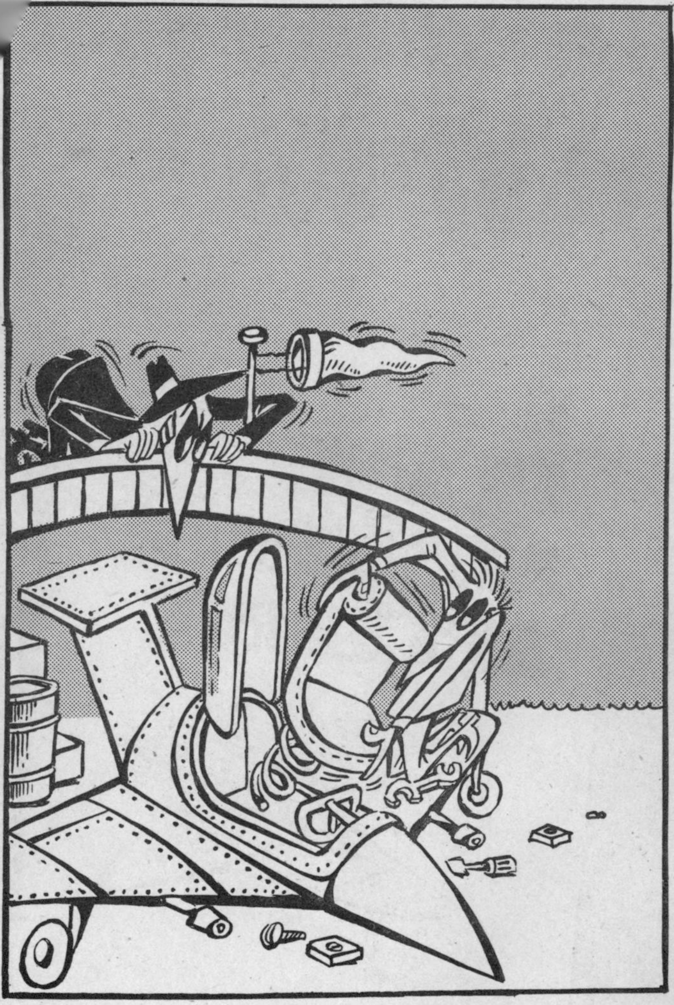

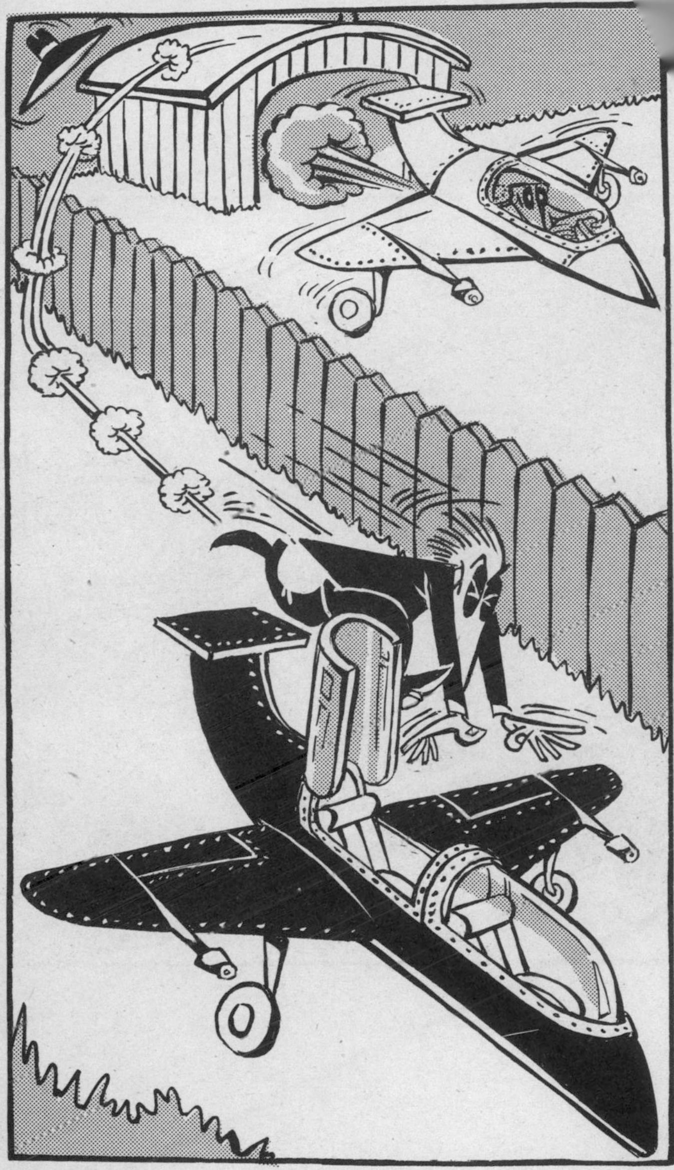

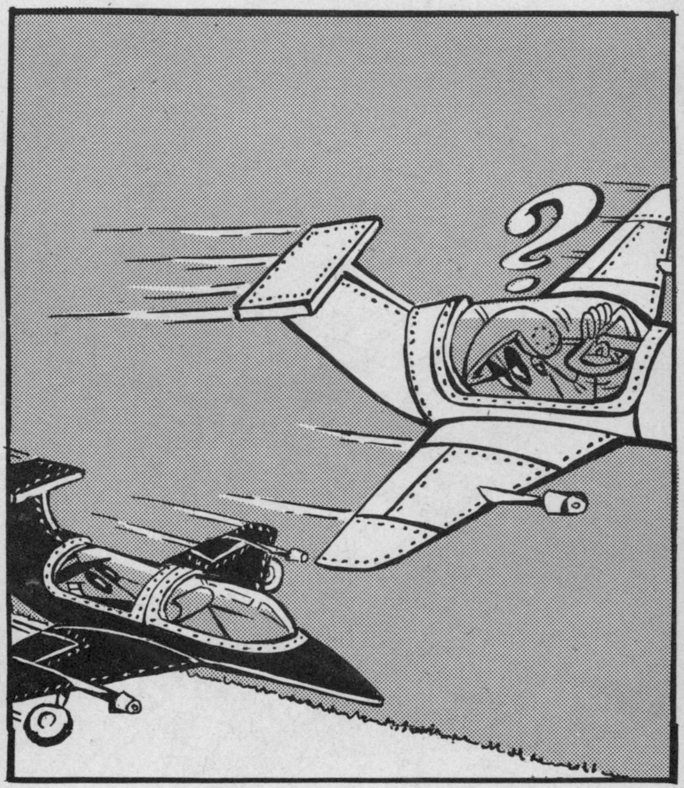

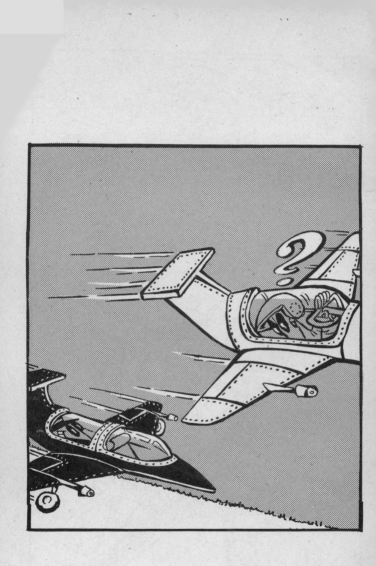

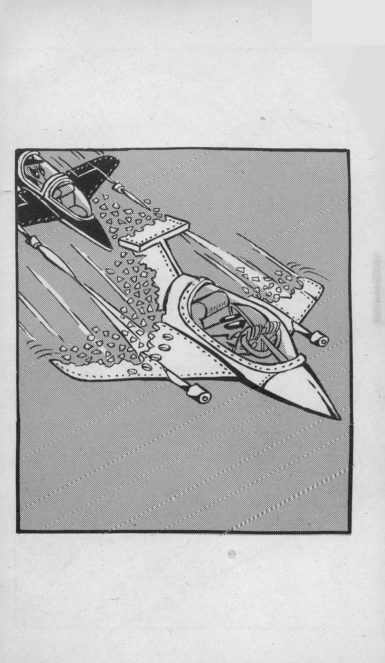

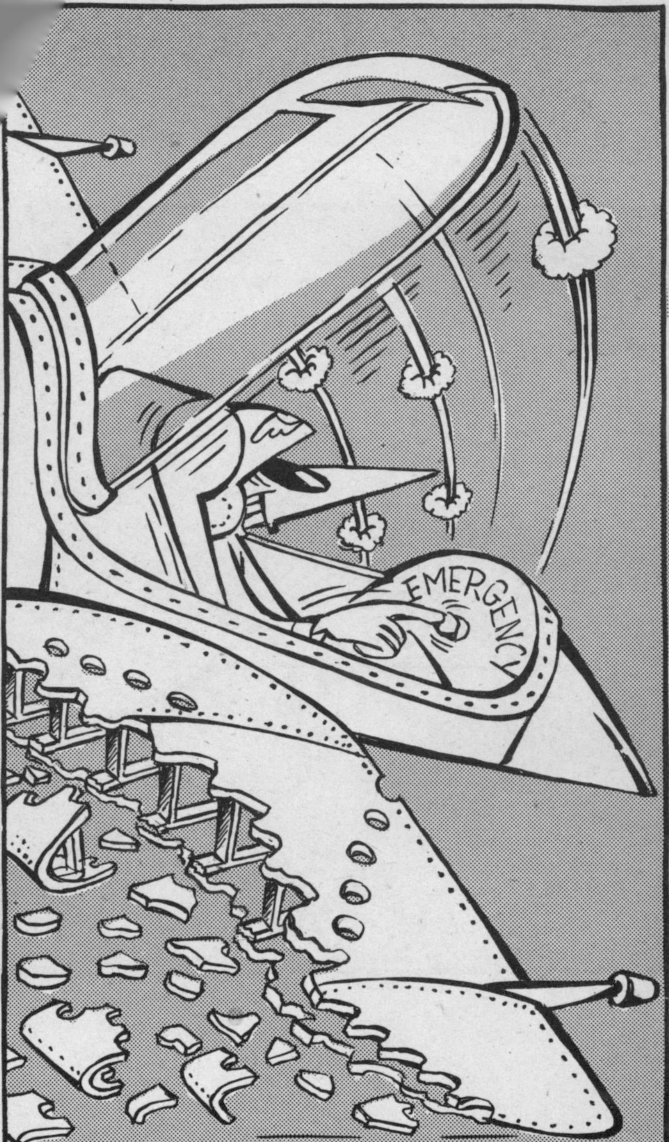
EMERGENCY

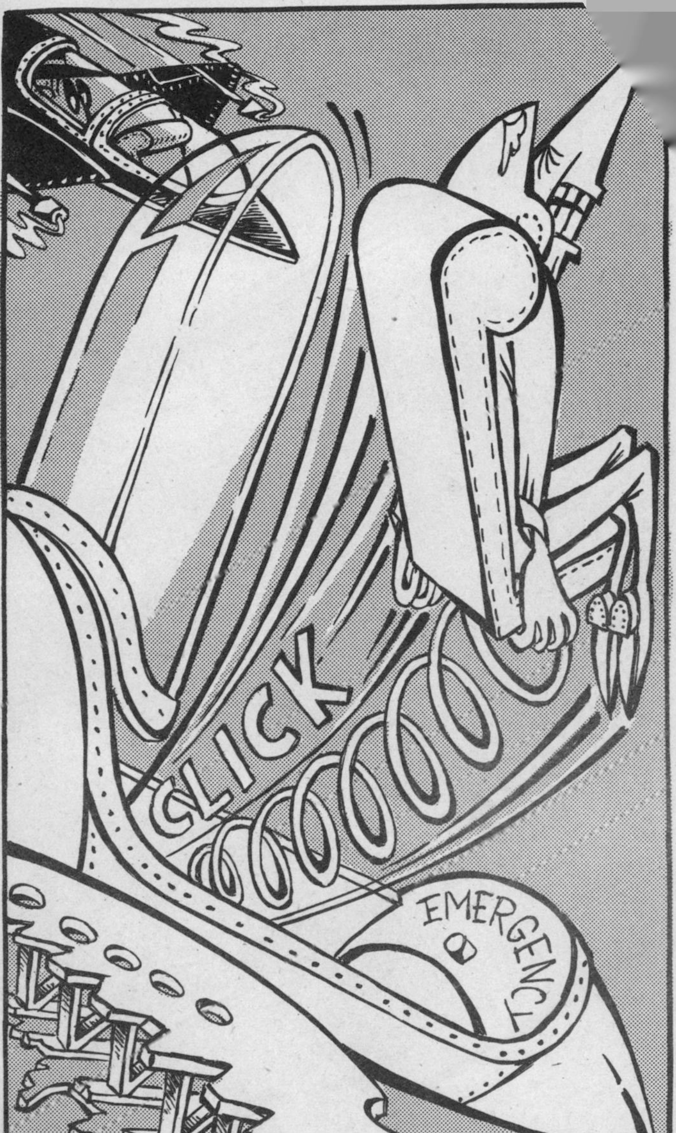
CLICK
EMERGENCY

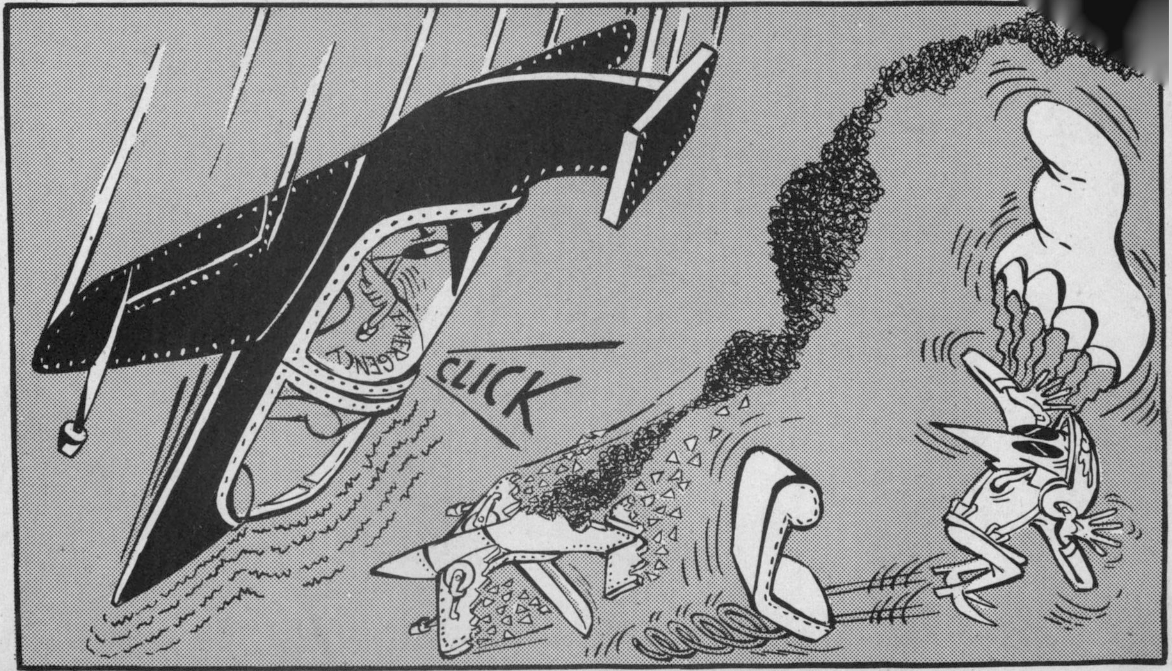
CLICK
EMERGENCY

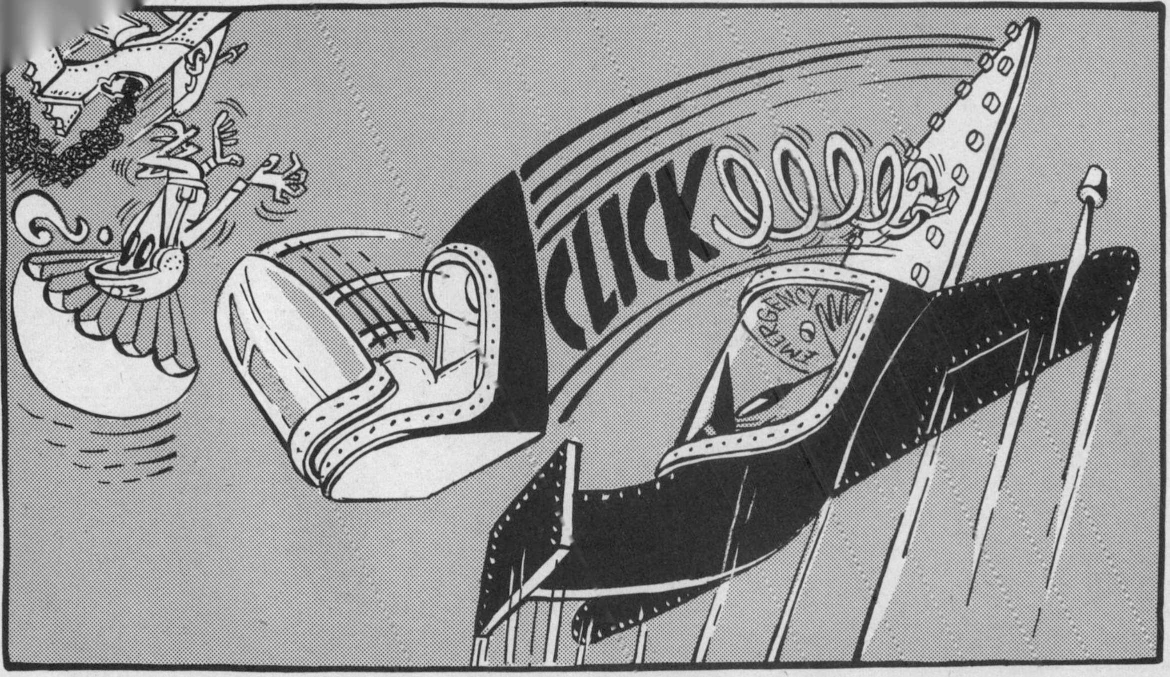
CLICK
EMERGENCY

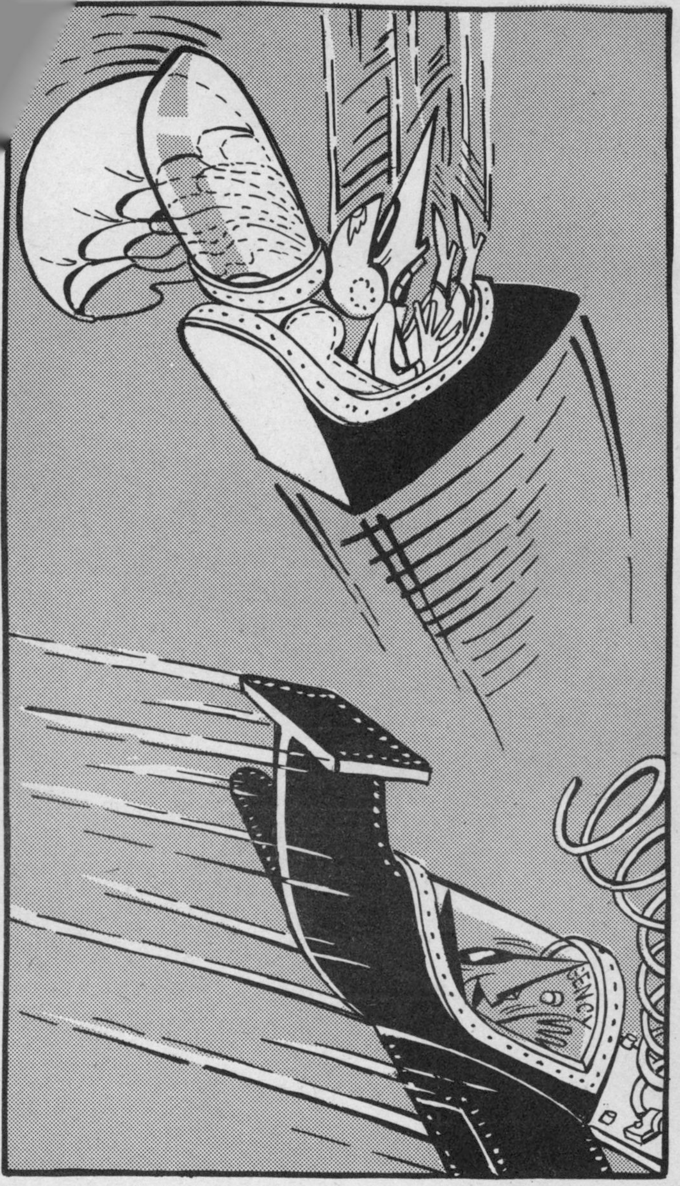

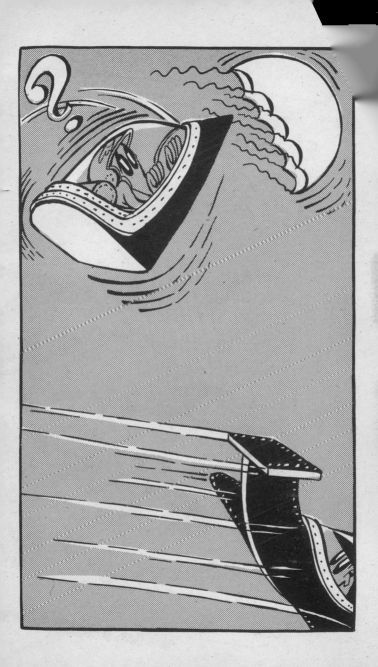

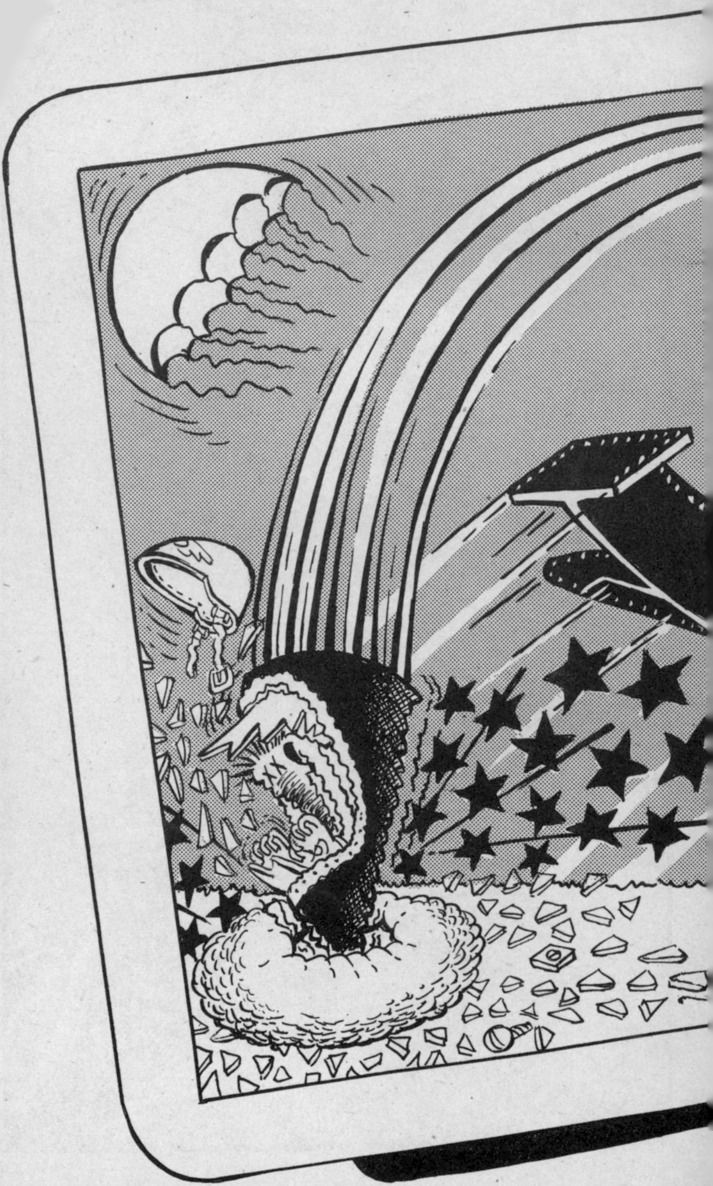

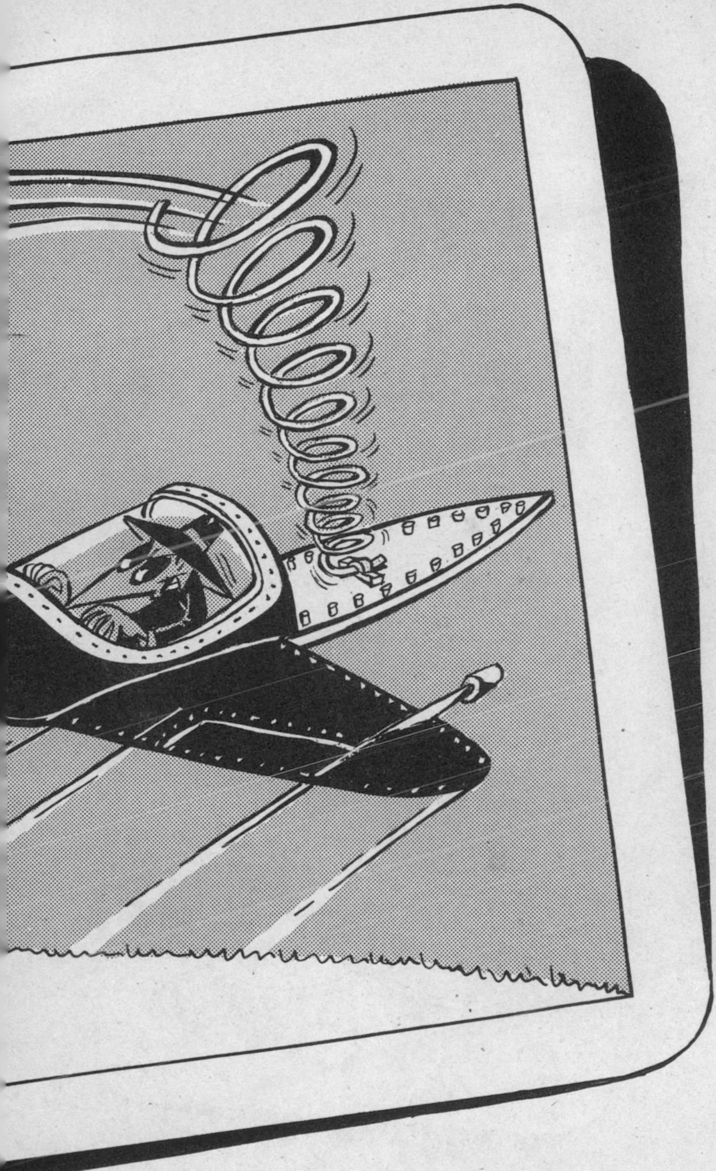

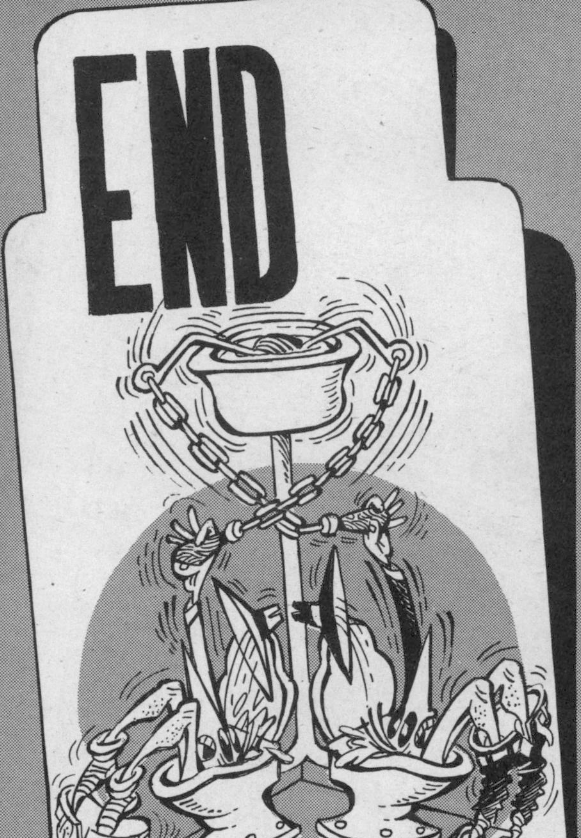
END

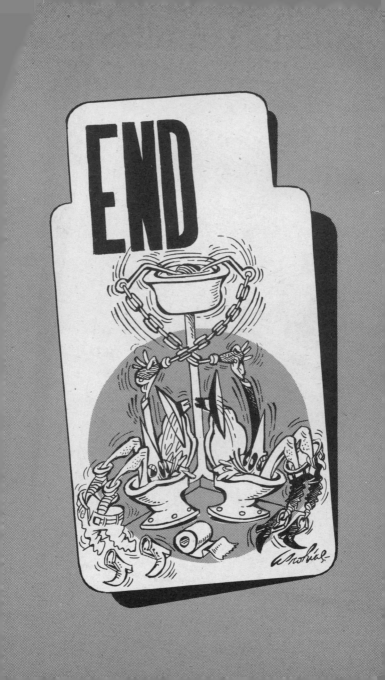

MORE **MAD** HUMOR FROM WARNER BOOKS

___30-430-1 **SHOOTIN' MAD,** $1.95
(In Canada 32-042-0, $2.50)

___88-731-5 **AL JAFFEE'S MAD MONSTROSITIES,** $1.50

___30-440-9 **GOOD LORD! NOT ANOTHER BOOK OF SNAPPY ANSWERS TO STUPID QUESTIONS,** $1.95
(In Canada 32-044-7, $2.50)

___90-528-3 **MAD'S AL JAFFEE FREAKS OUT,** $1.95

___30-441-7 **MAD'S SNAPPY ANSWERS TO STUPID QUESTIONS,** $1.95

___30-443-3 **STILL MORE SNAPPY ANSWERS TO STUPID QUESTIONS,** $1.95

___30-444-1 **DON MARTIN COMES ON STRONG,** $1.95
(In Canada 32-041-2, $2.50)

___30-446-8 **DON MARTIN DROPS 13 STORIES,** $1.95

___30-447-6 **DON MARTIN FORGES AHEAD,** $1.95

___30-481-6 **DON MARTIN GRINDS AHEAD,** $1.95

___30-448-4 **DON MARTIN STEPS OUT,** $1.95

___94-417-3 **THE MAD ADVENTURES OF CAPTAIN KLUTZ,** $1.75

___30-451-4 **MAD'S DON MARTIN CARRIES ON,** $1.95

___30-452-2 **MAD'S DON MARTIN DIGS DEEPER,** $1.95

___30-450-6 **MAD'S DON MARTIN STEPS FURTHER OUT,** $1.95
(In Canada 32-062-5, $2.50)

___30-453-0 **MAD'S MADDEST ARTIST DON MARTIN BOUNCES BACK,** $1.95
(In Canada 32-064-1, $2.50)

___90-819-3 **DON EDWING'S ALMOST SUPER HEROES,** $1.95

___94-190-5 **THE HOW-NOT-TO-DO-IT BOOK,** $1.75

WHEREVER PAPERBACKS ARE SOLD

WARNER BOOKS
P.O. Box 690
New York, N.Y. 10019

Please send me the books I have checked. I enclose a check or money order (not cash), plus 75¢ per order and 75¢ per copy to cover postage and handling.* (Allow 4 weeks for delivery.)

_____ Please send me your free mail order catalog. (If ordering only the catalog, include a large self-addressed, stamped envelope.)

Name _____

Address _____

City _____

State _____ Zip _____

*N.Y. State and California residents add applicable sales tax.   99